WELLINGTON'S LIGHT DIVISION AND THE DEFENCE OF PORTUGAL

WELLINGTON'S LIGHT DIVISION AND THE DEFENCE OF PORTUGAL

THE BATTLES OF 1811

ROBERT BURNHAM AND RON MCGUIGAN

FRONTLINE BOOKS

First published in Great Britain in 2024 by Frontline Books
An imprint of Pen & Sword Books Ltd Yorkshire – Philadelphia

Copyright © Robert Burnham and Ron McGuigan, 2024
ISBN 978 1 39906 057 8

The right of Robert Burnham and Ron McGuigan to be identified as Author of this work has been asserted by him in accordance with the Copyright, Designs and Patents Act 1988. A CIP catalogue record for this book is available from the British Library All rights reserved.

No part of this book may be reproduced or transmitted in any form or by any means, electronic or mechanical including photocopying, recording or by any information storage and retrieval system, without permission from the Publisher in writing.

Typeset by Lapiz Digital Printed and bound in the UK by
CPI Group (UK) Ltd, Croydon, CR0 4YY.

Printed on paper from a sustainable source by
CPI Group (UK) Ltd, Croydon, CR0 4YY

Pen & Sword Books Limited incorporates the imprints of Archaeology, Atlas, Aviation, Battleground, Digital, Discovery, Family History, Fiction, History, Local, Local History, Maritime, Military, Military Classics, Politics, Select, Transport, True Crime, Air World, Claymore Press, Frontline Publishing, Leo Cooper, Remember When, Seaforth Publishing, The Praetorian Press, Wharncliffe Books, Wharncliffe Local History, Wharncliffe Transport, Wharncliffe True Crime and White Owl.

For a complete list of Pen & Sword titles please contact

PEN & SWORD BOOKS LTD
47 Church Street, Barnsley, South Yorkshire, S70 2AS, England
E-mail: enquiries@pen-and-sword.co.uk
Website: www.pen-and-sword.co.uk

Or

PEN & SWORD BOOKS
1950 Lawrence Rd, Havertown, PA 19083, USA
E-mail: uspen-and-sword@casematepublishers.com

CONTENTS

Acknowledgements ix
List of Abbreviations xi
List of Maps xiii
List of Tables xv
Introduction xvii

Chapter 1   The Light Division, 1809–1810 1
Chapter 2   January and February 1811 11
Chapter 3   In Pursuit of the Withdrawing French, 1–9 March 1811 25
Chapter 4   Combats of Pombal and Redinha, 10–12 March 1811 39
Chapter 5   Condeixa and Casal Novo, 13–14 March 1811 53
Chapter 6   Foz de Arouce, 15 March 1811 69
Chapter 7   The Pursuit to the Border, 16–31 March 1811 81
Chapter 8   Sabugal, 3 April 1811 91
Chapter 9   The War of the Outposts, April 1811 105
Chapter 10 Battle of Fuentes de Oñoro, 3–5 May 1811 113
Chapter 11 The March to Badajoz, May–June 1811 129
Chapter 12 Misery in the South and Hunger in the North,
                June–August 1811 139
Chapter 13 Border Alarms and Sickness, September–October 1811 153
Chapter 14 Winter Quarters, November–December 1811 171
Chapter 15 What Happened to Them 183

Appendix I: Strength of the Light Division, January–December 1811 191
Appendix II: Strength of the 1st and 3rd Caçadores, 1811 201
Notes 205
Bibliography 221
Name Index 225
Place Index 229

*Dedicated to the memory of Captain Nicolas Frank Haynes,
Royal Green Jackets (1951–2021), the Dean of Light
Division Scholars*

ACKNOWLEDGEMENTS

Robert Burnham
When I decided to write this book I asked Ron McGuigan, with whom I had co-authored four previous books, to join me and I was very happy when he agreed! It is good to have the old team back together again. In many ways this book was a collaborative effort with several other people freely volunteering their time. They include: Moisés Gaudêncio, who translated old Portuguese strength returns and provided many of the photographs of the battlefields used in this book; Mark Thompson, the creator of all the maps we used; Gareth Glover, whose efforts to find and transcribe many diaries and letters from officers and men of the Light Division made writing this book much easier; Dr Michael Crumplin, who answered my numerous questions on sickness and disease in the British Army of 1811; and Zachary White, who shared much of his research on discipline and courts-martial of the period, as well as digging deep in the British National Archives to uncover long-lost Portuguese strength returns. Also, my two friends from 'Down Under', Steve Brown, who spent a day in the National Archives looking for further information on the Light Division, and Rory Muir, who answered my many questions on Wellington. Vic Powell provided images of the Sabugal battlefield. There are also three new names: Robert Pocock of the Tour Company 'Campaigns and Culture', who provided images of the battlefields; Major General Ashley Truluck, with whom I toured Fuentes de Oñoro in 2018 and who gave me much insight about the battlefield; and Michael Hopper, a designer of wargames scenarios, who pointed out many of the French sources used in this book. Last, but not least, I thank my wife of forty-five years Denah Burnham, who once again patiently sat through my recounting of anecdotes and stories of men long dead.

Ron McGuigan
I am honoured that Bob asked me to co-author this latest book. It is a pleasure to join him. I also join Bob in acknowledging the wonderful support and assistance freely given by those mentioned. It is deeply appreciated. Lastly, I must again thank Debbie, my wonderful wife of forty-nine years, for her usual patience, understanding and support.

LIST OF ABBREVIATIONS

AAG:	Assistant Adjutant General
ACG:	Assistant Commissary General
ADC:	Aide-de-Camp
AGC:	Army Gold Cross
AGM:	Army Gold Medal
Bn:	Battalion
CB:	Companion of the Most Honourable Order of the Bath
DAAG:	Deputy Assistant Adjutant General
DAQMG:	Deputy Assistant Quartermaster General
GCB:	Grand Cross of the Most Honourable Order of the Bath
G.O:	General Order
HQ:	Headquarters
KCB:	Knight Commander of the Most Honourable Order of the Bath
KGL:	The King's German Legion
km:	kilometre (s)
£:	Pounds
LTC:	Lieutenant Colonel
MGSM:	Military General Service Medal
NA:	Not Available
OR:	Other Ranks
QMG:	Quartermaster General
RHA:	Royal Horse Artillery

LIST OF MAPS

Note: We use standard NATO symbols for the units (see map legend).

Map 1.	Pursuit of the French, 6 March–2 April 1811	26
Map 2.	Combat of Pombal, 10 March 1811	40
Map 3.	Combat at Redinha, 12 March 1811	45
Map 4.	Combat of Casal Novo, 14 March 1811	56
Map 5.	Combat of Foz de Arouce, 15 March 1811	73
Map 6.	Sabugal, 3 April 1811	98
Map 7.	Fuentes de Oñoro, 3 May 1811	117
Map 8.	Fuentes de Oñoro, 5 May 1811	123
Map 9.	The march to Badajoz, June 1811	134
Map 10.	The march north, 30 July–9 August 1811	144
Map 11.	The Light Division, late August 1811	148
Map 12.	The Light Division, 2–16 October 1811	165
Map 13.	The Light Division, late October 1811	168
Map 14.	The Light Division, 28 November 1811	172
Map 15.	The Light Division, 31 December 1811	182

Map Legend

XX ⊠	Allied infantry division
Light XX ⊠	Light Division
1 ⊠ 43	1st Battalion 43rd Foot
1 ⊠ 52	1st Battalion 52nd Foot
2 ⊠ 52	2nd Battalion 52nd Foot
LW 1 ⊠ 95	Left Wing 1st Bn 95th Rifles
RW 1 ⊠ 95	Right Wing 1st Bn 95th Rifles
RW 3 ⊠ 95	Right Wing 3rd Bn 95th Rifles
1 ⊠ Caç	1st Caçadores Battalion
3 ⊠ Caç	3rd Caçadores Battalion
⊠	French infantry regiment
X ⊠	French infantry brigade
XX ⊠	French infantry division
XXX ⊠	French infantry corps
X ◤	French cavalry brigade

LIST OF TABLES

Table 2.1	Organization of the Light Division, 1 January 1811	11
Table 2.2	Light Division Other Ranks Sick, January–February 1811	12
Table 2.3	Light Division on Command, January–February 1811	13
Table 2.4	Light Division Effectives, January–February 1811	13
Table 3.1	Organization of the Light Division, 5 March 1811	29
Table 3.2	Light Division Effectives, 1 March 1811	30
Table 3.3	Organization of the Light Division, 11 March 1811	37
Table 5.1	Light Division Casualties at Casal Novo, 14 March 1811	65
Table 6.1	Light Division Casualties at Foz de Arouce, 15 March 1811	79
Table 7.1	March of the 2nd Battalion, 52nd Foot, 12–22 March	87
Table 8.1	Light Division Casualties at Sabugal, 3 April 1811	102
Table 10.1	Light Division Casualties at Fuentes de Oñoro, 3–5 May 1811	127
Table 11.1	Route of the Light Division, 8–9 June 1811	134
Table 11.2	Route of the Light Division, 11–23 June 1811	137
Table 12.1	Light Division, Other Ranks Sick, 24 July 1811	141
Table 12.2	Route of the Light Division, 1–9 August 1811	146
Table 12.3	Location of the Light Division, 10–20 August 1811	147

Table 12.4	Location of the Light Division, 21–28 August 1811	150
Table 12.5	Light Division, Other Ranks Sick, 24 August 1811	151
Table 13.1	Organization of the Light Division, 1 September 1811	153
Table 13.2	Light Division, Other Ranks Sick, 24 September 1811	162
Table 13.3	Organization of the Light Division, 1 October 1811	163
Table 13.4	Location of the Light Division, 2–16 October 1811	165
Table 13.5	Locations of the Light Division, 17–31 October 1811	167
Table 13.6	Light Division, Other Ranks Sick, 24 October 1811	168
Table 14.1	Location of the Light Division, 28 November 1811	173
Table 14.2	Light Division, Other Ranks Sick, 24 November 1811	174
Table 14.3	Organization of the Light Division, 5 December 1811	174
Table 14.4	Light Division, Other Ranks Sick, 24 December 1811	180
Table 14.5	Locations of the Light Division, 31 December 1811	181
Table AI.1	1st Battalion, 43rd Foot, January–December 1811	193
Table AI.2	1st Battalion, 52nd Foot, January–December 1811	194
Table AI.3	2nd Battalion, 52nd Foot, March–December 1811	195
Table AI.4	1st Battalion, 95th Rifles, January–December 1811	196
Table AI.5	2nd Battalion, 95th Rifles, January–December 1811	197
Table AI.6	Right Wing, 3rd Battalion, 95th Rifles, August–December 1811	198
Table AI.7	Brunswick Oëls, January–March 1811	199
Table AI.8	Approximate number of Brunswick Oëls Assigned to the Light Division Who Were Fit for Duty, January–March 1811	200
Table AII.1	1st Caçadores, 1811	203
Table AII.2	3rd Caçadores, 1811	204

INTRODUCTION

> Seven regiments of light infantry and riflemen defiled before us with their thread-bare jackets, their brawny necks loosened from their stocks, their wide and patched trowsers of various colours, and brown-barrelled arms slung over their shoulders, or carelessly held in their hands, whilst a joyous buzz ran through the cross-belted ranks, as their soldier-like faces glanced towards us to greet many of their old comrades now about to join in their arduous toils after a long separation.
>
> Lieutenant John Cooke, 43rd Foot[1]

One of the hallmarks of the Light Division was the camaraderie of its officers and men. They were truly a band of brothers, their bond forged in battle and shared hardship. This is their story, as told in the words of the officers and men of the division. It is the second instalment of a five-volume history of the most famous unit of the Peninsular War – Wellington's Light Division.[2] Like the first volume, which was a chronological look at the pivotal year of 1810, *Wellington's Light Division and the Defence of Portugal* takes the reader to the pivotal year of 1811 that saw the ejection of the French troops from Portugal. In it are described not only the many skirmishes and battles that the division fought, but also the trials and tribulations its men endured on a daily basis: the marches and counter-marches over mountainous terrain, the fickle weather that ranged between extremes of heat and cold, the chronic shortage of food, and the ever-present sickness and disease that decimated their ranks.

We are additionally fortunate that the officers and men were very literate for the time and a large number of their memoirs, letters and diaries still survive. Readers may be familiar with some of our sources, such as Harry Smith's *Autobiography*, George Simmons' journals and Edward Costello's *Memoirs*, but in this volume are many more known only to the most ardent historians. Furthermore every year new sources are discovered. In part, many of these are due to the tireless efforts of Gareth Glover, who for the past three years has searched numerous archives and libraries. He and I have transcribed five diaries[3] that have never been published before, as well as numerous accounts that were published in long-forgotten books and magazines. This new material, especially the diaries, provides a new perspective on the operations and battles of the division, and sometimes changes what we previously knew. But they are not just limited to actions on the battlefield. They are filled with more mundane, but equally important information about the life of the officers and men in their cantonment and on the march. Within them we were able to find such details as the daily location of the battalions, enabling us to track their movements; the arrival and departure of units, commanders and personnel; the impact of sickness and disease on the division's effectiveness; what they ate or often what they went without; the state of their uniforms and equipment; their living conditions; and how they entertained themselves.

Although our first volume included the monthly strength reports of the British units assigned to the division, it did not do so for its Portuguese caçadore battalions. Thanks to Zack White and Steve Brown, we now have never-before-published detailed strength reports for the Portuguese battalions in 1811. These numerous new primary sources and official records of the Portuguese Army have permitted us to fill the gaps present in so many histories of this period.

Like the previous volume, *Wellington's Light Division and the Defence of Portugal* is organized chronologically. It begins with the division manning outposts, under miserably cold and wet conditions, watching the French Army in Santarém. In March and April they were at the forefront of Wellington's Army, snapping at the heels of the retreating French, never allowing them to rest. Often this dogged pursuit found them catching up to the enemy well before the rest of the army and having to fight in unequal combat. Before long the division out-marched its supplies and was forced to halt, but not before capturing hundreds, if not thousands, of stragglers and the occasional baggage train. By the beginning of April they had chased the French out of Portugal and the division was once again in familiar territory along the Spanish frontier.

May saw the division distinguish itself during the three-day battle at Fuentes de Oñoro, where it made an epic withdrawal over open terrain pursued by thousands of French cavalrymen. Despite its victory, the division was not allowed to rest very long. By the end of the month the men were marching south to support the Allied siege of Badajoz. There they bivouacked for three months in the fever-ridden valleys of the Guadiana river, in merciless heat, living in ramshackle huts that occasionally caught fire, and on short rations. Not surprisingly, the health of the men began to fail and the hospitals were packed with the sick.

By September the division was back in the north, covering the ground they had guarded and fought over for many months the previous year. There they watched the approaches to Ciudad Rodrigo to interrupt any attempts to resupply the French garrison in the fortress. Matters should have been better since they were no longer on the march, but the men were still plagued by sickness and disease, while a breakdown in logistics caused them often to go hungry. Although they had left the oppressive heat of the south, they exchanged it for endless rain and very cold nights. The year took a heavy toll on them, and not just among the enlisted soldiers and junior officers. The senior officers shared their hardships and misery and in many cases paid for it with their lives. By the end of the year two of the division's brigade commanders had died from sickness, while a third went home broken in health.

About the Book

Images: Since most of the battles described in this volume are not well known, we focus on what those battlefields look like, for often a picture is worth a thousand words. These images show how the terrain appears more than two hundred years after the battle. Although much of the landscape would be recognizable to those who fought there in 1811, many of the towns and villages have expanded and now encroach on what were fields and orchards. Many of the hills that were covered with light woods in 1811 are now heavily forested. Perhaps the biggest change is at Sabugal, where the Côa river reservoir now floods the area that the Light Division marched through to reach the battlefield.

Chapter 1

THE LIGHT DIVISION, 1809–1810

On 22 February 1810 the Adjutant General's Office of the Anglo-Allied Army in Portugal and Spain issued a general order that reorganized the army. Paragraph Three of this order stated:

> The 1st and 2nd battalions of Portuguese Chasseurs[4] are attached to the brigade of General R. Craufurd, which is to be called the light division. These troops will be ordered to join the division to which they belong.[5]

And thus came into existence the most famous unit to serve under the Duke of Wellington. The Light Division had its origins in the formation of the Light Brigade in May 1809. The brigade was formed around a core of three British light infantry battalions: the 1st Battalions of the 43rd Foot, the 52nd Foot and the rifle-armed 95th Foot.

Prior to leaving England in April 1809, after receiving the command of the forces in Portugal, Wellington had a long discussion with Lord Castlereagh,[6] the Secretary of State for War and the Colonies, about his force's mission, and what he would need to accomplish it. One of his requests was more light troops, and Lord Castlereagh agreed with him. On 22 May he wrote to Wellington to inform him that 'The light brigade, under Brigadier-General Sir R. Craufurd, will embark at Harwich and Deal on the 24th instant. The Brigadier-General will be directed to join you by the shortest route, calling off Oporto, Aveiro, and Mondego, successively, for intelligence of your movements, or any orders you may have despatched to meet him at either of those places.'[7]

On 20 May the three battalions received orders to be ready to march on the 24th. This was the first time that the 1st Battalions of the three regiments would serve together under the command of Brigadier

General Craufurd. Little did they know that they would be together for the next sixty months.

Foul weather kept the ships from sailing until 3 June, when the winds finally changed. The convoy arrived off Lisbon on 29 June.[8] The troops remained on board until 2 July, when they boarded flat-bottomed boats and rowed up the Tagus river stopping at Santarém for four days. On 8 July the brigade marched 40km up the Tagus river to Golegã and then to Tancos. The next day they marched another 20km to Abrantes, where they crossed the Tagus on a bridge of boats. They entered Spain on 20 July.

At Navalmoral there were rumours that Wellington and his army were about to engage the enemy at Talavera. The Light Brigade left the town before sunrise on the next day (28 July) and soon could hear cannon fire in the distance. In accordance with their standing orders, Craufurd planned to halt at La Calzada and rest until the cool of the evening, before resuming the march. They marched the 22km to the village and arrived there about 9am. They had not been there long when a courier rode in with a dispatch from Wellington ordering them to move as quickly as possible to Talavera, since a battle was expected shortly. Craufurd immediately ordered the Light Brigade back on the road and they reached Oropesa about noon, having marched another 10km.[9]

The men were tired, and Craufurd ordered a short halt to rest. At 2am the brigade was back on its feet and moved out. This epic march was about 65km long, much of it over 'heavy sandy roads'.[10] The Light Brigade reached the centre of the position of the British army at Talavera about 6am on 29 July, having completed the forced march in 25 hours,[11] but arrived too late to participate in the battle. Instead, the men were sent forward to serve as a screen between the two armies.

On 1 August the Light Brigade was assigned to the 3rd Division, which had been commanded by Major General John Randoll Mackenzie until his death at Talavera on 28 July. Craufurd was now the senior brigade commander and thus took command of the division. Lieutenant Colonel William Gifford of the 43rd Foot probably took temporary command of the Light Brigade in his place.[12] Wellington soon realized that the longer he waited at Talavera, the more untenable his position became. On the night of 1 August he received intelligence that a French army under Marshal Jean Soult was at Plasencia and threatening his lines of communication with Portugal. The next day, Wellington ordered his army to withdraw back to Portugal.

On 5 August the 3rd Division was detached from the rest of the army and sent west through the mountains to take control of the bridge over the Tagus river at Almaraz. There they stayed until 20 August, when orders were received for the 3rd Division to withdraw back to Portugal. Upon arriving in Campo Maior they went into quarters for three months. On 21 August Craufurd was officially appointed a brigadier general on the staff, with a back date of 26 July.

On 11 December the Light Brigade received orders to march the next morning. They were moving to what would become their home for the next seven months: the Portuguese-Spanish border in the vicinity of Almeida and the Côa river. On 7 January the Light Brigade began deploying forward to the area between the Côa and Agueda rivers. Within ten days all three regiments were in forward positions. There they would sit for the next six months, observing the French who had moved into the vicinity of Ciudad Rodrigo from Salamanca.

In mid-February the British 3rd Division was located in the vicinity of Pinhel and along the Portuguese-Spanish border just to the east of the fortified city of Almeida. That month also saw Major General Thomas Picton's arrival in Portugal. His presence created a problem for Wellington since Picton was senior to both Major General Galbraith Cole, who commanded the 4th Division, and to Brigadier General Craufurd, who was temporarily commanding the 3rd Division. The only position Wellington had for Picton was as the commander of the 3rd Division. But if he appointed him commander of the 3rd Division, what was he to do with Craufurd, who had served so ably as the divisional commander for the previous seven months? Wellington's solution was to reorganize the army. On 22 February 1810 a General Order was issued in which Picton was appointed the commander of the 3rd Division and Craufurd was given command of the newly created Light Division, comprising three British battalions and two Portuguese caçadores battalions.

In the meantime, the French were making preparations to capture Ciudad Rodrigo. On 8 February troops of Marshal Michel Ney's 6th Corps marched from Salamanca towards Ciudad Rodrigo and three days later were spreading out around the city. A summons to surrender was made to the city's governor, Lieutenant General Don Andrés Péres de Herrasti, who refused. Ney had hoped to take the city without having to conduct a formal siege and had brought neither a siege battery nor sufficient supplies to feed a large enough force to effectively besiege the city. The next morning the French withdrew to Salamanca, but left a division in the vicinity of Vitigudino, to keep an eye on Ciudad Rodrigo.[13]

Craufurd was not aware of the movements of the French until they reached Ciudad Rodrigo on 11 February.[14] In accordance with his instructions, by 14 February he had redeployed the Light Brigade from the vicinity of the Douro river. All his units were west of the Côa river except for the 95th Rifles. The Division Headquarters was located in Pinhel.

On 18 March 1810 the 1st KGL Hussars were formally attached to the Light Division. This was the beginning of a long and close association between the Light Division and the KGL Hussars. The 1st Hussars were given the responsibility of screening the division's right flank along a 70km stretch of the Agueda river from Villar de Ciervo to El Payo, Spain.

The order creating the Light Division had made the Portuguese 1st and 2nd Caçadores Battalions part of its establishment. Craufurd also asked for the 3rd Caçadores Battalion to be assigned to him. Wellington considered this, but on 21 March wrote back stating, 'It [is] impossible to get Elder's[15] corps for you, otherwise you may depend upon it that I should have been happy to make your division so much stronger.'[16]

On 28 March word reached the division that the two caçadores battalions, with a combined strength of about 700 men,[17] were at Pinhel. From there they marched to Villar Torpim and were inspected by Craufurd on 5 April. He was not impressed with what he saw and wrote that night to Wellington about his concerns. Wellington replied on 9 April:

> I have ordered forward Elder's battalion, and when that arrives, the 2 others must return. But still Elder's battalion does not add sufficiently to your strength; and I doubt whether its services in front will compensate for the disadvantages of its advance from the rear, and the want of its example in the formation of the others.[18]

Craufurd chose to ignore the orders for him to send the 1st and 2nd Caçadores to the rear, correctly thinking Wellington would not notice it for a while.

It was quiet along the front during late March and early April. It had finally stopped raining on 25 March and the fords over the Agueda had become passable by the 28th. On 11 April the 95th Rifles received word to consolidate the men from two companies and send the officers and some non-commissioned officers home.

Now, in response to the French movements against Ciudad Rodrigo, Craufurd began moving his infantry units forward. By 30 April their new positions were along the Azaba river, about 15km further east and about 12km away from Ciudad Rodrigo. Although there was some French movement towards Ciudad Rodrigo at the end of April,

Wellington had no firm idea of when, or even if, a French invasion of Portugal was imminent. But he was not alone in this, for Ney did not know either. It was not until 16 April that Napoleon finalized his plans and appointed Marshal André Masséna to lead the invasion. On 17 April Napoleon created the Army of Portugal, composed of General Jean Reynier's 2nd Corps, Ney's 6th Corps and Junot's 8th Corps: in all, a force of about 75,000 men.[19]

Craufurd was spoiling for a fight and had contacted Wellington the previous month with a plan that would allow him to probe the enemy to keep them off balance. Wellington, however, would not give him permission to do so. Hence the Light Division had to sit and observe, not that there was much to see. It rained virtually every day in May, causing the Agueda river to flood and be unfordable much of the time.

Upon arriving in the vicinity of Ciudad Rodrigo, the French found secure cantonments for their troops and then began preparing for the siege. On 12 May a French staff officer approached the city under a flag of truce, bearing another summons for the governor to surrender. Herrasti's response was quite succinct and left no doubt in anyone's mind about his resolve. 'Since the answer I have given previously is final, it should be understood that no more representatives will be admitted in the future under a flag of truce. Now we have to talk only with guns.'[20]

As the rest of Napoleon's Army of Portugal began to arrive in the area, the Light Division saw an increase in the aggressiveness of the French outposts and reconnaissance patrols. Through early May it was relatively quiet, but by the middle of the month the French were patrolling in force. Craufurd was faced with a dilemma. The Agueda river was a natural barrier along which to set up his chain of outposts, but he had fewer than 5,000 troops to cover some 130km of frontage. The longer he kept his outposts in the vicinity of the city along the river, the greater the chance they would be trapped there by the French. But if he pulled back to the Azaba river, he would lose his ability to communicate with and resupply the city. The French completed a bridge over the Agueda at Molino Carbonero on 7 June and the next day French infantry and cavalry were seen on the west side of the river. Craufurd could wait no longer: he ordered his outposts to withdraw and form a new line along the Azaba river. The Agueda would only be picqueted from its confluence with the Azaba north to Barba del Puerco. What would follow became known as the 'War of the Outposts', as each side probed the other's lines and Craufurd tried to resupply the city.

By 27 June the situation in Ciudad Rodrigo was grim. A letter received by Craufurd the previous day from the governor of the city put a positive spin on the situation, but in truth it was only a matter of time before it would fall and the French could then turn their attention to the British. On 29 June Craufurd himself could see a sizeable breach in the city walls. The time had come to withdraw his troops. Ciudad Rodrigo finally surrendered to the French on 10 July.

***

The next major action for the Light Division would be the fighting at the Côa river on 24 July 1810. After the fall of Ciudad Rodrigo, the division was tasked with screening the Portuguese-held city of Almeida. Ney planned to attack the Light Division with his corps of three infantry divisions and a light cavalry brigade, plus an attached dragoon brigade. The British estimated that this force consisted of 22,000 infantry and 2,500 cavalry.

Due to the restricted terrain, Ney decided to attack on a very narrow front with only one infantry division and a cavalry brigade. The rest of the force would be held in support. The Côa river runs through a steep gorge, the western slope of which is steeper and some 100m higher than the eastern side. The river bed is very rocky with large boulders. The river flows quickly through the gorge and its width is no more than 10m. For much of the year it can be crossed on foot at several fords upstream. In the vicinity of the bridge, the river is a major obstacle that is impassable to formed troops and artillery. During the dry season it would not be much of an obstacle for light infantry, but heavy rains on the night of 23 July had turned the river into a raging torrent for several days, which made it impassable except at the bridge.

The French attacked at dawn on 24 July and the division's outposts were overrun after intense fighting. Craufurd rode forward to assess the situation and realized that his decision to stay on the east bank of the river in support of Almeida might result in the destruction of his forces. Their only route to safety was across a narrow bridge over an otherwise impassable river. Throughout the day there was desperate fighting and the Light Division nearly suffered a serious reverse when a large number of men were almost captured on the wrong side of the Côa, with only a single bridge for them to retreat across. The French then assaulted the bridge but were rebuffed, taking heavy casualties. They failed to capture the bridge and about 4pm the assault was halted. The Light Division suffered 316 casualties.

One major change came out of the fight on the Côa. Wellington finally realized that the Light Division was too large for one man to command without any subordinate command structure. In July Craufurd was trying to control five infantry battalions, three cavalry regiments and a horse artillery troop. He needed a brigade structure within his division, and so on 4 August 1810 Wellington issued a General Order creating one. Its new structure would comprise two infantry brigades, each commanded by the senior battalion commander: Lieutenant Colonels Thomas Beckwith of the 95th Foot and Robert Barclay of the 52nd Foot. Each brigade would consist of one British infantry battalion, one Portuguese caçadore battalion and four companies of the 1st Battalion 95th Rifles.[21]

Wellington's intention was to give the Light Division some well deserved rest. Most of its outpost duties were assumed by his cavalry, with the Light Division in support. On 26 July the French crossed the Côa river and on 15 August they opened the siege of Almeida, which surrendered on 27 August. Wellington knew that the time had now come to withdraw deep into Portugal. The Light Division was ordered to take the main road to Coimbra. Leaving Baraçal on 28 August, the division arrived at Busaço on 25 September. The next action for the division would be the Battle of Busaço on 26–27 September. There the division was involved in the fighting and assisted in the repulse and defeat of the French attacks. The division suffered a total of 177 casualties. Lieutenant Colonel Robert Barclay was slightly wounded just below the right knee and in the foot.

On 28 September it was confirmed that the French Army was marching to try to turn the Allies' left. The time to withdraw had come. Orders were sent out and once again the Light Division was instructed to cover the retreat with the cavalry. They fell back to Coimbra and from there continued withdrawing southward to Lisbon. After marching 250km in 13 days, they reached their destination: the Lines of Torres Vedras. The Light Division took up positions in the centre of the Lines between Sobral and Arruda. During the first few weeks in the Lines the Light Division had occasional contact with French patrols and foragers, but by late October most contact had petered out because the farms and houses in the area had already been thoroughly picked clean.

During the retreat Lieutenant Colonel Barclay's light wound had not healed and by the time the Light Division reached the Lines of Torres Vedras it was badly infected and he was forced to return to England in mid-October to recover. Barclay's brigade needed a new commander. The only possible candidate within the division was Charles McLeod, who had been promoted to lieutenant colonel on 16 August, but he was too junior to be given command of a brigade.[22] Wellington knew that he had got away with giving the brigades to lieutenant colonels in August, but several colonels had arrived in the Peninsula since then. On 14 November Brevet Colonel James Wynch was appointed the commander of Barclay's brigade.

Once within the Lines of Torres Vedras, Craufurd wrote to Wellington about expanding the Light Division. But again Wellington was faced with the problem that Craufurd was only a brigadier general, and there were seven major generals either on the staff or commanding brigades. Each of them had a valid claim to the command of the Light Division, by right of seniority. Wellington wrote to Craufurd on 23 October: 'I should be happy to make your division stronger, and I have had in contemplation various modes of effecting that object; but you must see the difficulty which is created by the arrival of General Officers, of rank superior to yours. However, I hope that I shall be able, in some manner, to increase your force.'[23]

Wellington did not forget his promise and on 12 November wrote again to General Craufurd to offer him the Brunswick Oëls Battalion, which was assigned to Wynch's Brigade.[24]

On the morning of 15 November word reached Wellington that the French Army before the Lines had withdrawn to Santarém. The Light Division moved north through the Lines and marched to Alemquer. They were up well before dawn and on the road in pursuit of the French. On the far side of Azambuja, they ran into a French piquet, which quickly retreated. After marching about 13km they came across a small French force on a ridge outside Cartaxo, consisting of three infantry battalions and a regiment of cavalry. Craufurd was planning to attack them when Wellington appeared and stopped him, because he did not know what was on the other side of the ridge. His caution was justified, because it turned out the ridge concealed the rest of a French corps. Wellington decided to force the French from their position and planned a concerted attack with the 1st and Light Divisions, and General Pack's Portuguese brigade. However, the attack was then cancelled because Wellington did not want to risk a battle that would cause heavy casualties. He knew that the scarcity of supplies in the area would eventually force the French to retreat.

In November Lieutenant Colonel Beckwith was incapacitated with a fever. Further compounding the chain-of-command problems, Colonel Wynch came down with typhus in late December and was thought not likely to survive. Craufurd himself was exhausted, both physically and mentally. More than anything he wanted to go home, and on 8 December he sent a letter to Wellington requesting permission to return to England to see his wife. But Wellington warned him that if he insisted on going, he might lose his command: owing to the 'number of General Officers senior to you in the army, it has not been an easy task to keep you in your command; and if you should go, I fear that I should not be able to appoint you to it again, or to one that would be so agreeable to you, or in which you could be so useful'.[25] Craufurd decided to stay.

By the end of December the Light Division's chain of command was a shambles. Its senior leadership had been decimated by death, injury and sickness. In addition to Craufurd, who did not want to be there, both brigade commanders were too sick to command, and had been replaced by the senior lieutenant colonels in their brigades. Of the division's battalions, only the 43rd Foot was still commanded by its lieutenant colonel. Fortunately for the division, both armies now went into winter quarters. With no operations likely in the foreseeable future, there would be time in the coming weeks for the Light Division to sort out its command problems.

Chapter 2

JANUARY AND FEBRUARY 1811

At the beginning of January 1811 the Light Division was located along the Rio Maior about 80km northeast of Lisbon. On the other side of the river, in the town of Santarém, was the French Army. Once again the division was manning outposts and screening Wellington's Army from the French. When not in the outposts, the men lived in cantonments about 8km from the Rio Maior near Vale de Santarém. Its organization was as shown in Table 2.1.

Table 2.1 Organization of the Light Division, 1 January 1811

Division HQ	Brigadier General Robert Craufurd	Commander
	Captain William Campbell 23rd Foot	ADC
	Lieutenant John Bell 52nd Foot	DAQMG
	Charles Purcell	ACG
1st Brigade	Lieutenant Colonel George Elder	Acting Commander
	Lieutenant Harry Smith 95th Rifles	Unofficial ADC
	Lieutenant James Stewart 95th Rifles	Brigade Major
1st Bn 43rd Foot	Lieutenant Colonel Charles McLeod	Commander
Right Wing 1st Bn 95th Rifles	Major Dugald Gilmour	Commander
Company 2nd Bn 95th Rifles	Captain Charles Beckwith	Commander
3rd Caçadores Bn	Major Manuel Pinto da Silveira	Commander

(Continued)

11

2nd Brigade	Lieutenant Colonel John Ross	Acting Commander
	Captain Charles Rowan 52nd Foot	Brigade Major
1st Bn 52nd Foot	Major Henry Ridewood	Commander
Left Wing 1st Bn 95th Rifles	Major John Stewart	Commander
1st Caçadores Bn	Lieutenant Colonel Jorge Avilez	Commander
Brunswick Oëls Regiment	Major Frederick von Hertzberg	Commander

The previous year had seen almost 12 months of continuous operations and the division was seriously understrength owing to casualties, sickness and exhaustion. Surprisingly, however, two of the three British battalions, which were authorized at 1,010 other ranks (that is, corporals and privates), were almost at full strength. In January 1811 the 43rd Foot was at 95 per cent of its authorized strength, the 52nd Foot at 96 per cent, while the 95th Rifles[26] was at 88 per cent. The Portuguese caçadores had an authorized strength of 564 other ranks. Both caçadore battalions were at 97 per cent of their authorized strength. However, this was the strength 'on the books'. When the men laid up in either the regimental or army level hospitals are factored in, the actual number of men available to fight was significantly less (see Table 2.2).

Table 2.2 Light Division Other Ranks Sick, January–February 1811

	January				February			
Unit	Strength	Sick	% Sick	Effectives	Strength	Sick	% Sick	Effectives
43rd Foot	958	153	16	805	950	130	14	820
52nd Foot	971	109	11	862	967	97	10	870
95th Rifles*	888	119	13	769	883	97	11	786
1st Caçadores	NA	NA	NA	NA	548	35	6	513
3rd Caçadores	NA	NA	NA	NA	552	55	10	497

Source: WO17/2466 and WO17/2467. We could not find the January numbers for the 1st and 3rd Caçadores Battalions.
* Includes the 1st Battalion and one company of the 2nd Battalion. This company, which had only been with the Light Division for a few months, had 25 per cent of its men reported sick.

The figures given in Table 2.2 only include those too sick to march with the battalion; they also do not include those individuals who were on command, i.e. detached from the units for duty elsewhere (see Table 2.3). Theoretically these men would be recalled to the colours when necessary, but often were not. We were not able to find accurate numbers for the Brunswick Oëls, because the monthly strength returns were for the whole regiment and did not differentiate between those companies assigned to the Light Division and those assigned to other divisions.

Table 2.3 Light Division on Command, January–February 1811

Unit	January Strength	On Command	February Strength	On Command
43rd Foot	958	24	850	29
52nd Foot	971	18	967	14
95th Rifles	888	16	883	12
1st Caçadores	NA	NA	627	28
3rd Caçadores	NA	NA	628	4

Sources: WO17/2466 and WO17/2467.

Those other ranks who were not sick, on command or absent for another reason were known as effectives. These were the men who would be available to fight (Table 2.4).

Table 2.4 Light Division Effectives, January–February 1811

Unit	January	February
43rd Foot	781	791
52nd Foot	971	856
95th Rifles	753	774
1st Caçadores	NA	470
3rd Caçadores	NA	481

Sources: WO17/2466 and WO17/2467.

Twelve months of campaigning had had a serious impact on the division's officers. Many of the company officers, including Captain Jonathan Leach and Lieutenant George Simmons, were so sick that they had to be evacuated to Lisbon to recover. And it was not just those on the front lines. Senior officers were especially hard hit. Colonel James Wynch, commander of the 2nd Brigade, died of typhus on 6 January. Lieutenant Colonel Thomas Beckwith, the 1st Brigade's commander, was sick in Lisbon and did not return to his command until 6 February.[27] Lieutenant Colonel Charles McLeod returned to England in January to recover his health. The senior officer in each brigade was temporarily given command, which left five of the division's six battalions commanded by a major. The only exception was the 1st Caçadores, commanded by Lieutenant Colonel Jorge Avilez. A replacement for Colonel Wynch was not appointed until 7 February, when Colonel George Drummond of the 24th Foot was given command.

Piquet Duty

During January and February the Light Division's mission was to serve as a screen for the army by manning outposts in the vicinity of Santarém. Private Thomas Garretty of the 43rd Foot described the terrain that the division covered:

> the light division, supported by a brigade of cavalry, occupied Valle, and the heights overlooking the marsh and inundation; the bridge at the end of the causeway was mined; a sugar-loaf shaped hill, looking straight down the approach, was crowned with embrasures for artillery, and laced in front with a zig-zag covered way, capable of containing five hundred infantry. Thus the causeway being blocked, the French could not, while the inundation was maintained, make any sudden irruption from Santarem.[28]

The piquets were set up to observe the two causeways that led to bridges over the Rio Maior, which was just south of a ridgeline occupied by the French. These bridges were about a kilometre apart, with the main road being on the left. The piquet duty rotated among the battalions and the duty battalion would set a company-size outlying piquet at each bridge and about a kilometre further away was a company-size inlying piquet which served as a ready reserve that would react to any incursion by the French. The companies were on duty for 24 hours. Captain Jonathan Leach, 95th Rifles, noted that on 'the bridge (which was mined and charged) we constructed an abattis; and to render our post at the causeway more secure, we made covert ways and traverses'.[29] Each morning the division would stand-to, where according to Lieutenant John Gurwood, 52nd Foot,

> every man, ... under arms at the time mentioned, two hours before daybreak; the guns are horsed, and baggage packed and loaded, all prepared for the battle or the march. The out-piquets are then relieved, so that the force may be double at all the outposts; the 'coming-off' piquet does not leave the ground until the Field Officer of the outlying piquet at the outpost reports 'All's well' – then the weary troops are turned in.[30]

Captain George Napier, 52nd Foot, left a detailed description of life on the outposts. He had orders regarding the blowing of the bridges:

> should the enemy attempt to force the passage to fire the mines and blow up the bridges, as everything was prepared for that purpose by the engineers. My company was posted at the lower one on the right, which was not that over which the great road passed, but there was a private road which led through the marsh to the enemy's position. One night, between twelve and one o'clock, I was visiting my sentinels and post in order to be sure all was quiet before I lay down to sleep, when suddenly I heard a shot, then another, and the noise of men as if coming down on our post. It was so pitch dark I could see nothing, and I was just going to blow up the bridge when I thought I would first venture a little way beyond on the enemy's side and listen if I could hear the noise of men marching, and be quite satisfied before I set fire to the mine. My company was drawn up in three minutes across our end of the bridge and I went over to the other side with two or three men, and placing our ears to the ground we listened attentively for a few minutes, when I felt assured there was no enemy approaching; and therefore bringing up an officer and ten men, I ordered him to remain there, and if the enemy should advance upon him to fire and instantly retreat as hard as he and his men could run across the bridge, as I should be ready the instant he passed to blow it up.[31]

Fraternization with the French

It was fairly common to see the enemy's piquets because 'the sentries of the two armies were so near each other on the bridge, and the videttes of the cavalry so closely advanced on the marsh on the right, that they might have conversed without exalting their voices much'.[32] Although fraternization with the French piquets was forbidden, it nevertheless occurred frequently. Rifleman Edward Costello wrote:

All this time, and for a great-part of that in which we were quartered here, a very friendly intercourse was carried on between the French and ourselves. We frequently met them bathing in the Rio Mayor, and would as often have swimming and even jumping matches. In these games, however, we mostly beat them, but that was attributed perhaps, to their half starved distressed condition. This our stolen intercourses soon made us more awake to until at length, touched with pity, our men went so far as to share with them the ration biscuits, which we were regularly supplied with from England, by our shipping; indeed we buried all national hostility in our anxiety to assist and relieve them. Tobacco was in great request; we used to carry some of ours to them, while they in return would bring us a little brandy. Their réveille was our summons as well as theirs, and although our old captain[33] seldom troubled us to fall in at the 'réveille', it was not unusual to find the rear of our army under arms, and, perhaps, expecting an attack. But the captain knew his customers, for though playful as lambs, we were watchful as leopards.[34]

Officers usually turned a blind eye to these activities. Lieutenant Gurwood remembered that

there existed not a little cordiality. On one occasion, for example, a sentry of the 52nd, being posted within a few yards of a French sentry, made his enemy understand, in a sort of Spanish gibberish, that he was very much in want of tobacco. The Frenchman, with national politeness, offered to supply his wants, if he would give him the money to buy some in the rear of his post; the five-frank piece was forked out, but, before given, it was necessary to have a guarantee for the fulfilment of this treaty, when the French man was about to leave his firelock in pledge; but here another difficulty took place: the French sentry said, 'But who is to keep my post?' The Englishman to this immediately answered, 'Oh! never mind that; I am the only one opposed to you, and I will keep your post until your return.' This assurance was perfectly satisfactory: but an hour passed away and the French man did not return: and it afterwards appeared that the vivandiere who sold the tobacco also had a bottle of brandy, and the change of the five-franc piece offered too great a temptation to resist, – the honor of the Frenchman got drowned in eau de vie,[35] and he was discovered dead drunk by his piquet. He was of course asked where his firelock was, or who had got it. His answer was thought hardly possible; but, on a communication between the Officers commanding the opposing piquets, the preliminaries of the amicable treaty were duly exchanged and ratified by a present of the tobacco.[36]

Officers also fraternized, but probably not as blatantly as the other ranks. According to Captain Leach,

> In these pastimes the French cavalry pickets, posted on the marsh, never interfered with us, nor interrupted our sport, although we frequently coursed hares, and shot quails, within half range of their carbines. On the contrary, their conduct was courteous, and, if I may use the expression, gentlemanly to a degree. One anecdote in particular deserves being mentioned. It was customary for our cavalry pickets to patrole every morning before daybreak, to ascertain if any change or movement had taken place in the French chain of cavalry posts. One morning, in a thick fog, a small patrole of ours suddenly found themselves close to a superior force of French cavalry, and instantly retired; but, in the hurry, one of our dragoons dropped his cloak. Our patrole had ridden but a short distance to the rear, when it was called to by the French, one of whom riding up to within a short distance, dropped the captured cloak on the ground and rode away, making signals to the English dragoon who had lost it, to pick it up. This was carrying on the war as it should be; and it is but justice to add, that we rarely found them deficient on this point.[37]

When not on piquet, life was good. The duty was not strenuous and quarters for the officers and men were comfortable compared to the previous year. The other ranks were billeted in whatever sheds, barns or buildings were available, while the officers had more comfortable billets. The quarters of Ensign William Hay, 52nd Foot, were in

> a sort of large farmyard surrounded by a low wall. A few houses which had been cleared of all furniture – even doors and windows taken from their frames – were allotted to the officers, the men being in a field in front. My bed was half an old window-shutter but on which I enjoyed most sound sleep, though my only covering was a camlet[38] boat-cloak; my clothes were never off my back, or my shoes off my feet any night during that winter.[39]

Lieutenant Kinloch had a few complaints and said that although they had made themselves 'as comfortable as the times will admit. . . . The only thing that annoys us is that from the vicinity of the army to Lisbon, all the necessaries of life are risen to a most extravagant pitch.'[40]

There was a shortage of firewood and the soldiers took to cutting down olive and fruit trees. Wellington noticed this and in a general order forbade the practice. A substitute had to be found, and Ensign Hay was astonished 'to see the camp-fires lighted up by the help of costly furniture, – the parties from each company sent to find fuel to cook the rations and dry the clothing, arms, etc. returning bearing chairs, tables, and all kinds of valuable articles which were broken up and used as if they were so much rotten wood'.[41]

Off-Duty Activities

A fortunate few were allowed to take leave in Lisbon, where they enjoyed, among other things, the luxury of being able to take off their clothes and sleep in a real bed. For those officers who remained on duty near Santarém there was a wide range of activities for entertainment. Horseracing was popular, and although exciting, it did not quite come up to the standards in England:

> six or eight half-starved devils, whose diet had for some months consisted principally of chopped straw and winter-grass, started, with *gentlemen riders*, for a sweepstakes. Before they had gone one hundred yards, the horse which was ridden by my friend T. of the 43rd regiment, came down heels over head, from sheer debility; and those in his wake, according to the nautical phrase, ran foul of him and his racer, who lay floundering on the earth. A greater burlesque on horse-racing never was witnessed: were I certain of seeing so amusing an exhibition at Newmarket, Epsom, or Doncaster, I verily believe I should seldom fail to attend their meetings.[42]

Many officers hunted in the marshes of the Rio Maior, where they found an abundance of birds such as golden plover, quail and snipe. Some had managed to bring over their hunting dogs and greyhounds and went coursing for hares.[43]

For the more intellectual, it was quickly noticed that the French put on musical performances on the heights above the outposts. Lieutenant Gurwood remembered that the

> first hint of day in all this stillness of darkness, when every ear was on the stretch, was the music of the French regiments relieving their outpost. They generally struck up at two hours before the first dawn of light was visible on the horizon, and almost always remained until day-break, playing those stirring airs for which French martial music is so justly celebrated; and although the causeway piquet was not sought after like an opera box, yet in fine weather it often became the favorite lounge for those Officers of the light division who were fond of music, and even to others, the time and place giving to this matin concert an interest which will never be forgotten by those who heard it.[44]

Amateur theatricals were also engaged in and the 95th Rifles had their own theatre,

> having converted an old house, in which olive oil had formerly been made, into a theatre: the blankets and great-coats of the soldiers made capital side-scenes; and had not too much wine and grog found their way behind them, no doubt the piece would have gone off with great éclat. But, as the truth must be told, they all forgot their parts; and it was a toss-up whether our attempt at horse-racing or play-acting was the most perfectly ludicrous.[45]

The other ranks' pursuits were less elaborate. There was not much to do in their free time and, as with all armies since the first was formed in ancient times, bored soldiers got into mischief. Rifleman Costello and his messmates set up a still using raisins, but it was discovered by his company commander and destroyed. At times there were incidents between the soldiers of the various regiments in the division. One day Costello

> crossed the hills to purchase some necessaries at the quarters of the 52nd Regiment, and on my return fell in with several of the soldiers of the 3rd Caçadores; one of them, a fierce looking scoundrel, evinced a great inclination to quarrel, the more particularly as he perceived that I was unarmed and alone. Having replied rather sharply to some abuse they had cast upon the English, by reflecting on their countrymen in return, he flew into a rage, drew his bayonet, and made a rush at me, which I avoided by stepping aside, and tripping him head foremost on the ground; I was in the act of seizing his bayonet, when a number of his comrades came up, to whom he related, in exaggerated terms, the cause of our disagreement. Before he had half concluded, a general cry arose of 'Kill the English dog', and the whole drawing their bayonets, were advancing upon me when a party of the 52nd came up, the tables were turned, and the Caçadores fled in all directions.[46]

Rumours

Rumours abounded. One of the most popular was that the Light Division would be relieved from their duties and rotated 'to the rear [so] that the soldiers might have some rest & respite from the outpost duty'.[47] Others concerned the French Army: 'Every day brought some rumour as to the intended movements of our adversaries, not one in fifty of which proved correct; for instance, "Massena would be reinforced immediately with thirty or forty thousand men from a distant part of Spain, and would instantly make a grand attack on our lines".' Two days afterwards, 'Massena and his legions were off in a canter out of Portugal.'[48]

Problems with the Brunswick Oëls

The Brunswick Oëls were assigned to the Light Division's 2nd Brigade on 12 November 1810 but they were not readily accepted by the officers and men of the division. They quickly became known as the 'Death and glory men' because of the skull and cross-bones badges that they wore on their shakos. The Oëls were mostly Germans, but a considerable number of them were former French soldiers who had been captured by the Spanish at Bailén in 1808, when General Dupont surrendered his army. Many of them were placed in prison hulks in Cadiz under horrific conditions. When recruiters offered them a chance to escape the death trap of the hulks by enlisting in the Brunswick Oëls, many took the opportunity to do so. It was unlikely that they had any loyalty to their new regiment, nor did they embrace the culture of the Light Division.

Wellington had a very low opinion of the Oëls almost from the time they arrived in Portugal. He wrote to Lord Liverpool, the Secretary of War, on 4 January:

> I wish to draw your Lordship's attention to the Brunswick Legion. This corps is composed generally of deserters from the French and other armies. The men are either very old or very young; and they are very sickly, infinitely more so than any of our Walcheren battalions. They are very irregular in their discipline and habits, and they desert to the enemy terribly. No fewer than six went from that corps yesterday. The officers are Germans, who have no experience of service (the Lieut.-Colonel, who is dead, may have had), but who have all the vanity of a great deal; they have no knowledge of the English language and customs; and upon the whole it would be very desirable that they and their men should pass a short time in Gibraltar or some other garrison before they should be brought into the field with an English army. I am not very fastidious about troops; I have them of all sorts, sizes, and nations: but Germans in our army in the Peninsula pass for Englishmen; and it is really not creditable to be supposed to be a soldier of the same nation with one of these people. I believe there is not an officer in the army who would not prefer to have under his command a Portuguese battalion of Caçadores.[49]

It was not long before the Brunswickers began to clash with men from the other regiments. Rifleman Costello of the 1st Battalion noted:

Among other attributes with which these allies were gifted, was a canine appetite, that induced them to kill and eat all the dogs they could privately lay hold of. By this means the different dogs of the division disappeared before the Germans with celerity truly astonishing, and we were in ignorance of their fate until the fact became openly proclaimed and acknowledged. Among other animals thus 'potted for consumption' was a dog which, from its having attached itself to our regiment, we had christened 'Rifle'. Rifle could never be induced to leave us, and upon one or two occasions when we had lost it, had always managed to rejoin us again. We used often to joke among ourselves at Rifle's antipathy to a red coat, and his decided preference to green; but although, poor fellow, he had survived many of our skirmishes, in which he used to run about barking and expressing his delight as much as a dog could, it was only, after all, to be devoured by the insatiable jaws of the Brunswickers.[50]

While this might be overlooked, the Oëls also quickly developed the reputation that they could not be trusted to perform piquet duty because of the likelihood of their deserting to their former comrades. Captain John Duffy, a company commander in the 43rd Foot, wrote in his diary on 19 January that: 'On piquet at the causeway 14 of the Brunswick Corps attempted to desert yesterday. 13 were taken, another wandered off from my piquet this evening. The men of this regiment have deserted in numbers since being attached to the division.'[51] These attempts were happening on a regular basis. Captain George Napier of the 52nd Foot was on piquet duty one night, when

> a sergeant came to tell me that the Brunswick Oels Corps . . . was deserting, and that I was to fire upon them and take as many prisoners as I could. I therefore sent some of my men on one side and some on the other, and we soon found these poor fellows swimming across. We were obliged to fire at some of them who had got over and were getting off to the enemy, and a great number were killed. However, as soon as daylight came, the greatest part were taken, and the rest returned to their quarters.[52]

These deserters caused problems for the men on piquet, especially when it came to officers. Corporal Patrick Fleming was in charge of an outlying piquet when he

> came in collision with one of the Brunswick officers, and suspecting his intentions to bolt to the enemy, knocked him down with his rifle, and otherwise maltreated him. The result was that Fleming was tried by a Brigade Court-martial, convicted for the assault, sentenced to

be reduced to the ranks, and to receive a corporal punishment of five hundred lashes.[53] This put us all on the alert, and the officers also, by whom he was very much liked. The division being formed, by order of General Crauford, the prisoner was brought to the centre of the square, and the minutes of the Courtmartial read aloud, Fleming proceeded to strip while the men stood attentively yet sullenly awaiting the result. The General now addressed him, saying,

'Prisoner Fleming, the offence which you have been guilty of, is of so heinous a nature, that could it be proved to be wilfully committed: it would be most unpardonable; but the excellent character for gallantry and honourable conduct, given of you by your officers, is such that I take the responsibility on myself, relying on the plea made by you, I shall not flog you, therefore, but your stripes will be cut off, and I trust your future conduct will testify that the discretion I now use, is not misplaced; and I here', proceeded the General, turning round to the division, 'take the opportunity of declaring, that if any of those gentlemen', (meaning the Brunswickers), 'have a wish to go over to the enemy, let them express it, and I give my word of honour, I will grant them a pass to that effect instantly, for we are better without such.'[54]

Wellington, frustrated by the desertions, wrote to Lord Liverpool on 19 January:

I am sorry to give you bad accounts of the Brunswick Legion. They continue to desert in large numbers; and on the night before last 14 deserted to go to the enemy; 11 were caught, one was shot while making the attempt, and only 2 got off. These were the men who had only joined the army 2 days before.[55]

Hoping to deter future desertions, Wellington initially took a light hand and on 11 (actually the 19th) January Privates J. Barnes [John Barens], C. Friefs [Gaspar Friess], W. Henricks [William Henrich], J. [Jacob] Knies, Contado Raffinetti and Jonathan Schneider were convicted of being 'concerned in a conspiracy to desert' and were sentenced to receive 200 lashes. Wellington was lenient and pardoned the prisoners 'in hopes that the example which will have been made of the others will deter soldiers from attempting to desert from their colours'.[56]

But leniency did not stem the flow of deserters, and on 17 January Private A. Husse was tried and executed by a firing squad. Also on 17 January a general court-martial was held in Cartaxo for Privates F. Gettmann [Frederick Getterman], Jonathan Lange [John Lange], F. Lieventhal [Francis Liebental] and William Mountz [William Morentye]. All were found guilty of 'quitting their quarters' and were sentenced to be shot.[57] After an incident of mass desertion on 18 January, Wellington showed no mercy. Their execution took place on 23 January.[58] Captain George Napier described the event:

> When led out for execution they requested not to be tied to the stakes, and one of them, who had been a 'sous-officier' in his own service, addressed his comrades who were drawn up to witness the execution, saying 'I know that by the laws of the service I am now in I deserve death, because desertion to the enemy is so punished in the English army; but I have been brought up in different notions, therefore it is no moral crime upon my part, who am not an Englishman but a German (Alsace). I have no fear of death, and am prepared to enter the presence of my Maker, being unconscious of having offended Him. I was compelled to enter the British service in order to escape the cruelty of the Spaniards, who had unlawfully kept me a prisoner contrary to the capitulation, and can it be wondered at, or can it be considered a crime that, when opposite my own countrymen and in daily sight of my old comrades, I should try to join them and once more fight under the colours of France? No, comrades! You who know me will consider me guiltless, and, like me, glory in death! When the English bullets have penetrated my breast, dip my handkerchief in my blood and distribute it among you as a relic of my devotion to France.' He then knelt down with the others in front of his grave, which in a military execution is always dug ready to receive the body of the culprit, and on the word being given to the party to fire, he and his unfortunate companions fell, but not dead (which sometimes happens, though very rarely), and he rose again and would have addressed the soldiers, had not a fresh party instantly stepped close up to these poor fellows and put a period to their existence by blowing out their brains. This fine fellow, for such he undoubtedly was, spoke in German, being an Alsacian, so that I may not have stated exactly all he said or the precise words he used, as the officer who told me, although he understood German, was not sufficiently master of the language to give a perfectly correct translation of the speech, but he said that as near as he could make out at the distance he was from him the above was the purport of it. When he was dead those whom he addressed ran forward and tearing off the handkerchiefs with which the poor victim's eyes had been bound, pressed them to the wounds, and when all wet with the blood of their dead comrade, tore them in pieces and distributed them among one another.[59]

Wellington had had enough and the Brunswick Oëls were sent far to the rear. On 6 March 1811 they were reassigned to the 7th Division.[60] Their punishment might be considered harsh by twenty-first-century standards, but it was effective. In January 1811 the regiment had thirty-six men successfully desert. In February there was just one.

General Craufurd Returns to Great Britain

General Craufurd was exhausted, both physically and mentally. At least one historian believes he was depressed.[61] On 24 January Craufurd again requested to return home, specifically on the next packet sailing for England. Wellington responded the next day, granting his permission, but also implied that Craufurd was abandoning the army, remarking 'I will just observe to you, however, that 7 Generals have gone, or are going, home from this army, and that there is not now one remaining in it, who came out with the army, excepting Gen. Alex. Campbell, who has been in England.'[62] Craufurd did not care and on 27 January wrote once again to Wellington, who replied the next day:

> I have received your letter of the 27th, and I see no reason why I should depart from the rule which I have laid down for myself in these cases. Officers (General officers in particular) are the best judges of their own private concern that cannot be settled by instruction and power of attorney, and that after all is not settled in this manner, I cannot refuse leave of absence to those who come to say that their business is of a nature that requires their personal superintendence. But entertaining these opinions, it is rather too much that I should not only give leave of absence, but approve of the absence of any, particularly a General officer, from the army.
>
> It is certainly the greatest inconvenience to the service that officers should absent themselves as they do, each of them requiring at the same time that when it shall be convenient to return he shall find himself in the same situation as when he left the army. In the meantime, who is to do the duty? How am I to be responsible for the army? Is Col. [Burgh Leighton][63] a proper substitute for Gen. Craufurd in the command of our advanced posts?
>
> I may be obliged to consent to the absence of an officer, but I cannot approve of it. I repeat that you know the situation of affairs as well as I do, and you have my leave to go to England if you think proper, as also Capt. Cotton.[64]

Although Wellington gave his permission for General Craufurd to return home, he did not guarantee him that he would still be in command of the Light Division when he returned. In any event, by early February Craufurd was on a ship heading to England. Colonel Drummond was left in temporary command of the division.

Chapter 3

IN PURSUIT OF THE WITHDRAWING FRENCH, 1–9 MARCH 1811

Overview of the French Situation

When Marshal André Masséna, the newly appointed commander of the French Army of Portugal, joined his army in May 1810, he had on paper about 130,000 men available for the invasion. His army consisted of three infantry corps, plus supporting cavalry and artillery.[65] Although this force appeared formidable, in fact large numbers of his troops were either detached on garrison duty to secure his lines of supply or were too sick to march. The actual number of effectives was closer to 85,000 men. Over the next three months Masséna had to conduct the sieges of the fortresses of Ciudad Rodrigo and Almeida. The latter had fallen on 28 August, and Masséna began preparing to move on Lisbon. Due to the need to garrison the two fortresses, and to casualties suffered during the sieges, the troops now available to him numbered about 65,000 men.[66]

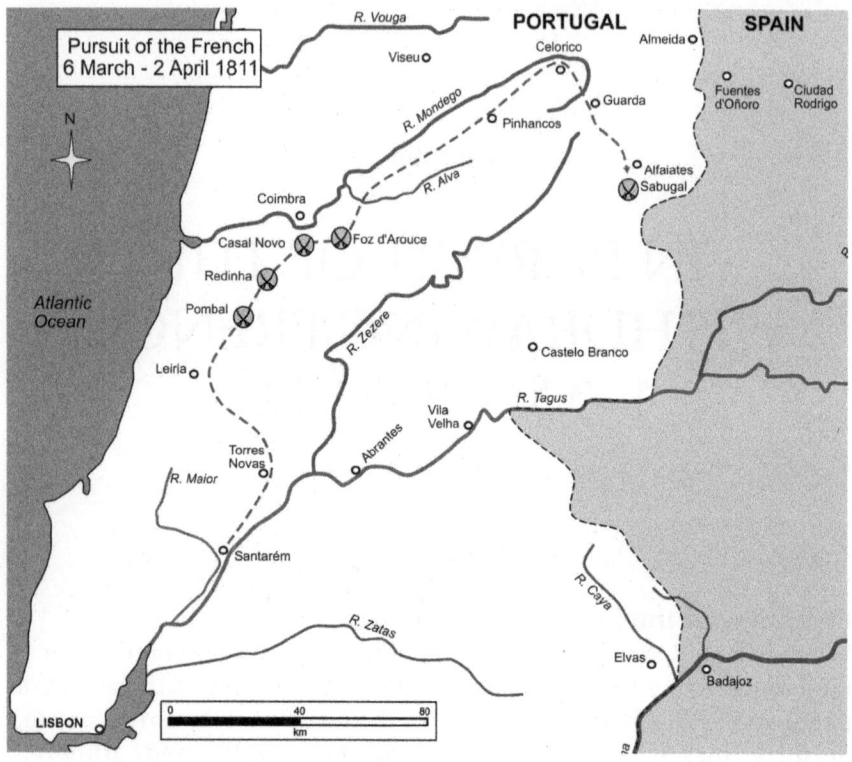

Wellington's Army conducted a fighting withdrawal from the Portuguese-Spanish border and fought Masséna at Busaco on 27 September. Afterwards, Wellington continued to withdraw and by 10 October his army was behind the Lines of Torres Vedras. One of the reasons for this retreat was that Wellington felt his army was not strong enough to defeat Masséna in a pitched battle, except under the most favourable conditions. Instead, his plan was to make it impossible for the French to live off the land by conducting a scorched earth operation. As his army retreated, therefore, they burned the crops, drove off the livestock and destroyed the mills to prevent the French from grinding any grain they found into flour for bread. The deeper the French drove into Portugal, the worse their supply situation would become, until eventually Masséna would have to retreat back to Spain or see his men starve.

When Masséna arrived before Lisbon he was shocked by what he found. His aide-de-camp, Chef-de-Bataillon Jean Pelet, described in his journal the sight that met them:

The English Lines, enveloping twenty or twenty-four thousand yards, barred the terrain between the Tagus and the sea. The right extended from Alhandra; the centre was at Monte Agraço, or mountain of Grace, facing Sobral; and the left reached through Torres Vedras to the sea. There was a very narrow defile in front of Sobral and beyond the mountain rose up again suddenly like a gigantic wall of rocks extending on both flanks; it was this formidable barrier that the English had crowned with works. On both sides of the passage two deep valleys full of ravines opened out and extended all the way to the sea and the Tagus. They served as the first obstacle of the primary defence line and as a kind of ditch at this line. These were the valleys where the rivers of Arruda and Torres Vedras flowed. Thus the terrain we occupied was joined at only one point to the range of mountains not covered by rocks or absolutely inaccessible, all the avenues, and all of the small detached abutments useful for observation or flanking the base and slopes, had been carefully entrenched to form their first line. One could find every type of field fortification among the thirty-two works. The works were armed with 141 pieces in position, manned by 10,040 Portuguese troops; and they were surrounded by with unattached militia and a multitude of ordenanza. Finally the first line was defended more particularly by the English army.[67]

Masséna maintained his army outside Lisbon until early November, when he finally accepted that he was not strong enough to take the Portuguese capital. Compounding his problems was the fact that his army had quickly depleted any food and forage that could be found in its vicinity. He decided to withdraw to Santarém, 80km to the north, where he hoped to find more plentiful supplies to feed his army. Foraging was better there than it had been near Lisbon, but he soon had trouble feeding his army. Furthermore, his lines of communication back to the Spanish border, now over 300km long, had been cut soon after he moved into Portugal so there was no hope of receiving supplies from Spain. In late December General Jean Drouet, commander of the 9th Corps, arrived with General Nicolas Conroux's Division, some 8,000 strong. These reinforcements were much needed and replaced some of the losses incurred over the previous months. However, there were not enough of them to significantly change the balance of power. More importantly, they were more mouths to feed from a rapidly dwindling food supply.[68]

By 1 January 1811 Masséna's army was down to 55,000 men and by the beginning of March he had fewer than 50,000 men able to fight.[69] With no choice but to withdraw to Spain, he had two options: the first was to cross the Tagus river and link up with Marshal Jean Soult's Army of the South in southern Spain; the second was to pull back to Spain over the route he had taken six months before. He chose the latter and in late February plans were made for the retreat.

Organization and Strength of the Light Division on 1 March

Three months of relative inactivity had done much to restore the health of the Light Division's officers. All the battalion and brigade commanders were present, but General Craufurd was still in England. Colonel Drummond, the 2nd Brigade commander, was temporarily serving as the division commander. Drummond had commanded the 24th Foot at Talavera in 1809, where he was severely wounded. He returned home to recover but was back in Portugal by early February 1811. Drummond was an unusual choice for Wellington. Prior to the Talavera campaign, he had no combat experience and had never commanded light troops. It was likely that Wellington had no other senior officers to appoint as brigade commander.[70] Whether Drummond was up to the task of commanding a division was yet to be seen, but his promotion impacted the 2nd Brigade. Its senior lieutenant colonel, John Ross of the 52nd Foot, had not joined the division until late December 1810. Ross had commanded the 2nd Battalion, 52nd Foot, at Vimiera and during the Corunna campaign, but he too was an unknown factor. While Ross commanded the 2nd Brigade, Major Henry Ridewood became the acting commander of the 52nd Foot. Ridewood had been with the battalion since it arrived in the Peninsula in July 1809 and fought with it in all its actions, and temporarily commanded it from November to December 1810.

Although the Brunswick Oëls had been sent to the rear in early February to prevent further desertions, they were still assigned to the Light Division. On 5 March, however, they were removed from the Light Division and reassigned to the 7th Division.[71] Word had been received from England that the 2nd Battalion, 52nd Foot, was en route. Reaching Lisbon on 5 March, it was assigned to the Light Division that same day,[72] but had arrived too late to participate in the pursuit of the French. This battalion would be a much-welcomed replacement for the Brunswick Oëls (see Table 3.1).

IN PURSUIT OF THE WITHDRAWING FRENCH, 1–9 MARCH 1811

Table 3.1 Organization of the Light Division, 5 March 1811

Division HQ	Colonel George Drummond	Acting Commander
	Captain William Campbell, 23rd Foot	ADC
	Lieutenant John Bell, 52nd Foot	DAQMG
	Charles Purcell	ACG
1st Brigade	Lieutenant Colonel Thomas Beckwith	Commander
	Lieutenant Harry Smith, 95th Rifles	Unofficial ADC
	Lieutenant James Stewart, 95th Rifles	Brigade Major
1st Bn, 43rd Foot	Major Christopher Patrickson	Commander
Right Wing, 1st Bn, 95th Rifles	Major Dugald Gilmour	Commander
Company, 2nd Bn, 95th Rifles	Captain Charles Beckwith	Commander
3rd Caçadores Bn	Lieutenant Colonel George Elder	Commander
2nd Brigade	Lieutenant Colonel John Ross	Acting Commander
	Captain Charles Rowan, 52nd Foot	Brigade Major
1st Bn, 52nd Foot	Major Henry Ridewood	Commander
2nd Bn, 52nd Foot	Major Edward Gibbs	Commander
Left Wing, 1st Bn, 95th Rifles	Major John Stewart	Commander
1st Caçadores Battalion	Lieutenant Colonel Jorge Avilez	Commander

The slow pace of operations also helped to restore the health of the men in the division. By 1 March the division had about 4,000 officers and men available for operations (Table 3.2). Unlike the previous year, it had no Royal Horse Artillery troop nor any cavalry attached to it.

Table 3.2 Light Division Effectives, 1 March 1811

Unit	March
43rd Foot	736
52nd Foot	768
95th Rifles	720
1st Caçadores	448
3rd Caçadores	557

Sources: WO17/2467 and PT AHM-DIV-1-14-12-3 ms 33.

The Departure of the French

The orders to withdraw were given in late February and the French began their preparations. Their departure from the fortifications was set for the evening of 5 March. Despite their efforts to keep their plans secret, word had reach Wellington's lines that something was happening, at least in Santarém. Captain Duffy, 43rd Foot, wrote in his diary on 1 March that there were 'reports of the enemy's intending to retreat', and three days later that the enemy was sending his sick to the rear.[73] Lieutenant Simmons, 95th Rifles, stated in his diary on 4 March: 'Two deserters came over; they report that the enemy are burning everything that they cannot remove, such as gun-carriages, carts, etc.'[74] This fire continued to blaze throughout 5 March and it looked like Santarém was on fire.

Wellington's forces knew something was up, but the enemy fortifications prevented them from confirming the French had withdrawn. Duffy's company had piquet duty on the night of 5/6 March. He was notified at 4am that something was amiss in the French positions. Two of his sergeants had crossed the causeway, and 'found the sentry was still at his post, however, not observing him walking about they suspected he was asleep. Went up and found that it was a uniform *stuffed with straw* erect with a pole for a firelock.' Duffy sent word back to his HQ and took the initiative to advance with his company. They went through a gap in 'the enemy's abbatis [sic] and moving a strong stockade. Passed on with the picquets to Santarem, found another abbatis in the enemy's line of defence. The tops of every hill & rising ground marked with bushes where guns were formerly placed. Amazingly strong.'[75]

The Light Division was given orders shortly before sunrise[76] to advance into Santarém. Rifleman Costello was one of the first to reach the city after Duffy's company from the 43rd Foot:

Ours being the senior captain of the regiment, the company, as was usual, were [sic] in the advance, when some of the front files suddenly came within a few yards of what appeared to be a French sentinel, leaning against a wall that ran along from the bridge. One of our fellows fired, but perceiving no movement made, we all rushed up, and discovered *him* to be, what our moneychangers at home have so great a horror of, 'a man of straw', or a piece of sacking stuffed and accoutred. This afforded a fit theme for joking, as we carried our 'prisoner' with us until we came to Santarem.[77]

When he entered the city Costello saw that

the streets and houses presented a mass of desolation and filth, which, in some degree, contaminated the air around, while to add to the picture, numbers of half-starved looking Frenchmen were grouped about in knots, and exhibiting the loathsome appearance of disease ... I fell upon a small fountain, close to which lay two or three murdered Portuguese; their brains and blood, which seemed freshly to have oozed from their mangled remains, had even streamed into the spring, and turned me away with disgust from the water ... As I, however, approached into the plaza, the desolation thickened; all the havoc that can possibly be imagined in so small a compass lay before me – murdered and violated women – shrieking and dying children – and, indeed, all that had possessed life in the village, lay quivering in the last agony of slaughter and awful vengeance ...[78]

Captain Jonathan Leach, 95th Rifles, wrote that

In the march of the Light Brigade from Lisbon to Talavera in 1809, we halted two days at Santarem, at which time its appearance was altogether extremely prepossessing. How utterly changed was it now! The extensive and valuable olive-groves, which clothed the sides of the hill on which the town stands, had long since been cut down by the French to construct *abattis*, and for firewood. For this act no blame can be attached to them, as no one will deny their right to strengthen their position by whatever means were nearest at hand, nor to their making as good fires as they were able, to keep out cold and the devil from their winter-quarters. But what defence can possibly be set up for the wanton destruction of houses, furniture, churches, convents and, in short, of every place and every thing in and about this unfortunate town, and that, also, under the immediate eye of Massena and his numerous staff? Here and there a wretched, half-starved, cadaverous Portuguese, with an appearance scarcely human, who had contrived to drag on a miserable existence during the winter, might be seen amongst the ruined habitations, thereby completing the sickening picture.[79]

And the destruction was not just in the town. On the advance from Santarém Private Garretty and his messmates from the 43rd Foot took time to explore a large building near the road. There they found

> a number of famished wretches crowded together, for no other conceivable purpose but to die in company. Thirty women and children had perished for want of food, and lay dead upon the floor; while about half that number of survivors sat watching the remains of those who had fallen. Of those who thus perished the bodies were not much emaciated, but the muscles of the face were invariably drawn transversely, giving the appearance of a smile, and presenting the most ghastly sight imaginable. Most of the living were unable to move; and it had been by great exertion that they had crawled to a little distance from the group of death. The soldiers offered some refreshment to these unfortunate persons, but one man only had sufficient strength to eat. The women seemed patient and resigned, and even in this distress had arranged the bodies of those who first died with decency and care.[80]

The division stopped for the night in Pernes, about 15km north of Santarém. There Lieutenant John Kincaid, 95th Rifles, saw that the

> few wretched inhabitants who had been induced to remain in it under the faithless promises of the French generals, shewed fearful signs of a late visit from a barbarous and merciless foe. Young women were lying in their houses brutally violated, – the streets were strewed with broken furniture, intermixed with the putrid carcasses of murdered peasants, mules and donkeys, and every description of filth, that filled the air with pestilential nausea. The few starved male inhabitants who were stalking amid the wreck of their friends and property, looked like so many skeletons who had been permitted to leave their graves for the purpose of taking vengeance on their oppressors, and the mangled body of every Frenchman who was unfortunate or imprudent enough to stray from his column, shewed how religiously they performed their mission.[81]

Captain Duffy also found that similar acts of violence had occurred in Pernes:

> The inhabitants of this place had been cruelly used by the French, having the whole of their property plundered and not even the means of subsistence left. Found several dead peasants in the different out houses starved. Several sheds filled with miserable peasants lying unable to move from mere want.[82]

IN PURSUIT OF THE WITHDRAWING FRENCH, 1–9 MARCH 1811

What the officers and men of the Light Division found in Santarém and Pernes horrified them, and they would see the same atrocities in almost every village the retreating French moved through. Despite witnessing so much destruction and cruelty by the French, the Light Division showed surprising compassion to the wounded and sick French soldiers they came across and even took steps to prevent reprisals against them by peasants seeking revenge. Rifleman Costello again:

> The faces of many of these poor fellows were dreadfully swollen and white. Our men were moved to pity at the scene, and threw them biscuits as we passed through the town . . . At every mile the enemy on their retreat had fixed finger posts with directions to the road the 'grande armée' had taken [and] they sufficiently directed us also. But after all, these were of little service, for straggling groups of the unfortunate enemy strewed the road as we advanced over it. The poor fellows, at first, would greet the English with a faint hope of protection, and turned up their swollen and pallid countenances to us with expressions that needed not words to explain them . . . Proceeding onward, [we] observed a gaunt ghastly figure in a cloak stealing towards a group of cadaverous looking Frenchmen – on his getting a little nearer to them, he suddenly spat in his hands and throwing his cloak aside, produced a heavy club, with which, I suppose, he was going to beat their brains out. Struck with horror, I instantly seized the stick from his half-famished grasp, drove him away, and assisted by one or two comrades got the poor men into a house . . .[83]

Some of the officers wanted to know why the French behaved as they did. During the pursuit to the Spanish border Captain George Napier, 52nd Foot, had the opportunity to interrogate a captured French colonel, who justified the ill-treatment of the peasants by saying that the troops had had no choice: they could either take the food from the peasants or starve.

> A French officer who was made prisoner during this retreat, and to whom I had it in my power to be kind, told me that after a few weeks from their first arrival at the Lines an order was given by Massena that every captain must provide his men with provisions in the best manner he could, which was generally done as follows. A captain and his company went off into the country, and on coming to a peasant's hut or cabin he demanded provisions, upon which the miserable father and his wife and half-starving children went down on their knees supplicating the officer not to take the miserable pittance they had left for their sole support. But this had no effect, and the father was told that he should be hung up to a beam; and if he made a sign, that was agreed upon,

that he would show where all his provisions were concealed, he would be instantly cut down, but if not, there he would hang till dead. Well, the wretched man, looking at his starving wife and helpless children, would determine on dying rather than tell where the little he had for their existence was hid. He was hung up accordingly, when in a few seconds the natural love of life and the shrieks of his distracted wife and children overcame the resolution to die. He gives the signal, is cut down, recovers his senses, and points out, with despair depicted in his haggard countenance, the spot where all he has to keep life in his wife and children is deposited, and he sees the ruthless plunderers depart without sparing him one morsel. But is this all? No! In a few hours afterwards comes a fresh party of soldiers in search of provisions, and finds this unfortunate family nearly exhausted, but will give no credit to their story of what had already taken place some time before, but instantly resort to the same barbarous measure of hanging up the father, who again, urged by the hopes of preserving his life a few minutes longer, makes the preconcerted signal. But, alas! when cut down, not being able to produce what has already been the prey of former robbers, is seized by the merciless soldiers and either shot or hanged, with the certainty that his miserable wife and children must perish with hunger. The French officer who told me this said it had often happened to him to witness such scenes during the stay of Marshal Massena's army opposite our lines, and very fairly said, 'But what could we do? If we did not find the provisions we must have starved ourselves; and you know soldiers will not do that, nor anyone else if he can possibly avoid it by any means.'[84]

The Pursuit of the French

After moving through Santarém, the division continued up the road to Pernes. The 1st Brigade led the advance, with the 2nd Brigade following. At Pernes they found the bridge over the Alviela river had been blown up by the French and they were forced to stop. Captain Alexander Todd, Royal Staff Corps, was tasked with repairing it.[85] The bridge was repaired by the next morning and the 1st Brigade was on road again by 8am heading to Torres Novas, where the French Army's headquarters had been located. The division had no encounters with the enemy, but the route was 'strewed with dead animals and several men left dead on the roadside . . . the Enemy abandoned two guns that they could not get through the mud near this. In one place today passed 5 or 6 men, some not dead, supposed to have been sick, left to their fate.'[86] They passed through Torres Novas after a 25km march and continued another 12km to Lamarosa, where the 1st Brigade halted for the night. The 2nd Brigade stopped in Argea.

The next morning, 8 March, the men were assembled at daylight to continue the pursuit. However, the roads had deteriorated so badly because of the rain and heavy traffic that the division was strung out for many kilometres. The 1st Brigade waited for a few hours until the 2nd Brigade arrived. While the men were waiting, a small group of French soldiers was captured. Among them was Lieutenant Richard Burke of the 45th Foot, dressed in a French uniform. He had gone missing from his regiment on 23 February:

> [he] had deserted a few weeks previously, and was, at the time he was missing from his regiment, supposed to have been made prisoner by some accident... He had been made aide-de-camp to the French general of division Loisson. We very soon delivered him up to the provost marshal, to be taken to Lord Wellington, in hopes he would have had him shot upon the spot; but his lordship, having made inquiries about him from the officers of his regiment, was inclined to think the miserable man was not right in his senses, having formerly been insane.[87]

There was consensus in the 45th Foot that Lieutenant Burke was mentally ill. Instead of being court-martialled, he was sent back to England and became a patient in the Newport Asylum.[88]

After their late start, the Right Wing of the Rifles, under the command of Major Dugald Gilmour, took the lead and the division marched for 8km or so until they caught up with the French rearguard in the village of Paialvo. Although pressed by the British cavalry and an RHA troop of guns, the enemy took the time to destroy four ammunition waggons and some artillery limbers.[89] The division continued the pursuit and ended the night in a miserable village called Caxarias.[90]

The division was back on the road again at daybreak on 9 March, with Gilmour's four companies of rifles again in the lead. They marched for 5 hours on the main road to Pombal. As on the previous days, the road was littered with broken French waggons and the sick and lame. By the end of the day the division had captured forty stragglers. Upon cresting a line of high hills they saw the retreating French crossing the plains below. The division's old friends, the 1st KGL Hussars, soon engaged the elite company of the 11th French Dragoons in a sharp skirmish near the road to Leiria. Rumours abounded that the

> French had taken two Hussars two days before, and, it was believed, had coolly sabred them. The Germans were so incensed at the report that they were going to put some of these men to death, but were luckily prevented and persuaded to desist. One of the enemy was a

very handsome man and an Italian. He had a narrow escape, as he was upon his knees and the sword uplifted to slaughter him when Colonel Gilmore begged him off.[91]

While the cavalry was skirmishing with the rearguard, the 1st Brigade moved down from the high hills and advanced across the plain for 5km. Then Colonel Drummond decided that the French were too strong and ordered the 1st Brigade to retreat back to the hills. It had been a long day for the division, having marched and counter-marched almost 40km. They did not arrive in their positions in the hills until 10pm.[92]

A Change in Command

As mentioned earlier, General Craufurd had returned to England in early February and Colonel Drummond was in temporary command of the division. This was not a problem while the situation was static but now that active operations had begun, Wellington had to find a more senior commander for the division. He fully intended to have Craufurd assume command again when he returned, but he could not wait for him. As a brigadier general, Craufurd was in any case too junior to command a division, since this was a lieutenant general's position. If Wellington temporarily appointed a major general to command the division in Craufurd's absence, this would raise the question of why the general was not given permanent command since he was senior in rank.

On 9 March Wellington decided to attach the Light Division to the Advanced Guard commanded by Major General Sir William Erskine. In effect, Erskine was given operational control of it. Yet this only appeared in daily orders regarding the movement of the army as it pursued the French. Erskine was never officially appointed the division commander in General Orders. This solved the problem of having a more senior officer in overall command of the division, but allowed Wellington to maintain the illusion that Craufurd was still its commander, with Erskine only filling in until he returned.[93]

The appointment of William Erskine was an odd choice, since Wellington had grave doubts about him initially. On 29 August 1810 he wrote to Lieutenant Colonel Henry Torrens at the Horse Guards that 'I have received your letter announcing the appointment of General Erskine . . . to this army . . . [whom] I have generally understood to be a madman'.[94] Torrens replied on 19 September 1810:

> Sir W. Erskine is, no doubt, sometimes a little Mad! But in his lucid intervals he is an uncommonly clever fellow, and I trust he may have

IN PURSUIT OF THE WITHDRAWING FRENCH, 1–9 MARCH 1811

no fit during the Campaign – though by the bye, he looked a little wild a few days before he Embarked! Sir David has a high opinion of Sir Wm who served with Him in Germany, and he thinks some of our Generals would not be worse for a little of his madness![95]

Wellington was also concerned that Erskine had very poor eyesight. He wrote to Marshal Beresford in April that 'He is very blind, which is against him at the head of the cavalry, but very cautious.'[96] Despite his reservations, Wellington wrote to Torrens on 4 October 1810 that 'I have seen Sir William Erskine, and I think he will do very well'.[97] Wellington may have thought he was acceptable, but Erskine proved to be very unpopular among the officers of the Light Division.

Table 3.3 Organization of the Light Division, 11 March 1811

Division HQ	Major General William Erskine	Acting Commander
	Captain William Campbell, 23rd Foot	ADC
	Major Henry Mellish, Sicilian Regiment	DAAG*
	Lieutenant John Bell, 52nd Foot	DAQMG
	Charles Purcell	ACG
1st Brigade	Lieutenant Colonel Thomas Beckwith	Commander
	Lieutenant Harry Smith, 95th Rifles	Unofficial ADC
	Lieutenant James Stewart, 95th Rifles	Brigade Major
1st Bn, 43rd Foot	Major Christopher Patrickson	Commander
Right Wing, 1st Bn, 95th Rifles	Major Dugald Gilmour	Commander
Company, 2nd Bn, 95th Rifles	Captain Charles Beckwith	Commander
3rd Caçadores Bn	Lieutenant Colonel George Elder	Commander
2nd Brigade	Colonel George Drummond	Commander
	Captain Charles Rowan, 52nd Foot	Brigade Major
1st Bn, 52nd Foot	Lieutenant Colonel John Ross	Commander

(Continued)

2nd Bn, 52nd Foot	Major Edward Gibbs	Commander
Left Wing, 1st Bn, 95th Rifles	Major John Stewart	Commander
1st Caçadores Battalion	Lieutenant Colonel Jorge Avilez	Commander

* Mellish was promoted to major on 7 March. It would be several months before word of the promotion would reach Wellington's HQ. On 11 May he was appointed an AAG but was still assigned to the Light Division.

Chapter 4

COMBATS OF POMBAL AND REDINHA, 10–12 MARCH 1811

When the French began to withdraw, their three corps took separate routes north. Junot's 9th Corps began in the vicinity of Torres Novas, reached Pombal on 9 March and continued north to the Mondego river. Ney's 6th Corps was in the vicinity of Leiria and slowly moved north following the 2nd Corps to Pombal, where it would become the French rearguard. Reynier's 2nd Corps left Santarém, followed the road to Tomar via Golegã and continued to Esphinal, and by 9 March was at Venda Nova. The Light Division initially pursued the 2nd Corps, but lost contact with it on 8 March when the French moved towards Tomar, and the division was ordered to follow the advanced guard towards Leiria. The next day they began pursuing the 6th Corps. Their route was now along the main road north to Coimbra. On 10 March Ney's 6th Corps was at Pombal and just to the north of him was the 2nd Corps.

The Light Division took up positions in a pine forest on the hills south of Pombal and spent the day observing the French. With the division was General Denis Pack's Independent Portuguese Brigade. Wellington did not believe he had enough troops in position to force the French to withdraw, so he ordered the main column of the army to close up to the advanced guard. Picton's 3rd Division led the march, followed by the 4th Division. While they waited for reinforcements, word had filtered down to the troops that the Light Division had a new commander, Major General William Erskine. Only a few of the men noted this in their surviving diaries and letters, and even those were mostly with indifference.

Combat of Pombal

Pombal was a small town situated along the north bank of the Arunca river.[98] The town was dominated by a ruined twelfth-century castle. During the night Ney withdrew his corps to the hills north of Pombal, leaving the 1st Brigade of General Jean Marchand's Division to hold the town. This brigade was commanded by Colonel Joseph Fririon of the 69th Line Regiment. Colonel Fririon deployed the two battalions of the 69th Line in the town and sent the two battalions of the 6th Léger about 2km away on the south side of the river to cover the road from Leiria.

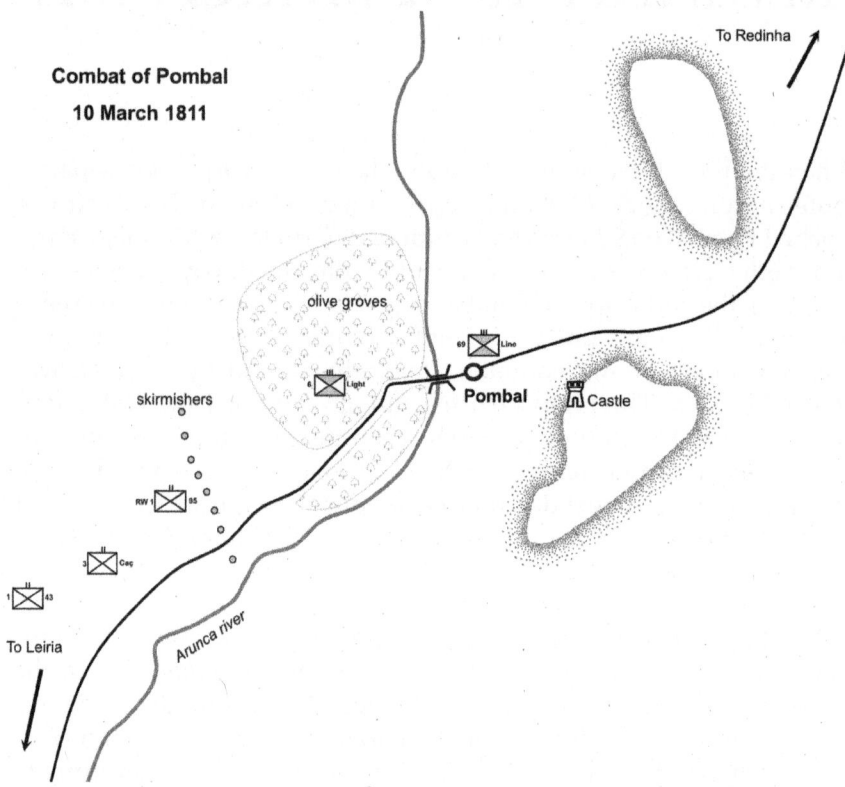

The Light Division was tasked to take Pombal, and its 1st Brigade was given the mission. In recognition of his confidence in his Portuguese troops, Colonel Beckwith ordered the 3rd Caçadores to be the assault force. Two rifle companies[99] under the command of Captain Peter O'Hare were to provide covering fire. The brigade moved towards the town about 9am. In order to get the covering party quickly to the front, the two rifle companies were hurried forward by the cavalry, each dragoon mounting a rifleman behind him on his horse – a method of riding peculiarly galling to the infantry, but which we frequently had to experience during the war. From the friction alone produced on the legs and seat by the dragoon's saddle-bags, it was some time before the foot-soldier, when placed upon his legs, could move with anything like despatch. Besides, this method of riding was generally attended by the loss of the men's mess-tins, which became shaken off by the jolting. There were, indeed, few of our men who would not have preferred marching twice the distance on foot to being thus carried.[100]

General François Fririon, Masséna's chief of staff, described what happened next:

The country which surrounds Pombal is very covered, the olive trees and the pines are there in great number. Towards eight or nine o'clock in the morning the enemy appeared, the 6th Light [Léger] immediately covered its retreat with a curtain of skirmishers against whom the enemy suddenly opposed more than 3,000 of its own; the brave men of the 6th Light were not intimidated by this multitude of adversaries; they permitted, by their firm countenance, their battalions to form a mass and to retire in order towards Pombal. These battalions, protected by the olive trees, effected their movement of retreat, leaving the high road free, in order to avoid the fire of two batteries which the English had succeeded in establishing, which took them by surprise and from behind; these batteries greatly inconvenienced them when crossing the Pont de Pombal, which is long and narrow.[101]

Ney, seeing the strength of the advancing Allies, ordered Colonel Fririon to evacuate Pombal. Fririon ordered his four battalions to withdraw to the north of the town, but even as they were withdrawing, the Allies attacked and many French were caught in the town.

The mounted British riflemen were followed by the 3rd Caçadores and the rest of the 1st Brigade. As the Allies moved towards Pombal, the French piquets withdrew into the town. The caçadores quickly moved across the bridge into the town, followed by the British riflemen. Rifleman Costello recalled that:

we had to sustain at a great disadvantage, a smart fire from the different houses, occupied by the rear guard of the enemy. As soon as we crossed the bridge we took possession of the houses opposite those held by the French, from which we kept up a brisk fire out of the windows. Tired, however, with this cross work, several of our men, headed by Lieut. [John] Hopwood, dashed into one of the French holds and found it crowded with the enemy, who to the number of thirty or forty quietly surrendered themselves prisoners. I recollect Sergeant Flemming,[102] who was the first to mount the stairs, bundling them neck and crop over the staircase. Lieutenant Hopwood, however, fell severely wounded in the thigh.[103]

In their eagerness to evict the French from the town, the Rifle officers lost control of their men and many continued to chase them into the fields outside the town:

> our men followed the enemy a considerable distance out of the town, galling them terribly in the streets, when perceiving how few our numbers were, being supported by a single troop only of our German Hussars, they turned round and made it a hard matter for us to escape the consequences of our temerity. Several of the men were out-flanked, and taken prisoners, and for myself, I had to run a great risk, and should certainly have been killed or captured, but for the gallantry of a German dragoon, who riding up, dragged me behind him, and galloped away amidst a volley of shots, unhurt.[104]

Ney had realized that by abandoning the town so quickly he was giving up a good position for his rear guard to protect the rest of the army as it withdrew to Redinha. He therefore ordered Colonel Fririon to retake the town:

> Marshal Ney then returned to the colonel and ordered the recapture of the castle, the town and the bridge, the burning of the main street of Pombal and the subsequent commencement of the retreat. The moment was critical: the enemy artillery was already bearing down on the opposite bank and firing at our troops. Fririon ordered the 1st Battalion of the 69th to charge and recapture the castle; this battalion acquitted itself of this mission with a boldness which was crowned with full success; on his side, at the head of the 6th Léger and another battalion of the 69th, Fririon entered Pombal, drove out the enemy and set fire to the narrowest passages of the main street. He then rallied his battalions on the one he had left in reserve and retired in order without being disturbed.[105]

British casualties from the fighting at Pombal were all in the Rifles, with 1 man killed, and 1 officer and 4 men wounded.[106] The initial Portuguese listing of casualties for the 3rd Caçadores was 10 men killed, and 1 ensign, 2 sergeants and 12 men wounded.[107] This was later amended to 8 men killed, 1 sergeant and 2 men died of wounds, 1 ensign, 2 sergeants and 12 men wounded, and 1 man missing.[108] French casualties were some 50 killed or wounded, with about two-thirds of them from the 6th Light Regiment.[109] Among the casualties in the 6th Léger were 1 lieutenant and 1 sub-lieutenant killed, and 2 sub-lieutenants wounded.[110]

Much to the delight of Captain O'Hare's men, they captured the baggage of General Pierre Soult,[111] commander of the 2nd Corps cavalry. This 'was mounted on a stately white horse with a Roman nose and a rat tail, which last I believe is rather an unusual appendage to a horse of that colour, but he was a waggish looking fellow, and probably had shaken all the hairs out of his tail in laughing at the contents of the portmanteau of which he was the bearer . . . Suffice it that it abounded in luxuries which we dreamt not of.'[112] That night there was auction of the contents and at O'Hare's insistence the proceeds were divided among the men of his company, with each receiving 6 dollars, the equivalent of 27 shillings.[113]

This combat also saw the rise of the making of a Rifle tradition:

> for the first time, I heard the words that afterwards became so common in our regiment, 'kill a Frenchman for yourself' . . . Two men of known daring, named Palmer and Tracey, during our approach to the bridge, seeing a French sergeant fall, ran up to claim the meed [sic] of conquest, by relieving him of any valuables he might be possessed of. They were quarrelling as to the appropriation of the spoil, when Palmer,[114] who was a known excellent shot, told Tracey[115] to go 'and kill a Frenchman for himself', as he had shot this man. This circumstance afterwards gave birth to a little gasconade in the regiment, that every rifle man could and ought to kill a Frenchman in action. From the period of the above occurrence, Palmer received the nick-name of the man-killer. . .[116]

After the French withdrew from Pombal, the rest of the Light Division moved across the river and occupied some high ground just outside the town. The Rifles bivouacked in a ploughed field near the castle, while the 43rd Foot were in a wooded area. No one got much sleep since the French piquets were very near – Lieutenant Kincaid of the 95th Rifles claimed the piquets were within pistol shot of each other. Adding to their discomfort was the heavy rain that fell most of the night.[117]

Battle of Redinha, 12 March

The enemy, having retired in the night, moved forward again at daylight on the road to Condeixa. The Light Division stood to before dawn and the men were surprised to find that the French had withdrawn northward. The 1st KGL Hussars led the advance through the hills, followed by the Light Division. The terrain soon became hilly and after marching about 8km they came upon a small French delaying force. Surprisingly, it was the 43rd and 52nd Foot who were called upon to clear the woods.[118] Among those tasked was Captain John Duffy's company of the 43rd Foot:

> The hussars came up with the enemy's rear in about a league, found them strongly posted in woods on the flanks of the road covered by several pieces of artillery. The Light Division ordered to clear the woods. The enemy had a natural defence in front of the left wood as the ground was almost perpendicular for about 40 paces and was very strong. The 43rd and 52nd Regiments after some skirmishing moved up in line and the enemy were driven from their ground.[119]

Captain William Mein's company of the 52nd Foot got into trouble when it followed the retreating French off the hill and onto the plain. They ran into a French battalion that was covering the withdrawal of their light troops and came under heavy fire. While Mein was organizing his men, a squadron of the French 3rd Hussars charged. Mein was able to stop the charge and his company quickly returned up the hill, but not without taking heavy casualties. Within a few minutes his impetuousness cost him 2 officers and 18 men killed or wounded – 20 percent of his company.[120]

The troops halted until the rest of the division came up. Orders were given to advance and after reaching the other side of the woods about 11am, they were spotted by the French a kilometre away and were brought under fire by two guns, but 'As the men were ordered to lay down but little injury took place.'[121] There the division halted and waited for orders. Lieutenant Simmons described the scene before them:

> his right resting on the river Soure,[122] protected in front by heights covered with wood, and his left beyond Redinha upon the river. The front part of his line was much intersected with deep ravines. In the centre was a beautiful plain filled with infantry, formed in good order but a motley-looking set of fellows in greatcoats and large caps, a body of cavalry supporting, and other bodies moving according to circumstances.[123]

The French position was relatively strong. The approach from the south was over a wide, open, heathland plain.[124] On the east of the plain was a line of low hills that rose about 25m above it. The western slopes of these hills were covered by pine forest, while the east side dropped down to the Anços river. On the west, the northern slope of the hills led down to the river about 500m away. Behind the hill was the village of Redinha, located on the south bank of the river, which was about 20m wide and unfordable owing to the heavy rains. The only way across the river was by a narrow medieval bridge on the far side of the town. From the north bank of the river a pass led through the mountains to Coimbra, about 40km to the north. These mountains towered some 200m above the river.

The French had made good progress in their retreat northwards but had stalled in the vicinity of Coimbra, since Portuguese militia had broken the bridge across the Mondego river at Coimbra. The river was too deep to ford and they needed to find another way to cross. Ney thus had to delay Wellington's army until a new crossing site could be found or a bridge constructed. Ney chose to make his stand at Redinha. He deployed Mermet's division on the low hills to the south of the village. With them were the 3rd Hussars and six cannon. On the north side of the river was Marchand's division. In all, Ney had about 12,000 men with him at Redinha. Another 12,000 men in Junot's Corps were at Condeixa-a-Nova, 20km further north.

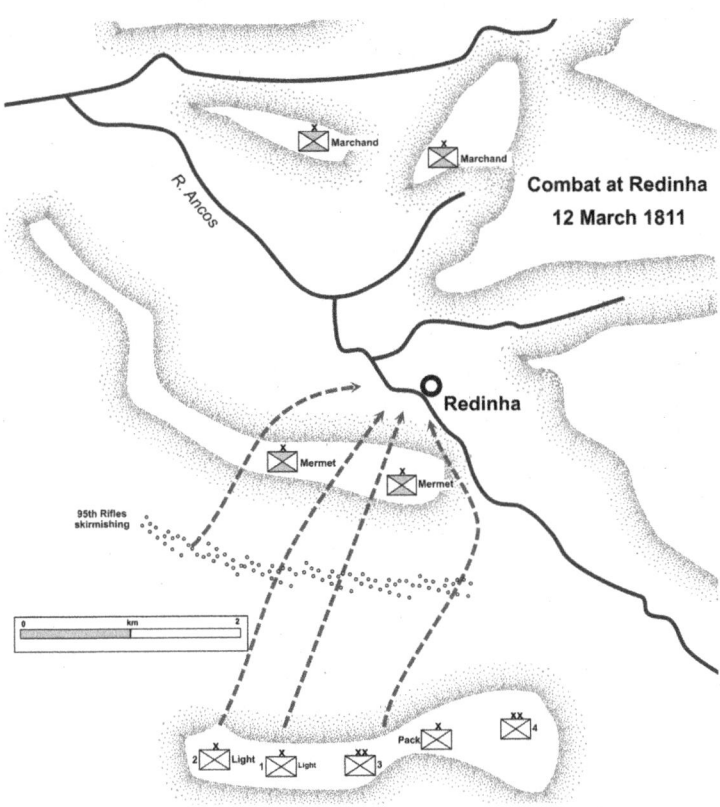

Wellington, thinking he had caught up with most of the French Army at Redinha, was reluctant to attack what he believed was close to 30,000 men with just the Light Division. Thus, he ordered most of his army up and by early afternoon had deployed the Light Division on the left. Next to it in the centre was the 4th Division and Pack's Portuguese Brigade. On the right flank was the 3rd Division. The 3rd and 4th Divisions, as well as the Portuguese, were formed in two lines when Wellington ordered the attack to begin at 2pm.

The Light Division deployed with the 1st Brigade on the right and the 2nd Brigade on the left. The whole army's advance was covered by the 95th Rifles. On the far left were the four companies of Stewart's Left Wing. The rifle company of the 2nd Battalion was to their right, and Gilmour's four companies of the Right Wing were further right. On their right were the light companies of the 3rd Division. This line of skirmishers extended for about 3km.

Behind this screen was the army, drawn up in columns. Rifleman Costello commented:

> I remember to have seen one of the finest views of the two armies I ever witnessed. The rifles were extended in the distance for perhaps two miles, and rapidly on the advance to the enemy's position. These were followed by our heavy columns, whose heads were just emerging from a wood about a quarter of a mile in our rear. Everything seemed conducted with the order and regularity of a field day. Meanwhile the rear columns of the French were slowly retiring, but in a few minutes the scene became exceedingly animated by our artillery opening their fire upon the retreating forces.[125]

Ney had no intention of engaging in battle but wanted to delay matters by forcing Wellington's troops to deploy into attack columns. Upon seeing them do so, he ordered his artillery, which had been firing at the advancing British and Portuguese, to withdraw, followed by the cavalry, and then the infantry.

The Rifles were under fire as they advanced into the woods. Lieutenant Harry Smith commanded Leach's 2nd Company during the advance.[126] His company was supported by O'Hare's 3rd Company. Smith was riding his horse Tiny as they approached the woods on the eastern side of the French position. He had paused to assess the situation when the

> Light Companies of the 3rd Division came up. I asked, 'Are you going to attack that wood?' A Captain of the 88th Light Company,[127] whom I knew, quite laughed at my question. I said very quietly, 'You will be

beat back, and when you are, I will move on the edge of the wood and help you.' How he laughed! My prediction was very soon verified: he was wounded, and picked up by my Company, which I moved on the right flank of the French and stopped them immediately. I sent to my support, O'Hare, to move up to me. The obstinate old Turk would not, and so I was obliged to come back, and had most unnecessarily five or six men wounded.[128]

The French were in the act of withdrawing when the battalion in front of Lieutenant Kincaid halted and turned to fight. Kincaid was at the front of his men when he found he was

> within a few yards of one of their regiments in line, which opened such a fire, that had I not, rifleman like, taken instant advantage of the cover of a good fir tree, my name would have unquestionably been transmitted to posterity by that night's gazette. And, however opposed it may be to the usual system of drill, I will maintain from that day's experience, that the cleverest method of teaching a recruit to stand at attention, is to place him behind a tree and fire balls at him; as, had our late worthy disciplinarian, Sir David Dundas, himself, been looking on, I think that even he must have admitted that he never saw any one stand so fiercely upright as I did behind mine, while the balls were rapping into it as fast as if a fellow had been hammering a nail on the opposite side, not to mention the numbers that were whistling past, within the eighth of an inch of every part of my body, both before and behind, particularly in the vicinity of my nose, for which the upper part of the tree could barely afford protection.[129]

Lieutenant Smith eventually made his way through the woods:

> A line of French infantry, concealed behind an alataza (or tower) on a hill good for the purpose, were lying down as my Company and the one commanded by that wonderful Rifleman, Willie Johnstone,[130] got within twenty yards of them. To our astonishment, up jumped the line, fired a volley (they did not hit a man), and went about. At them we all went like devils, a regular foot race, except for me and my little horse Tiny, from which I could not dismount. In the pursuit he carried me down a rock twelve feet high, and Johnstone and I got to the bridge and cut off half a Battalion of French.[131]

Soon the rest of the division entered the woods and the French continued their retreat to the village. O'Hare's company eventually moved up to support Smith. After clearing the woods and moving to the village, Simmons and Kincaid had a close brush with death:

Lieutenant Kincaid passed with me through a gap in a hedge. We jumped from it at the same moment that a Portuguese Grenadier, who was following, received a cannon shot through his body and came tumbling after us. Very likely during the day a person might have a thousand much more narrow escapes of being made acquainted with the grand secret, but seeing the mangled body of a brave fellow so shockingly mutilated in an instant, stamps such impressions upon one's mind in a manner that time can never efface.[132]

During the attack on the hill Private Garretty of the 43rd Foot witnessed one of those random events that seems unbelievable to those who hear about it. 'I remember that in the midst of the clangor and firing just described, a hare emerged from the woods, and for some time amused herself by sundry doubles and evolutions between the hostile lines; at length, as if satisfied that enough had been seen, she suddenly disappeared.'[133]

While the Light Division was attacking the right of the French position, the 3rd and 4th Divisions as well as the Portuguese Brigade were attacking its centre and left. The French 50th Line Regiment was the last unit to withdraw into the village. There, the French discipline began to break and many of the soldiers rushed to the bridge, desperate to reach the safety of the far side of the river. Before long the bridge became a chokepoint for those trying to cross it. Simmons observed:

> We pushed the fugitives so hard that the bridge was completely blocked up, numbers fell over its battlements, and others were bayoneted; in fact, we entered pell-mell with them. The town was set on fire in many parts by the enemy previous to our entering it, so that numbers of them, to avoid being bayoneted, rushed into the burning houses in their flight.[134]

Kincaid also witnessed the chaos on the bridge:

> When we reached the bridge, the scene became exceedingly interesting, for it was choked up by the fugitives who were, as usual, impeding each other's progress, and we did not find that the application of our swords to those nearest to us tended at all towards lessening their disorder, for it induced about a hundred of them to rush into an adjoining house for shelter, but that was getting regularly out of the frying-pan into the fire, for the house happened to be really in flames, and too hot to hold them, so that the same hundred were quickly seen unkennelling again, half-cooked, into the very jaws of their consumers.[135]

Eventually Redinha was taken and the Light Division moved across the river, halting after a few kilometres when it ran into Marchand's division.[136] The Rifles bivouacked 'on a range of heights, while the French lay below in a beautiful valley; the outlying sentries of both armies being not more than two hundred yards apart'.[137] Captains O'Hare and William Balvaird's companies had piquet duty.

Captain George Napier with the 52nd Foot occupied part of a village, while the French had the other half. The animosity displayed during the earlier fighting seemed to have been put aside for the night:

> It was my friend Captain [William] Mein of the 52nd who commanded our picket; and when all was quiet and his sentinels posted and no fear of any surprise, he asked the captain commanding the enemy's pickets to have some supper with him, which the poor fellow, who had been half-starved for some months, was delighted to accept. So he came to Mein's house, and after a good supper – for we had some sutlers come up to the army – and an hour or two of conversation, it was time for him to go back to his own picket; and he had not been gone above a quarter of an hour when he was ordered to retreat from his post.[138]

Soon the alarm was given that the French were pulling out, and the 52nd Foot quickly occupied the rest of the village for the night.[139]

For the Rifles, however, it was not a quiet night. The riflemen in Costello's company had begun cooking the meagre rations they had taken from their French prisoners when

> a man of the name of Humphrey Allen, a tall powerful fellow, whom we had also nick-named 'Long Tom of Lincoln', came up from the rear, where, during the preceding skirmish, he had been employed taking the wounded. On asking to be allowed to join one of the messes, he was immediately refused, on account of his having gone out of action with the wounded, when the care of them devolved upon the buglers or bandsmen alone. This, I must remark, was at first a common excuse for getting from under fire, and soon became marked with indignation by the braver men . . .[140]

Allen, having been rebuffed by his comrades, decided to take matters into his own hands:

> Taking up his rifle, very coolly observing that he would soon get something to eat if a Frenchman had it; [he] walked quietly down to our outlying picquets [sic], and taking deliberate aim, shot one of the French sentries on the spot: in an instant he was across the field to where he fell,

and having hoisted him on his shoulders, was in the act of bearing him back to our line, which the French perceiving, fired, pursued him, and compelled him to drop his prize.

The firing set off alarms and the brigade was quickly alerted. Colonel Beckwith came down to see what was going on. Allen was identified as the cause and before long was in front of Beckwith. Allen replied that 'Why, Zur, . . . I arn't had nought to eat these two days, and thought as how I might find summut in the Frencher's knapsack.' Beckwith reprimanded him and things quieted down for a time.[141]

About an hour later Costello was manning an outpost and was

> leisurely sauntering up and down, occasionally looking about me, and stooping to cull some flowers that grew in the field which divided us from the enemy. It was just at the close of the evening, or between the lights. The French sentry, who advanced occasionally seemingly for the same purpose, at last came so near, that I feared he was up to some manoeuvre, or about to fire at me; with this, I instantly cocked my rifle, and was awaiting his approach, when he suddenly rushed towards me, bellowing out in French, 'Déserteur! Déserteur!' Of course at the words I allowed him to approach, which he did, exclaiming, 'Je suis allemand', and instantly turning on his quondam[142] comrades, fired into them. The report of his fire caused the picquets [sic] of both parties to fall in, and the whole line of sentries to be engaged. However, he stuck by me all the time, shaking his fist at them, and loading and firing with all the jawbreaking oaths that the French and his native German could supply him with.[143]

Once again Beckwith showed up, swearing, thinking that the disturbance was caused by another hungry rifleman. He quickly calmed down when presented with the deserter.[144]

As shown above, the British soldiers were quick to loot the captured and dead French not just for food but for any valuables. During the fight in the village Rifleman Muckston[145] 'espied an officer endeavouring to get through the water he jumped in and brought him out by the neck. He gave the soldier thirty-six doubloons and a medal dedicated to the Legion of Honour. The soldier gave me the medal.'[146]

Costello witnessed a much darker episode:

> A French officer whom we had observed very conspicuously cheering on his men, had fallen by a rifle shot through the thigh, when two of our buglers ran forwards for the purpose of easing him of his money. This, I must observe, the French generally kept concealed in a kind of

belt round their waists. As soon therefore, as the buglers came up to him, they commenced quarrelling as to which of them should possess his property. The more readily to disencumber him of his belt, each of them had fallen on his knees over the poor Frenchman, and one of the buglers had drawn a knife to cut the strap that secured the hoped for treasure, when the other endeavouring to restrain him brought on a scuffle, during which, I am sorry to relate, the knife entered the body of the wounded man, and he expired on the spot. I had arrived just in time to perceive the occurrence, and could with difficulty restrain myself from shooting the owner of the knife, on the spot, until he told me it was purely accidental.[147]

The Light Division casualties were heavy. The 43rd Foot had 6 other ranks wounded; the 52nd Foot lost 2 other ranks killed, and 3 officers[148] and 21 other ranks wounded; while the 95th Rifles had 1 officer[149] and 24 riflemen wounded, with 1 rifleman missing.[150] The 1st Caçadores had 1 officer,[151] 2 sergeants and 23 other ranks wounded. The 3rd Caçadores had 6 other ranks killed, 10 other ranks wounded, and 1 other rank missing.[152]

French casualties are difficult to determine. General Fririon stated that in the first thirteen days of March Ney's 6th Corps lost only 291 men, of whom 179 were killed or wounded, 76 died of sickness, 34 drowned, 1 was taken prisoner, and another deserted.[153] Colonel Pelet states that the 50th Line Regiment lost about 60 men in the combat.[154] Martinien lists 4 officers killed and 19 wounded from the 6th Corps at Pombal and Redinha.[155]

Chapter 5

CONDEIXA AND CASAL NOVO, 13–14 MARCH 1811

The situation on 12 March was not good for the French. Most of their army was already in the vicinity of Condeixa-a-Nova about 15km south of Coimbra. Ney and the 6th Corps were slowly retreating northwards and within a day's march would also be at Condeixa, a key crossroads with a major road leading to Coimbra and another leading further east. The French needed to cross the Mondego river and were hoping to do so at Coimbra. A scouting force that was sent to the Coimbra bridge reported back:

> that the Mondego was extremely high and even touched the keystone of the bridge arches. The second arch nearest the city was broken and open for some forty feet; the preceding arch was half damaged. Planks placed across both of the arches served for the passage of a rather large number of people who went to the other side when they saw our troops. The Mondego then appeared to be almost four hundred yards wide near the bridge. On that day they saw very few troops and no cannon. The reports of these officers ... allowed us to believe that with some infantry we could have entered the city immediately behind the fugitives. However, the planks over the arches could have been very quickly seized and thrown into the water ...[156]

The terrain in the vicinity of Condeixa was good for defence and Masséna considered making a stand and offering battle. However, his army was short of supplies and running low on ammunition. If he lost, he would likely lose his baggage train and guns, and would have to abandon the sick and wounded. If he won, it would not significantly change the situation. He would still have to retreat towards the border with Spain. Left with no real choice, Masséna ordered the army to move east, to try to cross the Mondego further upstream.[157]

Condeixa was in chaos,

> full of artillery, baggage, herds, commissariat, sick, and the regiments. There was terrible confusion, but no remedy, at first because of our uncertainty about the direction to follow, the perilous roads, and then because of the nature of the terrain surrounding Condeixa. The terrain there was cut by a multitude of small irrigation canals and gardens which prevented the regular establishment of bivouacs and the parc [sic] and limited the number of passages, all of which were very narrow.[158]

It was up to Ney to buy the army time. At 8pm Masséna sent him a message: 'It is essential that we hold before Condeixa all day tomorrow in order to give our baggage time to file on the route to Miranda do Corvo.'[159] Ney promised he would hold the town for two days.

As was its practice, the Light Division stood-to at nautical twilight (5.15am) on the morning of 13 March. The men had begun marching by sunrise (6.14am), and halted when they reached a ridge overlooking Condeixa.[160] The terrain in the valley below them was perhaps best described by Pelet:

> Its slope was divided in two by a berm, and the road crossed it in a single straight line, embanked by the slopes and enfiladed from one end to the other. In front of this position was a stream about forty feet wide, running through difficult and cultivated ground. The left of the hill arrested firmly on the chain of mountains and the right dropped down two thousand yards; beyond it was extended a small rideau[161] to a bend in the stream about four thousand yards away.[162]

While the division observed the French below them in the valley, Wellington and his staff rode up. He spent some time planning how to evict the French from the town. He hoped to force Ney out of his position by threatening his line of retreat, and therefore avoiding a battle. Orders were issued for the 3rd Division to attack to the right and get behind Condeixa to prevent the French from retreating east to Miranda do Corvo. Pack's Portuguese Brigade was to attack in the centre, to the left of the 3rd Division. The Light Division was also to attack in the centre, to the left of Pack. On their left was the 4th Division and on the far left, against the French right flank, was the 6th Division.

The division's orders were detailed:

> As the ravine which the Light division will have opposite to it appears to be difficult, both on account of the rugged and rocky nature of its banks and by reason of the rivulet which flows in it, a large proportion of tirailleurs[163] should be thrown forward to cover the front of the division, and to get position of and reconnaitre [sic] the passes. And the division should not be pushed too much forward under the fire of the enemy on the opposite bank, until these previous steps have been taken.
>
> Some guns should be got up to the ground allotted for the Light division as soon as possible, to cannonade the enemy on the opposite bank of the ravine: these guns are to continue, however, in the position allotted to them on this side of the ravine, even after the attack has succeeded; and the artillery which has remained on the great road is to be moved forward to follow the enemy.[164]

Wellington and his staff stayed on the ridge near the Light Division long enough for a French officer in the buildings below to notice them. He sent up some light troops who, as Kincaid remarked, 'stole, unperceived, very near to him and began firing, but, fortunately, without effect. We immediately detached a few of ours to meet them, but the others ran off on their approach.'[165]

After observing Wellington's activity, Ney realized his intention and ordered his troops to retreat around noon.[166] In an effort to delay Wellington, he had his troops set fire to the town. About 3pm the Light Division received orders to advance and were in the village by 4pm There they found 'the town in flames, two or three beautiful chapels destroyed & all the convents'.[167] Simmons 'ordered some soldiers to remove several chairs and some straw under a staircase which was then on fire. By this timely removal, the house was saved, and most likely many others.'[168] Soon the division was fighting the fire. Rifleman Costello recalled:

> The main street was completely blocked by the flames darting across the road from the opposite houses. To enable the troops to pass, we were obliged to 'break' a way through some dry walls. This caused a temporary halt, during which the chief part of the division gallantly employed themselves extricating the unfortunate inhabitants from the burning houses. Tom Crawley . . . made use of his great strength to some purpose, and chucked some five or six old people, whom he had brought forth on his shoulders, over a wall as he supposed, out of immediate danger. Tom, however, who should have 'looked' before he

made the old ones 'leap', was not aware that close to their descent was a large well, into which, to their great terror, he had very nearly dropped the terrified and screeching sufferers.[169]

By the time the Light Division had extricated itself from the town, night was falling.[170] The men marched for a few kilometres and bivouacked in some woods on a hill.[171]

Combat of Casal Novo

Wellington's Quartermaster General spent the night writing and delivering new orders for the army. The main thrust would be to Miranda do Corvo, 20km away via the road to Vila Seca and Lamas.[172] The orders were quite specific on what each division would do. In the case of the Advanced Guard, which included the Light Division, 'Major Gen. Sir W. Erskine will put the advanced guard in motion soon after day-break, and will follow the enemy along the road towards Miranda do Corvo.'[173] Behind the Light Division was the 3rd Division, then the 6th, the 1st and finally the 5th. Interspersed in the column were cavalry and artillery. The order even went into detail concerning where in the march the trains would be: 'The baggage of the front divisions of the column will move in rear of the 5th division in the order of the column ... '[174]

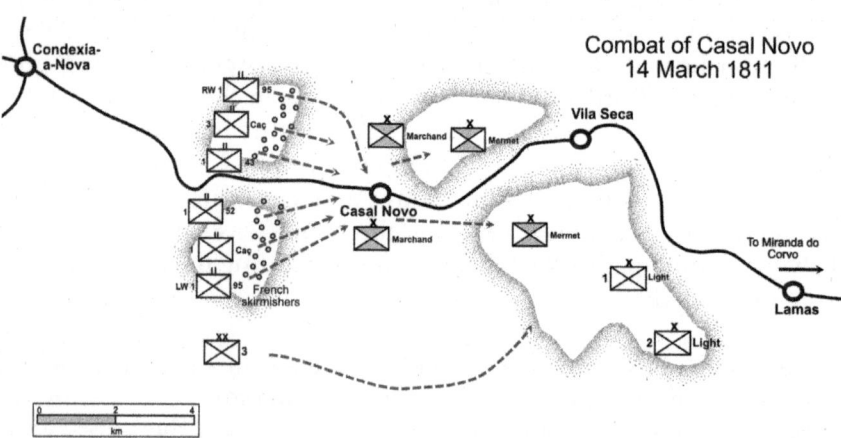

On a map, the route looks very compact and the Light Division's baggage train would thus be not too far behind. In reality, however, the troops were stretched out for kilometres. Marching four abreast, an 800-strong infantry battalion would be about 250m long. The Light

Division, with each brigade averaging about 2,000 men, would take up 1,500m of road. The four divisions that followed it would each be over 2km long. When the cavalry and artillery units were factored in, the Light Division's baggage was more than 10km to its rear. With the baggage was the division's ammunition caissons, a mistake that would cause problems later in the day.[175]

The morning of 14 March saw the Light Division standing-to and ready to march shortly after daybreak. As they descended from the hill they had bivouacked on, the weather became very foggy and it would remain so for several hours. The men knew the French were somewhere in front of them, but the heavy fog prevented them from identifying any enemy positions. The 16th Light Dragoons moved forward, but Harry Smith's company, which had been on piquet duty all night, kept its position and waited for orders. Soon he saw Beckwith and the rest of the 1st Brigade coming up behind him. The colonel

> moved up to where I was posted. He said, 'Come, Harry, get your Company together, and fall in at the head of the column.' At this moment two of the 16th Dragoons rode back, and Beckwith said, 'Where do you come from?' 'We have patrolled a league and a half in the front, and seen naught.' 'A league and a half, my friend,' says old Sydney, 'in a thick fog is a d– long way. Why, Harry, you said the vedettes were close to you.' 'So they are,' I said, 'and you will be fired at the moment you advance.' We had not gone fifty yards when 'Pop! Pop!' Oh, how old Sydney laughed! 'A league and a half!' But the fog was so thick we could not move, and the enemy, hearing our column on their rear, being clear, moved off.[176]

Before long the order came to move out. The rifle-armed 3rd Caçadores led the advance and soon came in contact with the French outposts. The Right Wing of the 95th Rifles deployed to the left to support the caçadores, while the 43rd Foot moved to their right, but staying to the left of the road.[177] The 2nd Brigade moved up to the right of the 1st Brigade, with the 52nd Foot to the right of the road, while the 1st Caçadores were to their right. On the far right flank of the division were Major Stewart's four companies of riflemen.

The fog caused serious command and control problems. Both brigades were skirmishing with the French and few knew what was happening on their flanks. General Erskine was at a loss and had no idea of the big picture. He came across the 52nd Foot waiting in column but not engaged. He approached their commander, Lieutenant Colonel John Ross, and asked why the regiment was not pursuing the retreating enemy. Ross replied that the enemy were not retreating and that Captain Joseph Dobbs, who commanded the piquets, had reported that the French were still on the hill to the front. This was supported by Captain William Napier, who commanded the 43rd Foot's piquets. Erskine did not believe them and lost his temper, 'swearing it was all nonsense and that the captains of the pickets knew nothing about the matter, and that there was not a man of them there'.[178]

Captain George Napier of the 52nd Foot described what happened next:

> the fog, which had been very dense, cleared away a little, and bang came a shot from a twelve-pounder which struck the head of our column and made a lane through it, killing and wounding many men; immediately a second and third, and then commenced a regular cannonade. Still the wise Sir William was sure it could be nothing but a single gun or two and a picket of the enemy and desired Colonel Ross to send my company to drive them in on the flank, at the same time sending an aide-de-camp to point out to me where I was to go to. We proceeded a short distance into some vine fields in a little bottom or valley upon the left flank of our column, the mist being very heavy, and just as we reached the bottom whiz came a few shots from some of the enemy close to us but whom we saw not. One of these shots went through my cap just grazing my forehead . . . I pushed forward immediately, and had just leaped with the men over a low wall into a narrow road, and was almost instantly charged by a squadron of dragoons which was waiting for us behind some trees. However, by this time it was broad daylight and the mist nearly dispersed; so perceiving what it was, and seeing the French officer commanding the squadron at its head, I had just time to form up half a dozen file and, giving the gentlemen a volley, down came the officer and a few of his men and horses, upon which the rest galloped off and I instantly made my company leap over the opposite wall into a vineyard where I knew I was safe from their cavalry; and forming a line of skirmishers, I advanced towards a French brigade which was drawn up at some distance in my front. However, they sent forward a cloud of sharpshooters to oppose me, and in a few minutes the action became very sharp. I continued advancing, but very slowly, for they were quadruple my strength . . .[179]

Erskine, seeing Napier's company in trouble, ordered Ross to take the 52nd Foot forward. It too got sucked into the mêlée. Erskine realized that the 52nd was badly outnumbered and ordered the 43rd Foot to support them. William Napier, the senior captain present, was sent forward with six companies to assist the 52nd. It did not go well at first. Napier wrote later:

When I arrived at a certain round hill under fire, which I judged a good point of support, I halted four companies to watch our flanks, and with the two others hastily descended a deep ravine on my right to join the left of the 52nd, whose charging shout I had just heard on that side, though an intervening ridge prevented my seeing them. Unfortunately for me, this charge was partial; a momentary effort to extricate the regiment from a dangerous crisis. Thus with two companies I suddenly found myself in the midst of the enemy, but I arrived just in time to save Captain [Joseph] Dobbs, 52nd, and two men who were cut off from their regiment. The French were gathering fast about us, we could scarcely retreat, and Dobbs agreed with me that boldness would be our best chance; so we called upon the men to follow, and, jumping over a wall which had given us over, charged the enemy with a shout which sent the nearest back. But then occurred the most painful event that ever happened to me. Only the two men of the 52nd followed us, and we four arrived unsupported at a second wall, close to a considerable body of French, who rallied and began to close upon us. Their fire was very violent, but the wall gave cover. I was, however, stung by the backwardness of my men, and told Dobbs I would save him or lose my life by bringing up the two companies; he entreated me not, saying I could not make two paces from the wall and live. Yet I did go back to the first wall, escaped the fire, and, reproaching the men, gave them the word again, and returned to Dobbs, who was now upon the point of being taken; but again I returned alone! The soldiers had indeed crossed the wall in their front, but kept edging away to the right to avoid the heavy fire. Being now maddened by this second failure I made another attempt, but I had not made ten paces when a shot struck my spine, and the enemy very ungenerously continued to fire at me when I was down. I escaped death by dragging myself by my hands – for my lower extremities were paralysed – towards a small heap of stones which was in the midst of the field, and thus covering my head and shoulders. Not less than twenty shots struck this heap. However, Captain [Thomas] Lloyd[180] and my own company, and some of the 52nd, came up at that moment and the French were driven away.[181]

About 11am the fog finally lifted and the situation became clear. About a kilometre away was the village of Casal Novo,[182] at the entrance to a defile between two high ridges. The approach to the village had numerous fields that were protected by stone walls and an occasional small hill. Deployed around the village was Marchand's division, and it would be very difficult to eject them from their positions.

Wellington did not want to fight, and preferred to force the French rearguard to retreat by threatening its flanks and rear. The Light Division was supposed to wait until the 3rd Division came up on line, while the 4th Division was sent on a different road to get to the French flank. However, Erskine ignored his orders and committed the Light Division into attacking before the 3rd and 4th Divisions were in position. Napier of the 43rd described the situation succinctly: 'The enemy's ground was so extensive, and his skirmishers so thick and so easily supported, that, in a little time, the division was necessarily stretched out in one thin thread, and closely engaged in every part, without any reserve.'[183]

The situation was chaotic and units were soon intermixed. Lieutenant Kincaid recalled:

> just as the mist of the morning began to clear away, a section of our company was thrown forward among the skirmishers, while the other three remained in reserve behind a gentle eminence, and the officer commanding it, seeing a piece of rising ground close to the left, which gave him some uneasiness, he desired me to take a man with me to the top of it, and to give him notice if the enemy attempted any movement on that side. We got to the top; but if we had not found a couple of good sized stones on the spot, which afforded shelter at the moment, we should never have got any where else, for I don't think they expended less than a thousand shots upon us in the course of a few minutes. My companion, John Rouse,[184] a steady sturdy old rifle man, no sooner found himself snugly covered, than he lugged out his rifle to give them one in return, but the slightest exposure brought a dozen balls to the spot in an instant, and I was amused to see old Rouse, at every attempt, jerking back his head with a sort of knowing grin, as if it were only a parcel of schoolboys, on the other side, threatening him with snowballs; but seeing, at last, that his time for action was not yet come, he withdrew his rifle, and, knowing my inexperience in those matters, he very good-naturedly called to me not to expose myself looking out just then, for, said he, 'there will be no moving among them while this shower continues'. When the shower ceased we found that they had also ceased to hold their formidable post, and as quickly as may be, we were to be seen standing in their old shoes, mixed up with some of the forty-third.[185]

In the centre the 52nd Foot was fighting for its life. Napier was reinforced with several other companies of the 52nd and then joined by the Left Wing of the 95th Rifles. Slowly the tide began to turn. Napier again:

> my commanding officer, who was following with the regiment, perceiving, sent several other companies to my support, and ere long we were four hundred strong, under Major [John] Stewart, of the Rifle Corps. We then made a grand push, and drove the enemy from vineyard

to vineyard, constantly advancing and keeping up a hot fire, the whole Light Division supporting us.[186]

Ney's goal was to force Wellington to deploy his army and attack his position. By doing so, he bought time for the rest of the French Army to get through the defile and make its way to Miranda do Corvo. By mid-afternoon the 3rd Division had joined the fighting and was supporting the Light Division on its right. When word reached Ney that the 4th Division was threatening his flank, he knew it was time to withdraw. Marchand began pulling back his troops and would soon be behind Mermet's division on the high ridge behind Casal Novo.

About this time the 52nd Foot was running out of ammunition and their momentum slowed. Napier had turned to speak to his lieutenant, Theophilus Gifford,

> when I saw some Frenchmen, who were concealed among the bushes, start up, and as poor Gifford's back was turned towards them while he was receiving orders from me, the muzzles of their muskets were within two or three yards of his head, when they fired, and he fell! I rushed forward, caught him up in my arms, when to my horror his head fell back and his brains literally splashed on the ground! My excellent and valued friend was a corpse! The back of his skull was blown off! Some of my men who saw the whole thing at the same instant, dashing forward, plunged their bayonets into the Frenchmen's bodies and revenged the death of their officer. I laid his body gently on the ground; the soldiers wrapped it up in his cloak, and under a heavy fire from the enemy dug a grave in the sandy soil, and in this rough but glorious sepulchre were deposited the remains of Theophilus Gifford, as honourable, generous, gallant, and guileless a soldier as ever the fate of war cut off in the prime of youth, health, and spirits! The soldiers then fired a volley over his grave, which volley carried death to some brave fellows in the enemy's ranks, and thus in the space of a quarter of an hour finished the life and funeral of my friend![187]

Erskine watched the advance falter, and saw to the front many Frenchmen on a small hill.[188] He rode over to Major Stewart and ordered him forward with words that implied he was a coward. Stewart angrily spurred his horse Tom into a gallop towards the French retreating towards Casal Novo. He was quickly followed by his four companies of the Left Wing of the 95th Rifles, and was joined by Major Gilmour and the Right Wing of the 95th Rifles. The fighting was intense and Stewart was seriously wounded by a shot through both lungs.[189] George Simmons, a former medical student, was there and recorded 'Major Stewart, as many others have done, asked me if he was mortally wounded. I told him he was. He thanked me, and died the day following.'[190] Stewart was 'led by two buglers to the rear, where he died shortly after'.[191]

The French continued to withdraw from the village but as the riflemen approached the far side they came across one man, who

> to our surprize remained loading and firing, as if he had a whole division to back him. I scarcely know what could have induced me to fire at this poor fellow alone, and exposed as he was, to at least twenty other shots; but my blood was up, through his having once aimed at me, his ball whizzing close by as I approached. Be that as it may, I had approached within fifty yards when I fired. In an instant I was beside him, the shot had entered his head, and he had fallen in the act of loading, the fusil lightly grasped in his left hand, while his right clutched the ramrod. A few quick turns of the eye as it rolled its dying glances on mine, turned my whole blood within me, and I reproached myself as his destroyer. An indescribable uneasiness came over me, I felt almost like a criminal, I knelt to give him a little wine from a small calabash, which hung at my side, and was wiping the foam from his lips, when a heavy groan drew my attention aside, and turning round my head I beheld stretched near him and close to the wall, another wounded Frenchman, a sergeant. 'Hélas', exclaimed the wounded man, the big tears suddenly gushing down his sun burnt countenance, as he pointed with his finger, to my victim, 'avez tué mon pauvre frère' (you have killed my poor brother), and such indeed was the melancholy fact. The sergeant, a stout heavy man, had fallen, his thigh broken by a shot. The younger brother, unable to carry him off the field, had remained, apparently with the intention of perishing by his side.[192]

After abandoning the village, Marchand moved past Mermet's division through the defile until he met a staff officer who pointed out the next position he was to defend. Often these positions were only suitable for a brigade. The other brigade would move further east to the next position. Once the division was in place, Ney would order the rear division to quit its position and move past it. He continued to 'leapfrog' his divisions in this manner all the way back to Miranda do Corvo.[193]

It took time for the Light Division to move through Casal Novo. Once it did, it ran into Mermet's division on the ridge above. Artillery was brought forward and began shelling the French positions. With Marchand's division having safely escaped through the defile, Mermet ordered his men to retreat. The Light Division followed them, and sometimes the leading units were able to engage the French before they had a chance to pull back. At one point Beckwith and his brigade had attacked the rearguard of the retreating French, while two companies[194] of the 52nd Foot got on their flank and fired as the enemy soldiers moved down the road.[195] It was not, however, a one-sided fight, and British and Portuguese casualties were heavy. George Napier was one of them:

> We drove the enemy from hill to hill with great slaughter, and about three o'clock, while leading on my men to charge a strong body of French which was a few yards before me, and which I thought I might be able to take prisoners, I received a shot in my right wrist which completely shattered it and forced me to go to the rear, as I was also very much fatigued, having been incessantly engaged with the enemy from three o'clock in the morning to past three o'clock in the day.[196]

The Rifles also lost Lieutenant John Strode, who was shot in the thigh. He turned to Lieutenant George Simmons, who was in his company, and 'called to me to take his rifle, exclaiming, "This, Simmons, may be of service." I had no time to stand on ceremony, but moved on.'[197]

During their advance the men of the Light Division found several destroyed villages. Lieutenant Henry Dawson of the 52nd Foot wrote that as they 'passed their camp, we found ammunition waggons innumerable burnt & destroyed. Every village we have passed has been burnt to the ground, I suppose with the intent of burning their dead, as well as to deceive us in the immense quantity of baggage as well as of every other equipment they have been obliged to abandon.'[198]

A captured French colonel told George Napier that 'he had the execution of orders to burn every town and village they passed, and boasted of the regular and expeditious manner in which he performed it, placing all the furniture in the houses in the rooms below and then setting fire to it by soldiers who were placed in each house with firebrands, and all by sound of bugle so that every house was in a blaze at the same moment'.[199]

As the division reached the village of Lamas, night began to fall and the fighting ended. The troops were exhausted, having fought for almost 10 hours over a distance of 12km. Kincaid was on piquet duty in the village:

> Our post that night was one of terrific grandeur. The hills behind were in a blaze of light with the British camp-fires, as were those in our

front with the French ones. Both hills were abrupt and lofty, not above eight hundred yards asunder, and we were in the burning village in the valley between. The roofs of houses every instant falling in, and the sparks and flames ascending to the clouds. The streets were strewed with the dying and the dead, some had been murdered and some killed in action, which, together with the half-famished wretches whom we had saved from burning, contributed in making it a scene which was well-calculated to shake a stout heart, as was proved in the instance of one of our sentries, a well known 'devil-may-care' sort of fellow. I know not what appearances the burning rafters might have reflected on the neighbouring trees at the time, but he had not been long on his post before he came running into the piquet, and swore, by all the saints in the calendar, that he saw six dead Frenchmen advancing upon him with hatchets over their shoulders![200]

Kincaid and Simmons took the time to explore the village. It had been the scene of many atrocities. 'They went into a house where an old man was seated; he had been lame in both legs for many years. A French soldier, on leaving the house, had given him two deep sabre wounds on the head and another on the arm.'[201] In another they

> were shocked to find in it a mother and her child dead, and the father, with three more, living, but so much reduced by famine as to be unable to remove themselves from the flames. We carried them into the open air, and offered the old man our few remaining crumbs of biscuit, but he told us that he was too far gone to benefit by them, and begged that we would give them to his children. We lost no time in examining such of the other houses as were yet safe to enter, and rescued many more individuals from one horrible death, probably to reserve them for another equally so, and more lingering, as we had nothing to give them, and marched at day light the following morning.[202]

It was a hungry night for the troops, for the division had outmarched its baggage trains. Lieutenant Dawson of the 52nd Foot was lucky enough to come upon some French troops who were cooking dinner. 'We drove them from their woods & from their dinners, which were great prizes to those who were fortunate enough to get them.'[203]

The division's efforts were recognized in Wellington's dispatch on the battle: 'In the operations of this day, the 43rd, 52nd, 95th Regiments, and 3rd Caçadores, under the command of Colonels Drummond and Beckwith and Major Patrickson, Lieut. Colonel Ross, and Majors Gilmour and Stewart, and Lieut. Colonel Elder particularly distinguished themselves.'[204]

Ney's performance during the battle was masterful. His use of the terrain to delay Wellington and the timing of the withdrawal of his troops before they could be pinned in place was superb. He bought his army time, and paid with minimal casualties. The French claimed to have lost only 55 men. Oman disputes this, saying they were more likely 100–200, and puts the Allies' losses at 155.[205]

The Light Division's casualties were the heaviest since the battle of Busaço on 26 September 1810. George Napier claimed that he 'went into action with sixty-six soldiers, three sergeants, and three subalterns, and I lost one officer, one sergeant, and ten or twelve soldiers killed; myself, two sergeants, and about fifteen or sixteen wounded, so that of my original number nearly half were killed and wounded.'[206] Napier's figures disagree with the official number of casualties, but not significantly (see Table 5.1).

Table 5.1 Light Division Casualties at Casal Novo, 14 March 1811

	Killed Officers	Killed Other Ranks	Wounded Officers	Wounded Other Ranks	Missing Other Ranks	Total
43rd Foot			3	11		14
52nd Foot	1	8	3	52	1	65
95th Rifles		3	2	10		15
1st Caçadores		1	1	3		5
3rd Caçadores		1		7		8
Total	1	13	9	83	1	107

Sources: Oman, vol. 4, p. 615; PT AHM-DIV-1-14-12-3 ms 33.

Among the officer casualties were:

- 43rd Foot: Captain William Napier and Ensign Richard Carroll severely wounded, and Captain Robert Dalzell slightly wounded
- 52nd Foot: Lieutenant Theophilus Gifford killed, Captains William Jones and George Napier severely wounded, and William Mein slightly wounded
- 95th Rifles: Major John Stewart[207] and Lieutenant John Strode[208] wounded
- 1st Caçadores: Lieutenant Joaquim Manuel da Fonseca wounded

The combat of Casal Novo was unusual because it was fought over a distance of 12km. As the division was moving forward from one position to another, the wounded were left where they fell. Wellington had realized this and a General Order was sent that night to address the problem. The 5th Division was told to send Staff Surgeon Henry Emery to set up a collection station at Condeixa and the 1st Division was to provide an assistant surgeon. 'Each Division of infantry, and brigade of cavalry, will send out a fatigue party, consisting of 1 subaltern, 2 serjeants, and 30 rank and file, to collect the wounded; those found are to be brought to the nearest part of the road leading from the respective divisions to Condeixa.'[209]

William Napier was left behind, presumed dead, while his regiment moved forward. He was found by Captain John Wilson of the 1st Foot:

> We were advancing towards the enemy, when I saw an officer at the distance of about eighty yards stretched on the ground beneath an olive-tree, to the right of my company. Believing him to be either dead or badly wounded, I ran towards him and said, 'I hope you are not dangerously wounded,' at which he shook his head. 'Have you been attended to by a surgeon?' I said; and he again shook his head, but did not utter a word. He looked deadly pale, and I was deeply impressed with the classical outline and beautiful expression of his handsome countenance! I told him I had some cold tea and brandy in my flask, and asked if I should give him a little of it; at which he raised his head, a sudden beam of pleasure sparkled in his eyes, – he stretched out his hand, and I gave him a tumblerfull [sic], which he drank with a most interesting expression of unexpected enjoyment – so much so, that I gave him a second dose; and when he had finished, he seized my hand and grasped it several times, as much as to say, 'I don't know who you are, my good fellow, but I feel most gratefully thankful for your kindness.' I then said, 'Heaven protect you!' and ran off to join my company. I had not the slightest knowledge who he was, and amidst the firing and excitement of the moment I did not notice his uniform.[210]

While William Napier's brother George was being evacuated, he 'saw some men carrying an officer in a blanket who seemed badly wounded, and when I came up to them I found it was my brother William, who had received a shot in the back while giving orders to his company. I and everyone who saw him thought it was a mortal wound, but it proved otherwise, thank God!'[211] They had to wait along the side of the road while the other divisions were moving to the battlefield. While they waited, their older brother, Major Charles Napier, 50th Foot, passed by with his regiment:

He was sorry to find us both wounded so severely, and was himself suffering from weakness and want of food, as he had not been able to get anything to eat for the last two days and had been continually on horseback pushing on to join the army, being one of those who never remained behind when the troops were advancing unless forced to do so by wounds and sickness, and not even then unless in so weak a state as to preclude his sitting on his horse. While waiting with us under the tree, one of his own officers came up and said, 'Major, here is our surgeon, who is very clever at *taking off an extremity*; if you like him to try his hand on your brother's arm he will do it elegantly,' upon which Charles swore that if the little doctor came near me he would shoot him! I laughed immoderately at Charles's rage and assured him he need not be afraid for I would not let anyone take it off.[212]

After the road finally cleared, the two brothers continued to Condeixa. En route they were joined by other wounded officers and upon reaching the village they found one of the few remaining intact buildings. There they were

all examined by the surgeons, and on probing William's wound they told me they feared it might prove mortal; mine they said would be very tedious and most probably I should lose the use of several of my fingers. Poor Major Stewart died that night holding my hand; and he blamed an officer high in rank as the cause of his death, this person having said something to him in the execution of his duty which made Stewart gallop forward, when he was immediately shot by the enemy. The conduct of that officer was quite unwarrantable, but as he is also gone I shall not mention his name, but merely say he never had the character of a brave man while in our division, notwithstanding he said that which caused the death of as fine, enterprising, and gallant a soldier as ever faced the enemy.[213]

During the night Lieutenant William Light of the 4th Dragoons was passing through Condeixa with his regiment when he heard that there were 'several wounded officers in a house without much to eat or drink; he came up to us and said he had brought all the provisions he had with him and requested our acceptance of them; and he would not hear of our leaving him a morsel for himself, and wishing us a speedy cure, he went after his regiment leaving bread, wine, tea and sugar, &c'.[214]

Within a few days the two Napier brothers were moved by cart to Coimbra, where their medical treatment continued.

Chapter 6

FOZ DE AROUCE, 15 MARCH 1811

We have not had bread served out for these 3 days past, so that the men are suffering much.

Captain John Duffy, 43rd Foot[215]

Masséna's army had been retreating on two axes, with the 6th and 8th Corps on one axis and the 2nd Corps further east. The three corps finally joined up in the vicinity of Foz de Arouce on 14 March. Although this brought all of Masséna's troops together, he now had to move 40,000 men and thousands of waggons and pack animals along the same road. The column would stretch for 40km along poorly maintained roads over mountainous terrain through hostile territory. It could only move as fast as its slowest waggon.

Another factor that would slow the column was the need for the army to supply itself from local sources, so it needed to send out parties to search for food and forage. This was not an easy task because many of the villages and farms had been abandoned by the population the previous autumn. The fields lay fallow and any livestock had long disappeared. Troops from the 2nd Corps, which was at the head of the lengthy column, would snap up any food that was easy to find, and its animals would eat the forage close to the route. The 8th Corps, in the centre of the column, had to send its search parties further and further away from the route to forage. These parties were then vulnerable to guerrillas, and sometimes returned to find that their units had moved on without them. The 6th Corps had the worst of it, with little time to search for supplies owing to the enemy troops following hot on its heels. Morale among the troops was low and desertions were rampant. Those sick, injured or too exhausted to go on often fell prey to the Portuguese peasants. The fortunate ones were picked up by Wellington's men. Costello recalled the tale told by one of the prisoners they had taken:

> The troops were in a most distressed state, reduced to half their numbers, almost naked and without provisions, for most of them consumed in a few days the whole of their scanty allowance. They could not expect aid from any of their comrades, for all were without, and the country around us devastated by both parties; our wants, however, urged us to plunder, and we wandered in strong parties from the regiment, and meeting with every species of resistance, gave blow for blow.
>
> The Guerillas followed us everywhere; they fled in the front, and harassed us on our flanks, so that not an hour passed but we were obliged to be on the alert to save our lives; out of this arose every cruelty which ensued, and made our retreat almost unparalleled for devastation and blood-shed. Meanwhile the British troops came on in our rear, their light divisions harassing us night and day, and completing the wreck that never will be forgotten while Portugal retains its name.[216]

At 10pm on 14 March Ney ordered his aide-de-camp, Chef de Bataillon Emmanuel Sprünglin, to burn Miranda do Corvo. Sprünglin had four companies of voltigeurs and five troopers from the 3rd Hussars to carry out the task. At 1am he set the village on fire and the troops marched away to Foz de Arouce, some 12km distant.[217]

The Defence of Foz de Arouce

Foz de Arouce was a small village of no significance other than its bridge across the Ciera river, which was 'sixteen to twenty yards wide, was deeply embanked and its bottom was full of rocks, resulting in some difficult fords. The bridge had a large arch in the middle and two smaller ones on each side; the one toward the right bank was damaged a little. There was a ford above the bridge, and a quarter of a league above and below it we found two others so poor that many men were drowned there.'[218]

Ney arrived in the village early in the morning of 15 March. There he met with Masséna to decide what to do. The problem was although the bridge was passable, it was a natural chokepoint. It would take hours, if not all day, to pass the 6th Corps and its baggage over it. Furthermore, it was very obvious that the army's baggage train was slowing them down and would have to be abandoned. Orders were given to the whole army that only waggons and carts carrying food and ammunition would be permitted to continue on. The wounded and sick would have to fend for themselves or be left behind. Sprünglin wrote: 'To get rid of everything that might have delayed his march, he [Ney] burned his own cars and ordered that, following his example, everything that was useless or of luxury should be burned, and that the soldiers employed in transporting the baggage should return to the ranks. This necessary order was carried out with such severity that more than 500 donkeys laden with the soldiers' sacks were cut off.'[219]

A guard was placed on the bridge to enforce this order. Soon 'crowds of isolated men moved towards it and were pushed back by the guards... The unfortunate wounded grenadiers, mounted on donkeys with their feet dragging on the ground and caps on their heads, waited sadly for their turn to cross. The poor sick men dragged themselves along on their guns and asked for a piece of biscuit.'[220]

Even the herds of cattle and flocks of sheep that fed the army were not permitted to cross the bridge. They were driven to the fords and 'pushed into the middle of the current and we often saw sheep (like snowballs) rolling about in the current'.[221] Rather than abandoning the donkeys to Wellington's troops, an order was given that they be hamstrung rather than killed. This caused a panic among the French soldiers who were using the animals for their own baggage. There was a mad rush to the river where it

> had as its first result the drowning of some men who ventured to save the companions of their hardship; they were carried away by the rapid waters of the Ceira, although we attempted vainly to save them. The men fled in all directions with their donkeys and threw themselves into the water to shield them from their murders. Since the poor beasts were of a very small species in general, they could not cross the fords themselves as their drivers did; two soldiers would get together and carry them by the head and tail. The cantinières[222] fought to defend their donkeys and several of them, their heads covered with feathers, gathered their silk or velvet dresses above their hips and carried their mounts across the river. On these donkeys were beautiful parrots, infants, monkeys and Japanese liquor services used as bottle cases. Beside them were mules with parade horse-cloths, grotesquely loaded with baggage.[223]

The terrain around Foz de Arouce was good for defence. The river offered a natural barrier with few ways across it. Pelet gave a clear description:

> The hills on the right bank were abrupt and the slopes very uniform with few cuts. Towards our right, some two hundred yards away to the north, was a difficult ravine which turned a little behind the position. Immediately beyond the position, the ground was rather practicable and the road leading to Ponte de Murcella[224] was generally favourable. Above the bridge and halfway up the slope was a rather rounded berm, suitable for the establishment of a few small pieces that would advantageously overlook the river and the bridge, while the heavy artillery could be placed on the crest of the height. The first needed to be covered with a breastwork because the berm was dominated somewhat by the left bank. Some 200 yards away was Foz de Arouce. On the north of this village, toward the Ciera, was a hill covered with woods which ended on a plateau dominating the berm. However, this hill was dominated by those on the other bank, on which some works had once been constructed to defend the crossing at the bridge. These heights extended towards the west and cut the road on which we had come. To the south of the village, the plains and terrain stretched out, inundated by a river which must have been the Arouce. All these factors covered and limited the approaches for a position on the right bank.[225]

Masséna ordered Ney to defend the river from the right bank to give the army time to move out. He was to destroy the bridge to prevent Wellington from using it. Ney, thinking he had time, ignored the part of the order about defending the river from the right bank, and only sent Loison's division to the hills above the right bank. The rest of the 6th Corps was formed in a semi-circle around the village. On the right on a wooded hill were the 6th Léger and the 69th Line of Fririon's brigade of Marchand's division. In support behind them was the 76th Line. In the centre was an ad hoc force formed on 12 March and commanded by General of Brigade Claude Ferey. It consisted of the 39th Line[226] from Marchand's division, General of Brigade Marital Bardet's brigade with the 25th Léger,[227] the 27th Line[228] of the 2nd Division, and three light artillery pieces and a howitzer commanded by Captain Binner.[229] On the left was General Mathieu Delabassée's brigade of Mermet's division. The brigade consisted of the 50th and 59th Line, with the 27th Line behind them. Near the bridge was General Auguste Lamotte's Light Cavalry Brigade. Ney's failure to obey the order to move his men to the right bank of the Ciera would cost him dearly.[230]

FOZ DE AROUCE, 15 MARCH 1811

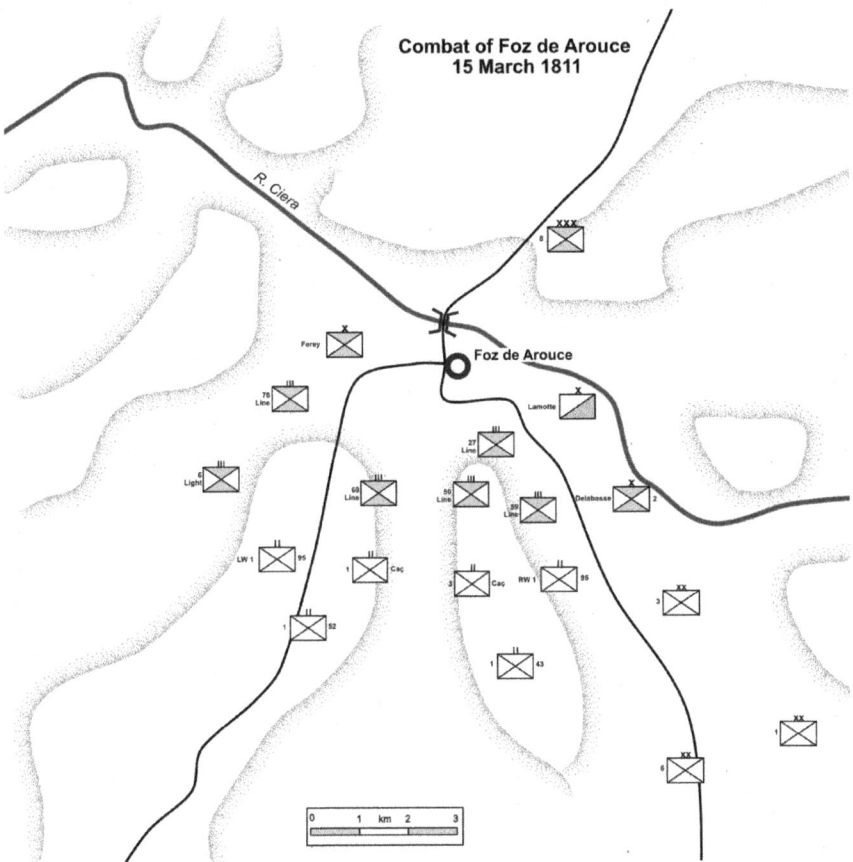

The Light Division was exhausted. It had marched over 175km in nine days, fought in three separate actions, and left its supply trains far behind. The men were very hungry and had not been issued bread in three days.[231] Orders to move out were slow to come and the division did not resume the pursuit until 10am. In every village they passed through they came across scenes of destruction worse than anything they had encountered before. Simmons wrote in his diary that night:

> At every step this morning we found sick and dead Frenchmen, gun-carriages, waggons, baggage; horses, mules, and donkeys abandoned by their masters, not being able to carry their loads farther, some from frightful sore backs, others from lameness and starvation. We passed through Miranda do Corvo in pursuit of the enemy. The town was almost filled with sick, wounded, and dying men, abandoned to their

fate, and dead. The rascally French had even plundered this place and committed every sort of wanton atrocity upon the inhabitants, and then left many of their helpless countrymen for the infuriated inhabitants to wreak their vengeance upon. Luckily for these poor wretches, we followed the French so rapidly that they fell into our hands, and were put in charge of British soldiers, or they would have been butchered indiscriminately.[232]

At Miranda do Corvo Captain Duffy of the 43rd found

a vast number of dead lying about and several peasants. Village destroyed by fire. This is a very strong pass & I should think an admirable place for any force retiring towards Lisbon to make a stand at. Found several pits filled with ammunition, gun carriages burned & every sign of a flight. Several dead bodies of officers even lying in uniform uninterred so that their retreat must have been very rapid.[233]

One of the Light Division's caçadores had grown up in this village and his parents still lived there:

He rushed to the house where they resided. On reaching the doorway, the soldier hesitated a few seconds, but the door was open, and stretched across the threshold he beheld the mangled bodies of his father and mother, the blood still warm and reeking through the bayonet stabs, while an only sister lay breathing her last, and exhibiting dreadful proofs of the brutality with which she had been violated. The unhappy man staggered, frenzied with grief, and stared wildly around him; till suddenly burying all other feelings in the maddening passion of revenge, he rushed forth from what had probably been once a happy home. His first act was to dash at some French prisoners that unfortunately were near the spot, guarded by some of our dragoons. These he attacked with the fury of a madman. One he shot and another he wounded, and he would have sacrificed a third, had not the guard made him prisoner. On the circumstances being made known to the General, he was liberated.[234]

By mid-afternoon the division had reached the high ground overlooking the village of Foz de Arouce, just 2km away. There the men stopped and waited for orders. None came, so the troops assumed that they would be bivouacking for the night. Fires were lit and shelters were constructed. The 1st Brigade occupied an area that the French had vacated upon their approach. Costello was one of the lucky ones when it came to food. He noticed a goat, which by its frisking and jumping about, I supposed to have been a pet of some French officer. Whenever we went near, it would step aside, until some of the men levelled their rifles and shot it; swords were out in a moment, and the little animal, skin and all, dissected. I was just apportioning the hind quarter, when who should ride near, but Lord Wellington and staff; for a while, I felt as if the noose were already round my neck,[235] until our old Colonel coming up, re-established my serenity, and congratulated us on our lucky chance; for this kindness we shared our booty with him that same night. We had suffered dreadfully throughout the previous week; many of our men from weakness, and through want of rations, having been unable to keep up with their regiments, Colonel Beckwith, in the hearing of many of us, took this opportunity of making it known to the Commander in Chief, who immediately promised we should have the first rations that came up.[236]

Although the officers and men were ready to call it a day, Wellington had other plans. After speaking with Colonel Beckwith, he inspected the French positions and saw that they too had halted their retreat for the day and set up camp. Furthermore, he noticed that Ney had left most of his corps on the near side of the river, with only a single bridge for them to retreat across. Wellington knew that he had the opportunity to inflict a crushing defeat on them. Before long the Light Division received the order to attack:

> The Light division (left in front) will move by the high ground on the left of the great road, slanting up to it, so as to gain possession of the heights near Foz de Aruçe. One troop of horse artillery will accompany the division. The 3d division (right in front) will continue its march, in the first instance, along the great road, and will afterwards incline to the right, so as to gain possession of, and hold the wooded hills in that direction in sufficient force to secure the right flank of the attack. The 1st division, including Major Gen. Nightingall's brigade, will follow the 3d, and the 6th will follow the Light division, and both will act as circumstances may require in support of the troops preceding them.[237]

The division formed up with the Rifles and Caçadores in the front, and the 43rd and 52nd Foot in columns. While they were waiting for word to advance, Captain Peter O'Hare decided to speak to the new men in his company. He called forward

> a fresh batch of recruits from England, a number of whom had been drafted into our company. These fellows' rosy cheeks and plump appearance, with their new dresses, formed a bright relief and amusing

contrast to our fierce embrowned visages, covered with whisker and moustachio, as we then were, and our clothing patched and of all colours. As these newcomers were now about to go through the ordeal of fire, for the first time in their lives, Major O'Hare[238] thought proper to say a few words by way of advice to them, on so momentous an occasion; accordingly, he gave the command, 'Recruits to the front!' Some ten or twelve immediately stepped forward, wondering, no doubt, what they were wanted for. 'Do you see those men on that plain?' asked the Major, as he pointed to the French camp. On several of the men answering 'Ees, Zur!' Major O'Hare, with a dry laugh, continued, 'Well then, those are the French, and our enemies. You must kill those fellows, and not allow them to kill you. You must learn and do as these old birds here do,' pointing to us, 'and get cover where you can. Recollect, recruits, you come here to kill, and not be killed. Bear this in mind: if you don't kill the French they'll kill you.'– 'Ees, Zur!' said they again.[239]

The division began to advance about 4pm The skirmishers pushed the French outposts from the pine forest to their front and continued to chase them down the hill. The 43rd and 52nd Foot moved through the woods in column and formed into line after they cleared the woods. As they were changing formation the 52nd Foot was brought under fire by Binner's light guns and took some casualties.[240]

Soon all of the Light Division was under fire. Simmons wrote:

The enemy opposed to the company (Captain Beckwith's) I was with, were behind a low wall. The approach was through a pine wood, and the branches were rattling about our ears from the enemy's bullets. Lieutenant Kincaid got shot through his cap, which grazed the top of his head. He fell as if a sledge hammer had hit him. However, he came to himself and soon rallied again. Lieutenant M'Cullock was shot through the shoulder.[241]

Kincaid's version of what happened was slightly different:

About the middle of the action, I observed some inexperienced light troops rushing up a deep roadway to certain destruction, and ran to warn them out of it, but I only arrived in time to partake the reward of their indiscretion, for I was instantly struck with a musket-ball above the left ear, which deposited me, at full length, in the mud.

I know not how long I lay insensible, but, on recovering, my first feeling was for my head, to ascertain if any part of it was still standing, for it appeared to me as if nothing remained above the mouth; but, after repeated applications of all my fingers and thumbs to the doubtful parts, I, at length, proved to myself, satisfactorily, that it had rather increased than diminished by the concussion; and, jumping on my legs, and hearing, by the whistling of the balls from both sides, that the rascals who had got me into the scrape had been driven back and left me there, I snatched my cap, which had saved my life, and which had been spun off my head to the distance of ten or twelve yards, and joined them, a short distance in the rear, when one of them, a soldier of the sixtieth, came and told me that an officer of ours had been killed, a short time before, pointing to the spot where I myself had fallen, and that he had tried to take his jacket off, but that the advance of the enemy had prevented him. I told him that I was the one that had been killed, and that I was deucedly obliged to him for his kind intentions, while I felt still more so to the enemy for their timely advance, otherwise, I have no doubt, but my friend would have taken a fancy to my trousers also, for I found that he had absolutely unbuttoned my jacket.[242]

Wellington's attack caught the French in their bivouacs, but they quickly responded. Fririon sent skirmishers from the 6th Léger and the 69th Line to support the outposts, while Ferey, seeing the outposts falling back, sent forward the 25th Léger to support them. Even so, the Allies' four-division attack on the French began to overwhelm them.

Lamotte, rather than supporting the infantry with his light cavalry, ordered his regiments to withdraw. That in itself would not have been a major problem if he had directed them to cross the river at the fords. However, he sent them back through the village and over the bridge. About this time Binner abandoned his guns and was trying to get back across the river via the bridge with his caissons.[243] The several hundred cavalry and the ammunition caissons all trying to move quickly through the streets leading to the bridge caused a massive traffic jam. On the French left flank, Mermet had given the order to withdraw and at first it was orderly. The retreat was led by the 59th Line, followed by the 50th Line. Spotting the French artillery withdrawing at a trot, the soldiers of the 50th Line, 'believing that our artillery had been brought back by the enemy, was seized with panic terror and dragged the 59th into the disorder that one can imagine, up to the bridge where, by the excess of their fright, these unfortunate soldiers rushed at the same time, while several others drowned while trying to cross the river by swimming'.[244] During the chaos Mermet was stabbed in the thigh with a bayonet by one of his own men.[245]

Before long the French outposts were forced back. In the centre Ferey had ordered the 39th Line up to support the withdrawal of the outposts, but disaster awaited them. The commander sent out skirmishers, but they panicked at the sight of the advancing enemy troops and ran away:

> Colonel [François] Lamour, commander of this regiment, ran forward to determine what caused his soldiers to flee. He was wounded and taken prisoner without his regiment knowing about it. The battalion commander who was in command dared not take it upon himself to give the orders which were becoming urgent; he wanted to wait for his colonel. The 39th retreated and was soon routed. It ran in disorder towards the bridge.[246]

In the village there was complete chaos as fleeing soldiers tried to force their way across the bridge. It was every man for himself. The eagle bearer of the 1st Battalion, 39th Line, fell off the bridge and drowned.[247] Others ran for the fords where 'whether they knew how to swim or not, threw themselves inconsiderately into the river to cross it, and in this scene of terror, two hundred soldiers remained engulfed under the waters'.[248]

On the far right of the French line was Ney with Fririon's brigade of Marchand's division. They too saw the collapse of the rest of the 6th Corps. But instead of panicking, Colonel Fririon ordered the 69th Line to turn and face to the left. This brought them close to the riverbank. Dark was falling and the French troops on the far side of the river opened fire, thinking they were British trying to ford the river. Captain Pierre Guingret of the 69th Line wrote later that

> The troops of the right bank believed that the two regiments which were near the Marshal belonged to the enemy; the fugitives, as they moved away, had the same idea, and we were fired on from all sides. Several people and a few horses were killed or wounded in the group of the Duke of Elchingen ... We then saw the devotion of a few officers who, sacrificing themselves to the general interest, competed from ardour to rushing in front of the bullets to warn of a mistake, and to put an end to the fire.[249]

Ney faced losing Fririon's brigade, so he ordered chef de battalion Dutoya to take the 3rd Battalion, 69th Line, and three companies of voltigeurs from the 6th Léger to clear a path to the bridge. Captain Marcel, a company commander in the 3rd Battalion, 69th Line, wrote that 'In an instant, our battalion was under arms and beat the charge; the 27th of the line, in line, fired from two ranks on a Portuguese column which wanted to approach the bridge; it fired with the same coolness as on drill. Under the protection of this fire, we marched, bayonets forward, with such assurance that the enemy was routed.'[250]

This attack, supported by artillery on the right bank, was so fierce and unexpected that it stopped the Allies' advance and Fririon's brigade was able to move into Foz de Arouce. The brigade was able to rescue Binner's guns as they moved into the village. By this time, it was getting dark[251] and the fighting ended.

For the Light Division, halting an attack was unusual. In this instance it may have been due to the hunger and exhaustion of its troops. Lieutenant Kincaid, reflecting on it years later, put it down to the confusion in the orders they received:

> I have often lamented in the course of the war that battalion officers, on occasions of that kind, were never entrusted with a peep behind the curtain. Had we been told before we advanced that there was but a single division in our front, with a river close behind them, we would have hunted them to death, and scarcely a man could have escaped; but, as it was, their greatest loss was occasioned by their own fears and precipitancy in taking to the river at unfordable places – for we were alike ignorant of the river, the localities, or the object of the attack; so that when we carried the position, and exerted ourselves like prudent officers to hold our men in hand, we were, from want of information, defeating the very object which had been intended, that of hunting them on to the finale.[252]

The Light Division's casualties were not heavy (see Table 6.1).

Table 6.1 Light Division Casualties at Foz de Arouce, 15 March 1811

	Killed Officers	Killed Other Ranks	Wounded Officers	Wounded Other Ranks	Missing Other Ranks	Total
43rd Foot	–	–	–	–	–	–
52nd Foot	–	2	–	3	–	5
95th Rifles	–	–	2*	17	–	19
1st Caçadores	–	–	–	2	–	2
3rd Caçadores	–	–	–	3	–	3
Total	–	2	2	25	–	29

Sources: Oman, vol. 4, p. 615; (1st Caçadores) PT AHM-DIV-1-14-12-3 ms 33; (3rd Caçadores) PT AHM-DIV-1-14-256-03_m013.
* Lieutenants John McCullock and John Kincaid.

French casualties are hard to determine. Ney remarked: 'The loss we experienced yesterday was not more than 100 killed or wounded by the enemy; the 59th, which had to suffer the most in drowned men, since it was pushed by the 50th, only lost 60 men; I suppose that if the 50th lost as many, the total loss does not exceed 220 men.'[253]

The Light Division occupied the French bivouacs, where they came across half-cooked meals. Many ate quite heartily. Simmons and his men found

> their cooking utensils were left upon their fires for strangers to enjoy their contents. Such are the chances of war! I was quite exhausted and tired, and was with about fifteen of the company in the same state, when we made a great prize. One of the men found a dozen pots upon a fire, the embers of which were low and caused the place to escape notice. Here we adjourned, and soon made the fire burn brightly. We found the different messes most savoury ones, and complimented the French for their knowledge of making savoury dishes, and many jokes were passed upon them. The men looked about and found several knapsacks; they emptied them at the fireside to see their contents and added to their own kits, shoes and shirts of better quality than their own. In every packet I observed twenty biscuits nicely rolled up or deposited in a bag; they were to last each man so many days, and he must, unless he got anything else, be his own commissary.[254]

Chapter 7

THE PURSUIT TO THE BORDER, 16–31 MARCH 1811

> The place we occupied was a little village called Melo, where we remained during the following day, having had one ration only for the last four days. Never let it be said that John Bull cannot fight upon an empty stomach.
>
> Rifleman Edward Costello, 24 March 1811[255]

The Light Division had outmarched its supply trains and could go no further. Wellington recognized this and allowed his men to rest for the day. The night of 15 March was not a comfortable one for either the officers or the men. For the officers, their personal gear was far to the rear with the division's baggage train:

> As our baggage was always in the rear on occasions of this kind, the officers of each company had a Portuguese boy, in charge of a donkey, on whom their little comforts depended. He carried our boat-cloaks and blankets, was provided with a small pig-skin for wine, a canteen for spirits, a small quantity of tea and sugar, a goat tied to the donkey, and two or three dollars in his pocket, for the purchase of bread, butter, or any other luxury which good fortune might throw in his way in the course of the day's march. We were never very scrupulous in exacting information regarding the source of his supplies; so that he had nothing to dread from our wrath, unless he had the misfortune to make his appearance empty-handed. They were singularly faithful and intelligent in making their way to us every evening, under the most difficult circumstances. This was the only night during Massena's retreat in which ours failed to find us; and, wandering the greater part of the night in the intricate maze of camp-fires, it appeared that he slept, after all, among some dragoons, within twenty yards of us.[256]

The troops were none too happy with the supply situation as they 'continued to occupy the same spot the whole of the following day; waiting very anxiously for the promised supply of rations, one day's rations however, to our exceeding joy, made their appearance in the evening'.[257] The reduced rations were taking a toll on everyone, and one officer noted that

> our jackets, which had been tolerably tight fits at starting, were now beginning to sit as gracefully as sacks upon us. When wounds were abundant, however, we did not consider it a disadvantage to be low in flesh, for the poorer the subject the better the patient! A smooth ball or a well polished sword will slip through one of your transparent gentlemen so gently that he scarcely feels it, and the holes close again of their own accord. But see the smash it makes in one of your turtle or turkey fed ones![258]

At 10pm on 15 March Ney ordered his troops still on the left bank of the river to withdraw through Foz de Arouce to the right bank. The bridge was blown up at 1am. Plans were made to continue the retreat, but because Wellington was not making any offensive moves, Ney chose to wait. During the day Captain Guingret of the French 69th Line regiment spotted 'Lord Wellington on the opposite bank; he was followed by a numerous staff, and advanced to reconnoitre our positions.'[259]

The pursuit was about to go through very mountainous terrain and the roads were not very wide. In anticipation of the roads becoming clogged with long columns of troops and wagons, Wellington issued a general order about how the troops were to march:

> The Commander of the Forces requests that for route marches each company in every battalion of infantry may be told off in threes; when the column is to be formed for the march the companies must be wheeled up or backward by threes, and each stand in column of three men in front, which is as large a number as the greater proportion of the roads in Portugal will admit. This front can easily [be] increased or diminished as circumstances may render expedient.

> The Commander of the Forces refers the officers particularly to his orders regarding the march of companies or smaller divisions through a defile or any other difficulty; the soldiers cannot make the march with ease to themselves, if they are obliged or allowed to close up intervals the difficulties of the road may occasion, by running.[260]

Movement orders for 17 March were drawn up but not issued until 5am. 'The Light division (left in front) will pass at a ford immediately below the village of Alça Pema,[261] which is on the right bank of the river, a little lower down than Foz d'Arouce.'[262]

That night the French withdrew eastward towards the Alva river. There they found Portuguese militia defending the bridge. They quickly brushed them aside, but not before the militia blew an arch in the bridge. The French were able to repair the bridge and cross it the next day. Once their troops were across, Ney ordered the bridge to be destroyed. The position was a strong one and Massena initially contemplated forcing a battle on Wellington if he kept up the pursuit, but he decided it was not a good idea and ordered the retreat to continue. Ney was left to guard the bridge while the rest of the army resumed its march.

The next day was St Patrick's Day and the riflemen both 'English and Irish duly celebrated the event, by a proper attention to greens, and not having shamrocks, leaves, grass and boughs of trees were substituted; thus ornamented we commenced our march.'[263] At 10am the order was given to ford the river and continue the advance.[264] The difficulty each unit encountered in crossing the river depended on timing. Lieutenant Kincaid, who was among the first to cross, found 'the fords were still so deep, that, as an officer with an empty haversack on my back, it was as much as I could do to flounder across it without swimming. The soldiers ballasted with their knapsacks, and the sixty rounds of ball cartridge, were of course in better fording trim.'[265] Captain Duffy of the 43rd Foot found that the water level dropped during the morning and did not mention having any trouble fording the river.[266]

The men of the Light Division marched for only a few hours, then bivouacked in a pine forest. Although they had received some food the previous day, there was some concern they might out-march their supply trains, so they halted after marching about 10km. For the first time since the pursuit began, they encountered French deserters in large numbers.

The morning of 18 March was very foggy, and the division did not move until 9am. After marching for several hours, they approached the hills above the Ponte da Mucela, where they saw the French rearguard. As the Light Division

> ascended the mountain near it and when the fog cleared up discovered the enemy in great force upon the hills covering the village of Murcella. About 3 o'clock having got up 4 brigades of artillery, the light cavalry & General Campbell's Division. Our division moved down the road for

an olive grove near the river not entering to pass. The enemy as soon as he perceived us descending the mountain commenced his retreat in the greatest confusion. We observed guns, baggage, women & columns of soldiers all intermingled in the greatest confusion. A movement that would disgrace an Arab army. Our nine pounder brigade was brought down about 5 o'clock as about 1,000 men stood fast as a rearguard above the village. As soon as the artillery opened these moved off as precipitately as possible. Remained all night in the olive ground [sic].[267]

Wellington did not want to assault across the Alva river. Instead, he planned to force the rearguard to retreat from Ponte da Mucela by sending the 1st, 3rd and 5th Divisions further east to cross the Alva at Pombeiro. If Ney did not withdraw, he risked being cut off from the rest of the French Army. Ney ordered his corps to continue their retreat and by nightfall the final elements of the French army had withdrawn from Ponte da Mucela.

The British Royal Staff Corps moved to the Alva river and found a spot to build a bridge near the destroyed Ponte da Mucela. They spent the night erecting a temporary bridge and by the next morning[268] the Light Division started crossing it. The bridge was reserved for the infantry, while the cavalry and artillery crossed at a nearby ford.[269] The Light Division halted about a kilometre from the bridge to protect the bridgehead until the 6th Division crossed. It then marched through Sobreira and for another 5km before stopping for the night.[270]

There was some confusion about the orders given to the 6th Division. They were originally told that the whole left column was to 'halt before descending to the bridge, and wait for further orders. If however, the enemy has abandoned the ground on the opposite side of the bridge, the advanced guard of the left column will take possession of it, and the General officer at the head of the column will cause the bridge to be repaired without delay ... the baggage of each column is to follow, in rear of the troops, in the order of the column.'[271] Kincaid remarked that there was a long delay before the 6th Division began crossing the bridge, and in obedience to his orders the commander of the division refused to let the Light Division's baggage train cross before his division:

> The late Sir Alexander Campbell, who commanded the division next to ours, by a wanton excess of zeal in expecting an order to follow, would not permit anything belonging to us to pass the bridge, for fear of impeding the march of his troops; and, as he received no order to march, we were thereby prevented from getting any thing whatever to eat for the next thirty-six hours. I know not whether the curses of

individuals are recorded under such circumstances, but, if they are, the gallant general will have found the united hearty ones of four thousand men registered against him for that particular act.[272]

On the march they came upon many French stragglers. Most had been taken prisoner by the cavalry of the advanced guard, who handed them back to the infantry behind them. Among them was the 'aide-de-camp of General Loison, together with his wife, who was dressed in a splendid hussar uniform. He was a Portuguese, and a traitor, and looked very like a man who would be hanged. She was a Spaniard, and very handsome, and looked very like a woman who would get married again.'[273] Captain Duffy noted that they had 400 passed to them and rumours had it that as many as 800 had been taken that day.[274]

By 20 March food continued to be an issue for the Light Division. This was not just a problem for the troops in the advance guard: all along the march Wellington's men were going hungry. Some units were taking matters into their own hands and seizing any supplies moving on the road, regardless of who owned them. The problem became so bad that Wellington intervened and in a strangely worded General Order appealed to his army's honour:

1. The Commander of the Forces is concerned to hear that some of the regiments coming up in the rear have forcibly seized on the supplies on the march for those in front, in consequence of which these last have been deprived of them.

2. Those who stopped and seized those supplies should reflect that it is most easy to supply the troops nearest to the magazine, while those nearest the enemy require the supplies with the greatest urgency. It is besides quite irregular, and positively contrary to the orders of this army, for any Commanding officer to seize supplies of any description; there is a commissary attached to every part of the army, and there is no individual, much less regiment, for whom some commissary is not obliged to provide.

3. It is necessary that this practice should be avoided in future, otherwise it will become impossible to carry on any regular operation.[275]

The officers were as hungry as the troops and Lieutenant Kincaid went exploring to see what he could find:

[He] had now been three days without anything in the shape of bread, and meat without it, after a time, becomes almost loathsome. Hearing that we were not likely to march quite so early as usual this morning,

> I started, before daylight, to a village about two miles off, in the face of the Sierra D'Estrella, in the hopes of being able to purchase something, as it lay out of the hostile line of movements. On my arrival there, I found some nuns who had fled from a neighbouring convent, waiting outside the building of the village-oven for some Indian-corn-leaven, which they had carried there to be baked, and, when I explained my pressing wants, two of them, very kindly, transferred me their shares, for which I gave each a kiss and a dollar between. They took the former as an unusual favour; but looked at the latter, as much as to say, 'our poverty, and not our will, consents'. I ran off with my halfbaked dough, and joined my comrades, just as they were getting under arms.[276]

The division marched for 30km and stopped for the night at Galizes.[277] They were preceded by the light cavalry, so the march was quiet. The road was littered with dead French soldiers and the occasional Portuguese peasant who had been shot by the French. The men came across many abandoned carts and wagons broken down and abandoned by the French.[278]

The morning of 21 March started off well. The baggage trains finally caught up with the division and the men were issued with three days' supply of bread. They marched for about 20km and stopped in the vicinity of Santiago. The next day's march was about 15km through Pinhanços to Moimenta da Serra, where they bivouacked for the night. There they found

> the principal houses as usual burnt to the ground. In some of the villages on the side of the Estrella the enemy has indiscriminately murdered the inhabitants. In a village a short distance from this 40 people are hanging & lying dead. The cruelty practised upon the females is beyond belief. A party of my company returning yesterday from escorting prisoners to the rear fell in with 3 French soldier stragglers and on one acknowledged to have found 15 doubloons, 2 watches & some dollars. All the French soldiers' knapsacks are filled with the plunder of the unfortunate natives.[279]

That night much-needed reinforcements arrived when the officers and men of the 2nd Battalion, 52nd Foot, linked up with them.[280] The new battalion was assigned to the 2nd Brigade. It had disembarked its troops at Lisbon on 6 March and moved by boats 36km to Vila Franca de Xira. Over the next ten days they marched 300km, averaging 28km per day. The soldiers were issued eight days of rations at Vila Franca but by the time they linked up with the Light Division on 22 March they were on half rations.[281] This march had taken its toll on the unit. It had left Lisbon with 562 other ranks but by 25 March it had only 489 with the colours: a 13% reduction in its effective strength just from sickness (see Table 7.1).

Table 7.1 March of the 2nd Battalion, 52nd Foot, 12–22 March

Date	End Location	Distance (Kilometres)
12 March	Vila Franca de Xira*	36
13 March	Almoster	40
14 March	Rio Maior	21
15 March	Carvalhal Benfeito, Portugal	27
16 March	Leiria	50
17 March	Pombal	27
18 March	Condeixa a Nova	27
19 March	Miranda do Corvo	20
20 March	Ponte da Mucela	30
21 March	Poços–Galizes**	35
22 March	Pinhanços	28
Total		341

* By boat. ** Galizes, Nogueira do Cravo.

The supply of food continued to be an issue, and it affected the Light Division's ability to cover long distances. On 23 March the men advanced 10km to São Paio and on the following day moved a further 4km to the vicinity of Melon. There they halted for two days and waited for their rations to come up. The farmers who had remained in the area and had successfully hidden their animals from the hungry French soldiers now began selling them to Wellington's Army. Captain Ewart of the 2nd Battalion, 52nd Foot, was able to buy a goat for 5 dollars,[282] which was the equivalent of 22 shillings. Kincaid was so happy to be fed that he was once more, able 'to rejoice under the load of a couple of biscuits, and made me no longer ashamed to look a cow or a sheep in the face, now that they were not required to furnish more than their regulated proportions of my daily food'.[283]

After resting for two days, the division marched 20km to Celorico on 26 March. There they found much of the town had been set on fire by the French. They bivouacked there for two days and on 28 March moved to the vicinity of Baraçal, about 10km distant. The division was ordered to send some men to Alverca da Beira to help man the outposts. The Right Wing of the 95th Rifles, under the command of Major Gilmour, was chosen for this, and duly force-marched another 25km to the village. Once there, the men received word that French foragers were at Freixedas:

> A party of Rifles (100), under the command of Captain [Charles] Beckwith, was sent to dislodge a body of the enemy from a mill in the front of Freixeda [sic], at which mill, Johnny[284] was busily employed grinding flour, and another body of the enemy was baking it in the town. The enemy were driven from the mill, and twenty prisoners captured, but we had to regret the loss of a gallant fellow in Brigade Major Stewart,[285] who was killed on incautiously entering the town, some French soldiers firing at him quite close, from a window.[286]

Lieutenant Kincaid was not with Beckwith's company but observed the action from a church in Alverca da Beira:

> Our rejoicings on the flight of the enemy were quickly turned into mourning by observing in the procession of our returning victorious party, the gallant adjutant's well-known bay horse with a dead body laid across the saddle. We at first indulged in the hope that he had given it to the use of some more humble comrade; but long ere they reached the village we became satisfied that the horse was the bearer of the inanimate remains of his unfortunate master, who but an hour before had left us in all the vigour of health, hope, and manhood.[287]

Lieutenant Simmons

> was requested to examine his wound by Colonel Beckwith, and report how he came by his death, as his head was deeply cut in the forehead and it was feared by some that when wounded he had been deliberately murdered. I gave my opinion that from a musket ball having entered his left breast, and passed through his heart as he rode forward, he had instantly fallen upon his head. The place he was riding over being granite rocks, and he being a heavy man, the fall had scarred his head as it then appeared. My supposition satisfied every one.[288]

At dawn on 29 March a funeral was held for Lieutenant Stewart. It was well attended: 'the officers composing the advanced guard, dragoons, artillery, and riflemen, were seen voluntarily assembled in front of Sir Sidney Beckwith's quarters, and the body, placed in a wooden chest, was brought out and buried there amid the deep but silent grief of the spectators'.[289]

Shortly after dawn the division was on the road towards Guarda, and spent five hours marching via Rocamondo through the mountainous terrain to the north. About 1pm it was deployed on the high ground above Guarda, with the 5th and 3rd Divisions to its right.[290] The appearance of Wellington's Army so close to the town caught the French by surprise and the British troops saw 'several strong columns of French in full retreat towards Sabugal. Reported near 20,000 under Massena, having left Guarda in great haste and confusion. . .'[291]

The 3rd Division was ordered to occupy Guarda, while the Light Division was quartered in villages about 10km north of the town in the vicinity of Avelãs de Ambom. The villages were small and few could hold a complete battalion, so the men were split between several villages, which they would occupy for the rest of the month. During the last days of March some officers explored the surrounding countryside and rode into Guarda. Many of the villages were in ruins as a result of French depredations. Numerous atrocities against the local populations were discovered. One of these hit the men of the 95th Rifles hard:

> I saw a woman laid in the street near her own door, murdered. The ruffians had placed upon her bosom a huge piece of granite taken from the market cross, so heavy that it took me and six men to remove it. The blood was running from her ears and mouth. Her dress upwards was most respectable, but her lower habiliments had been dragged off her. A peasant informed me that she was the wife of the juiz de fore of the village (that is the Mayor).[292]

The three days' rest were a welcome break for the division. For most of the last twenty-six days they had been in the army's vanguard, having marched over 450km and fought in five different combats; overall, they had incurred 65% of all casualties in Wellington's Army. All this while living on short rations. Wellington recognized the efforts of the Light Division on 20 March when he issued a General Order thanking his officers and remarking upon 'their excellent conduct in the operations of the last 10 days against the enemy'. He singled out the Light Division and requested 'the Commanding officers of the 43d, 52d, and 95th regts. to name a serjeant of each regiment, to be recommended for promotion to an ensigncy, as a testimony of the particular approbation of the Commander of the Forces, of these three regiments'.[293] Thus three NCOs were removed from their regiments and promoted to ensign: Sergeant Major James Kent, 43rd Foot, to the 60th Foot on 11 April;[294] Sergeant Major James Mitchell, 52nd Foot, to the 88th Foot on 8 May;[295] and Sergeant Major Andrew Simpson, 95th Rifles, to the 2nd Foot on 25 April.[296]

Chapter 8

SABUGAL, 3 APRIL 1811

I consider the action that was fought by the Light Division, by Colonel Beckwith's brigade principally, with the whole of the 2nd corps, to be one of the most glorious that British troops were ever engaged in.

Wellington[297]

By 1 April the French Army had crossed the Côa river and were within a day's march of the Spanish border. Much to Wellington's surprise, Masséna halted his exhausted army for two days along the Côa river. While they rested some units were resupplied from the army magazines at Ciudad Rodrigo and Almeida. It was not a good position for the army, spread out along a 60km front, with Drouet's 9th Corps in the vicinity of Almeida; the 6th Corps, now commanded by Loison, at Bismula,[298] some 45km to the south; Junot's 8th Corps at Alfaiates, 13km southeast of the 6th Corps; and Reynier's 2nd Corps at Sabugal. The 2nd Corps was in an especially exposed position, with its nearest support, the 6th Corps, at Bismula, 13km to the north. The 8th Corps was 15km to the east.

Wellington, learning about the isolated 2nd Corps, made plans to destroy it. The Light, 3rd and 5th Divisions were ordered to march towards Sabugal. Thus on 1 April the Light Division, after three days' rest in their quarters near Guarda, marched southeast towards Sabugal. The troops were up and on the road by 3am on a very dark and rainy night.[299] The 1st Brigade marched for about 7 hours and halted at Pega.[300] After resting for an hour, they moved another 10km to Quintas de São Bartolomeu, where they stopped for the night. This village lies about 3km from Sabugal.[301] The 2nd Brigade followed the 1st Brigade, and bivouacked for the night about 8km behind them.[302]

The 95th Rifles were responsible for setting piquets for the night along the Côa river. Due to the poor visibility caused by heavy rains, the officers commanding the piquets were given orders 'never to quit the post, in case the enemy attacked ... during the night, and to be very vigilant indeed'.[303] Lieutenant Kincaid, who had temporary command of his company, was also on piquet duty and had his men deployed on the left front of the brigade. Although the French were bivouacked on the east side of the Côa river, they had outposts on the west side. Kincaid 'was ordered if they were civil to me not to interfere with them, but in the event of the reverse, to turn them over to their own side. My stomach was more bent upon eating than fighting that evening, and I was glad to find that they proved to be gentlemen, and allowed me to post my sentries as close as I pleased without interruption.'[304] These orders, combined with the dismal weather, caused problems for the sentries. Kincaid noted that his sentries were

> within half-musket shot of theirs: it was wet, dark, and stormy when I went, about midnight, to visit them, and I was not a little annoyed to find one missing. Recollecting who he was, a steady old soldier and the last man in the world to desert his post, I called his name aloud, when his answering voice, followed by the discharge of a musket, reached me nearly at the same time, from the direction of one of the French sentries; and, after some inquiry, I found that in walking his lonely round, in a brown study, no doubt, he had each turn taken ten or twelve paces to his front, and only half that number to the rear, until he had gradually worked himself up to within a few yards of his adversary; and it would be difficult to say which of the two was most astonished – the one at hearing a voice, or the other a shot so near, but all my rhetoric, aided by the testimony of the serjeant and the other sentries, could not convince the fellow that he was not on the identical spot on which I had posted him.[305]

The night passed without any major incidents. At dawn, the division, now joined by the 2nd Brigade, stood to.[306] At 9am the division marched about 5km southwest and went into bivouacs near Aldeia de Santo Antonio.[307] The 3rd Division occupied the positions that the Light Division had vacated, while the 5th Division moved onto the heights opposite Sabugal. The 2nd Battalion, 52nd Foot, had responsibility for providing two companies for their brigade's piquets along the left of the division. Captain Ewart was among those on piquet duty; he wrote in his diary that 'some of the British sentries were posted within 200 yards of those of the French, and some shots were fired by the former, but the night passed quietly. My company being on picquet I heard the French bands play very distinctly.'[308]

Wellington, upon learning that the French still occupied Sabugal, issued orders that night to attack Sabugal the next day. The 5th Division was to attack down the main road from Pega across the bridge into the town. To its right, the 3rd Division was to attack about 1.5km south of the town. On the right of the 3rd Division was the Light Division, which was to form 'in close columns behind the top of the heights which form the left bank of the Côa above Sabugal, so as to be prepared at 8am to move down towards the river (if so ordered), and to pass it about one mile above the little chapel'.[309] Erskine with two cavalry brigades moved across the Côa upstream of the Light Division in order to protect the right flank of the attack, which was to begin at 8am.

The weather continued to be bad and on the morning of 3 April it was very foggy. Poor planning also caused problems. The Light Division had moved away from the river the day before and although they had outposts to their front, no route reconnaissance was made, nor were any guides left to point the way to the ford where the men were supposed to cross the river. At 8am the division formed into company columns and began to advance towards the river, with the 1st Brigade leading. In the heavy fog and almost constant rain, however, they took the wrong road and headed upstream. When they reached the heights above the river, they halted in compliance with their orders. In the meantime, the 3rd and 5th Divisions did not advance because of the heavy fog.

It was at this point that problems with the chain of command came to a head. Erskine, instead of being with the division, was off to the right with the cavalry of the advanced guard, and assumed that Beckwith would attack across the river. However, Beckwith's orders were to cross it only when told to do so. After waiting for some time, a staff officer sent by Erskine arrived and asked Beckwith why he had not crossed the river, to which Beckwith replied he was awaiting orders from Erskine.[310] He then ordered his brigade to cross the river.

Unfortunately, the 1st Brigade was lost. The original plan was to cross the river 3km upstream of Sabugal and then turn the flank of the French, which would force them to withdraw. Instead, the brigade advanced without any guides, took the wrong road and arrived at a ford about 3km upstream from their planned crossing point. Beckwith realized this and ordered his brigade to march downstream for 3km and cross at a ford closer to Sabugal, although it was not the one designated in the original orders. It was after 11am before the crossing began.[311]

The five Rifles companies were the first to cross, followed by three companies of the 3rd Caçadores, the 43rd Foot and finally the rest of the 3rd Caçadores. They were followed by Ross's and Bull's troops of the Royal Horse Artillery, and two cavalry squadrons.[312] It was not an easy passage. The banks were steep and covered with brush, and the three days of heavy rains had turned the river into a raging torrent. 'Many of the men were up to their middle in water; and a dark, heavy rain coming on, it was impossible for some time to distinguish friends from foes.'[313]

The crossing was unopposed and the riflemen and caçadores moved quickly to secure a height about 500m to the north. Upon reaching the heights and entering a chestnut grove, they were surprised to encounter a piquet line of voltigeurs from the 4th Léger, part of General Pierre Merle's division. Instead of making an unopposed crossing and turning the French flank, the brigade, by taking the wrong ford, hit the front of the left division of the 2nd Corps. Soon the eight companies of rifles and caçadores were engaged in a firefight.

According to Captain James Fergusson, the 43rd Foot crossed in company columns 'and as each company gained the opposite bank of the river it moved rapidly forward in support of the riflemen, each company getting into line as it arrived. We had scarcely formed when the riflemen were driven in and passed silently through our line, when immediately two strong columns of the enemy appeared in view. We were aware (by the peculiar noise of musquetry when near) that they were approaching but the weather was so thick we could see but a few yards before us.'[314] The two strong columns were the four understrength battalions of the 4th Léger moving up to support their outposts.

After crossing the river, the three companies of the 3rd Caçadores that crossed after the 43rd Foot were sent with the cavalry and most of the artillery about 5km to the right to serve as a screen for the division.[315] A section of four guns, two each from the two RHA troops, were left with the 1st Brigade. To the front was a skirmish line of riflemen from the 95th Rifles and the 3rd Caçadores. About 100m to the rear of them was the 43rd Foot in line. On both sides of the 43rd Foot were two 6-pounder guns of the RHA.[316] The riflemen of the 95th Rifles and the 3rd Caçadores brought the French under fire but were forced to fall back by the advancing enemy. The skirmishers passed through the lines of the rest of the brigade and formed up on the left flank. Before the 4th Léger could shake out into a line, Beckwith ordered his troops to fire a volley at them and to charge.[317] Captain Duffy and the rest of the 43rd Foot, as well as the rifles and caçadores, 'moved on with a cheer & charge under a heavy fire of grape, musquetry & some shells till we perceived the heads of 3 or 4 columns of infantry with a body of cavalry moving to support their front line, which had taken post behind some walls of an inclosure to our front'.[318] By this time the heavy fog had begun to clear and Beckwith saw the masses of French troops before him. He ordered the brigade to retreat up the hill to the chestnut grove.[319]

At the beginning of the attack, Lieutenant John Hopkins and his company[320] were on the extreme right of the 43rd and thus the right flank of the 1st Brigade. He noticed that

> a strong detachment of the French from Rovena[321] were directing their march to the ford. I saw all the danger of our being so turned and immediately requested Captain Duffy, commanding the next company, to allow me to take mine to oppose the attempt of the enemy, who were gaining fast upon our rear. He replied that he could not take upon himself such a responsibility as allowing the separation of my company from the regiment. I said no time should be lost, and that I would take the responsibility at such a moment on myself; and instantly I marched off the company, by bringing up their left shoulders, advancing rapidly to the right towards an eminence at some distance, on which I placed the company in position, fronting the enemy, who were marching round the right flank. I was now quite separated from the regiment, which was fiercely engaged with the French. I had above 100 men in the company, as several of Duffy's men had followed.[322]

Sergeant Samuel Harrison, 43rd Foot, was in the fight and was happy when the order came to fall back because 'In this charge, twenty-seven men of my own company were cut down, thirteen of whom were killed, and the others, myself among the number, wounded. Under these circumstances the leading battalion would probably have been sacrificed, had not Colonel Beckwith, with great promptitude, retreated behind some stone enclosures, which enabled him to maintain his ground.'[323]

While waiting for the next French attack, Beckwith noticed Hopkins' isolated company on the far right. He rode over to it and met Lieutenant Hopkins, who 'reported all that had occurred and that the French had brought up two guns in rear. I requested his instructions. He spoke most handsomely to me, approving and thanking me for what I had done and said that he should give me no orders, but leave me to act entirely on my own judgement, in which he had perfect confidence; that he would not forget me and that he would bring me to the notice of Lord Wellington.'[324]

The French troops that Beckwith saw in the distance were the two other regiments from Merle's division: the 2nd Léger and the 36th Line. They had seven battalions between them and totalled about 3,000 men. With them were two howitzers. These 'columns of the enemy moved forward with drums beating and the officers dancing like madmen with their hats frequently hoisted upon their swords'.[325] Duffy described how the ground over which the French were advancing 'gradually descended through a wood for about 200 yards to the first part of the square field that was surrounded by a wall about 4 feet high, but broken in many places & then ascended for about 150 yards to a higher & more commanding ridge of hills in which the enemy's guns were placed'.[326]

The 1st Brigade waited in line for the French. Fergusson of the 43rd wrote, 'We remained firm and steady under a heavy fire of grape & musquetry until the enemy's columns neared us, when we again charged them, routed them, drove the enemy from the wall and took the howitzer that had so much annoyed us. Our soldiers were so much excited and advanced with such rapidity that our front was rather scattered.'[327]

The fight see-sawed back and forth. The French attacked again, forced the 1st Brigade off the position and recaptured the howitzer. This would not do, and the 43rd Foot counterattacked to take it back. Private Garretty was in the fight for the howitzer, and described how one of his 'comrades, having previously passed the howitzer, took a piece of chalk from his pocket, and, as he said, marked it as our own, and we were determined to keep it'.[328] However, French fire forced the British to retreat and the howitzer sat between the two lines for some time as heavy firing from both sides prevented either side from taking the gun.

Lieutenant Hopkins, in self-imposed isolation on a hill to the right, saw, 'the body of French, who were marching towards the Coa, halted on seeing us and despatched a body of infantry against us. I reserved my fire until they neared the summit of the hill, when I opened upon them, causing them to retire in some disorder to the plain. They again formed and advanced as before, but were checked, retreating to a greater distance.'[329]

Beckwith was now badly outnumbered and could only hope for either the 2nd Brigade to come up or the 3rd and 5th Divisions to begin their assault across the river near Sabugal. The fighting often broke down to company-size actions and sometimes Beckwith took companies forward in a local counterattack.[330] The battalion commanders also did not wait for orders. When necessary, they took the initiative and charged to throw back the French. During the fight Beckwith was everywhere encouraging his troops:

> [He] was the life and soul of the fray; he had been the successful leader of those who were then around him in many a bloody field, and his calm, clear, commanding voice was distinctly heard amid the roar of battle, and cheerfully obeyed. He had but single companies to oppose to the enemy's battalions; but, strange as it may appear, I saw him twice lead successful charges with but two companies of the 43d, against an advancing mass of the enemy. His front, it is true, was equal to theirs, and such was his daring, and such the confidence which these hardy soldiers had in him, that they went as fiercely to work single-handed as if the whole army had been at their heels.
>
> Beckwith's manner of command on those occasions was nothing more than a familiar sort of conversation with the soldier. To give an idea of it I may as well mention that in the last charge I saw him make with two companies of the 43d, he found himself at once opposed to a fresh column in front, and others advancing on both flanks, and, seeing the necessity for immediate retreat, he called out, 'Now, my lads, we'll just go back a little if you please.' On hearing which every man began to run, when he shouted again, 'No, no, I don't mean that – we are in no hurry – we'll just walk quietly back, and you can give them a shot as you go along.' This was quite enough, and was obeyed to the letter – the retiring force keeping up a destructive fire, and regulating their movements by his, as he rode quietly back in the midst of them, conversing aloud in a cheerful encouraging manner – his eye all the while intently watching the enemy to take advantage of circumstances. A musket-ball had, in the meantime, shaved his forehead, and the blood was streaming down his countenance, which added not a little to the exciting interest of his appearance. As soon as we had got a little way up the face of our hill, he called out, 'Now, my men, this will do, let us shew them our teeth again!' This was obeyed as steadily as if the words halt, front, had been given on parade, and our line was instantly in battle array, while Beckwith, shaking his fist in the faces of the advancing foe, called out to them, 'Now, you rascals, come on here if you dare!'[331]

General Reynier noticed that the 1st Brigade was isolated and without support, and decided to make another attack. This time he threw in the seven battalions of the 17th Léger and the 70th Line Regiments from General Étienne Heudelet's division. They were supported with artillery and Soult's cavalry brigade on its left flank. The attack began about 2pm.

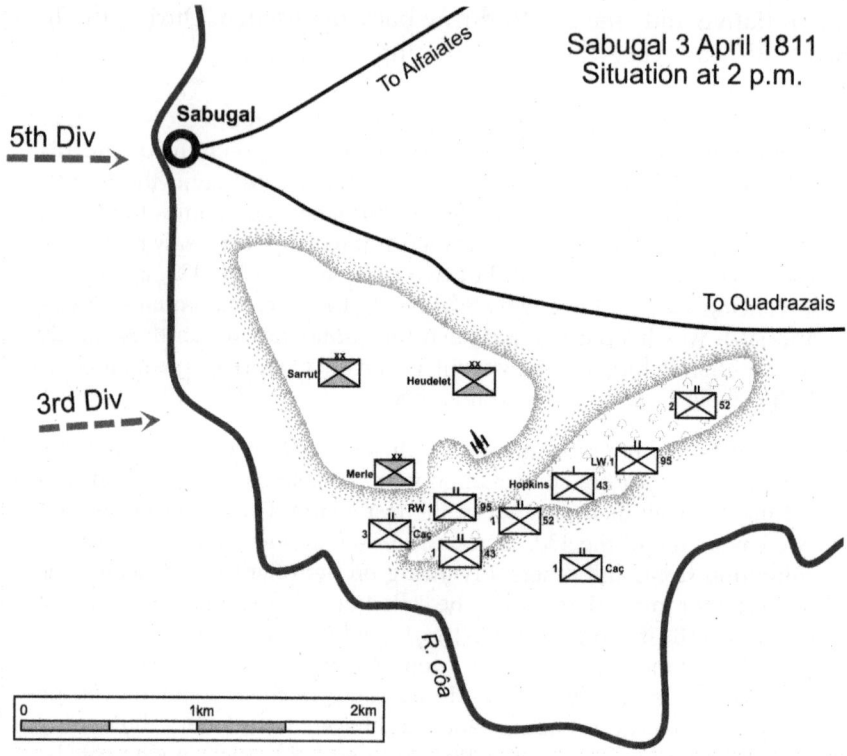

As the French advanced, their 'guns were discharging showers of grape but fortunately too high to do much mischief. Two heavy columns of the enemy now moved to our right to charge or break through and some other columns opposite our left made their appearance on the ridge. The columns came on to within 30 yards of our guns & we expected every moment that their weight would press through our line.'[332]

The situation was dire, and the 1st Brigade was about to be overrun when the 2nd Brigade finally arrived. They marched up in columns with the 1st Battalion, 52nd Foot, leading, followed by the 2nd Battalion, 52nd Foot, and the 1st Caçadores. The 1st Battalion, 52nd, formed to the right of the 43rd Foot. On the right of the 1st Battalion, 52nd Foot, was Lieutenant Hopkins and his company. On their right were the four companies of the Left Wing of the 95th Rifles. The 2nd Battalion, 52nd Foot, was placed behind the two RHA guns to the right of the line,[333] and the 1st Caçadores were kept in reserve behind the 1st Battalion, 52nd Foot.

SABUGAL, 3 APRIL 1811

The arrival of the 2nd Brigade was a welcome sight to the battered 1st Brigade. Captain Duffy, who was now the right company of the brigade's line, was the first to link up with them. They 'had just reached our rear in good line and extended to our right. We then sprung up, cheered again & charged & drove their columns completely over the ridge to the right & got possession for an instant of the walls of the field within 40 yards of the mouth of the howitzer; it was intended we should halt here but the impetuosity of the soldiers impelled them over the walls to secure the howitzer (which had just been rendered unmovable) and thereby exposed them to the fire of the enemy's columns.'[334]

It was now the cavalry's turn. Two regiments of French dragoons charged and hit the line at the junction of the right flank of the 43rd Foot and the left flank of the 52nd Foot. 'Luckily the 4 right companies of the 43rd and 2 or 3 of the left of the 52nd jumped the walls, took post behind them and opened a fire which upset most of the cavalry & completely preserved the flanks of both regiments that were so broken as to be perfectly at the mercy of the enemy.'[335] The French dragoons got in among the rest of the 1st Battalion, 52nd Foot, but did little damage.

> Private Patrick Lowe, a well known character for hardihood, was in advance with skirmishers, and being a little stout man, and not one of the fastest runners, particularly when forced to turn his back, was soon almost overtaken by a French trooper. Finding that he had no time to get to the walls behind which the greater part of his comrades were now making cover, he took refuge behind an old stump of a tree; came to the right about; down on one knee, and deliberately covered the trooper with his piece on rest, and the butt to his cheek. The dragoon at once reined up, and not liking the look either of Pat or his muzzle, began to curvet right and left, hoping to induce him to throw away his fire. Lowe, however, remained steady as a rock, and cool as on parade, still covering his man. Some of his comrades from the wall wished to bring down the dragoon, but were stopped by others, who called out that he was Pat's lawful game, and ought not to be taken away from him ... to the surprise of every one Lowe allowed his friend to ride off unharmed. When he was roundly taxed by the leading officer for such conduct, as being 'a fool not to shoot him', the reply was irresistible. 'Is it shooting ye mane, Sir? Sure how could I shoot him when I wasn't loaded?'[336]

Meanwhile the 2nd Battalion, 52nd Foot, was given orders to advance and was posted to the right of Hopkins' company. Lieutenant John Dobbs was with the battalion when 'we came up on the right of our 1st battalion, which had been waging an unequal battle with a powerful adversary. We advanced in line, being received with a heavy cannonade and volleys of musketry, which we returned with interest, the enemy retreating before us . . . A heavy downfall of rain occurring in the middle of our advance, the firing on both sides ceased on the instant – not a musket would go off.'[337]

Hopkins, seeing the enemy coming up,

> went to the commanding officer,[338] pointing out the enemy near and we agreed it would be best for him to form his regiment on the right of my company and make an immediate advance upon the French, which we did. As we advanced, they retired, forming themselves into a line perpendicular to our left and in continuation of their line to Sabugal, where their chief body was posted. I therefore brought up my right shoulders to front them, extending all my men as skirmishers; the 52nd doing the same to my right, we all commenced skirmishing amid the trees in unabated rain. The French showed fight, in their new line, mingling several dragoons with their skirmishers; their sudden debouch from behind the trees at first shook ours and severely wounded several. One man, close to me, was cut in the face, but he would not leave the field. A marksman, of the name of Cassan, was taking his aim at a dragoon riding towards him, when another horseman appearing suddenly on his right, he turned his firelock and shot him dead, the other dragoon instantly galloping away.[339]

This fight had now reached a critical point. If the French succeeded in pushing back the 2nd Brigade, it would expose the flank of the 1st Brigade. Beckwith, seeing the danger, rode over with Major Henry Mellish, the DAAG assigned to the division, to ensure the men stood fast. Mellish was

> seen in every post of danger, loudly and gallantly cheering the men. Colonel Beckwith, also with the blood streaming down his face, encouraged the men to stand fast against the enemy. Our whole line preserved their ground for some time, until a few of the horsemen getting amongst the skirmishers on the right, a sudden cry, 'The cavalry! The cavalry is in the midst of us!' caused the 52nd to retreat in confusion. I was with the skirmishers on the left and did not retire my men, seeing that the horsemen who had got into the line were so few. Some men of the 52nd remained on the left with my company. It was fortunate that we remained skirmishing, as it prevented one of the colours of the 52nd falling into the hands of the French, owing to the firmness of the men. The officer bearing the colour came up to thank me, at the same time highly praising the gallantry of my men.[340]

SABUGAL, 3 APRIL 1811

It was not only the 2nd Battalion of the 52nd Foot but also its 1st Battalion that made the initial advance. Lieutenant John Gurwood, the 1st Battalion's Adjutant, wrote that the

> whole then advanced under the command of Colonel Beckwith, assisted by Colonel Mellish, of the A.A.G.[341] Staff of the division. The 52nd passed the closure and the howitzer was recovered from the enemy who endeavoured to carry it off. The left centre of the 52nd on its advance came up to the howitzer being without horses at some distance in front of the enclosure; but immediately afterwards a fresh column of the enemy, supported by cavalry, charged the two regiments which were broken. The 52nd took refuge in the enclosure, when Captain Dobbs rallied his company and others and lined that part of the wall immediately opposite the howitzer (not a hundred yards from it), the remaining part of the battalion, under Colonel Ross, defending the other side of the enclosure . . .[342]

Lieutenant Robert O'Hara, who was in Lieutenant James Love's company, was with the men when they took the howitzer:

> We (the 52nd) advanced in line across a ravine towards the enemy in a position on some high ground opposite to us. We had nearly reached the height, when I made a rush with part of Dobb's company and took a large sized howitzer.[343] A considerable body of French cavalry were posted below the height and were at first, unobserved by us. We retired to a stone enclosure which fortunately was very close (about a 100 yards distant). We then with the remainder of the regiment, which had been under cover, threw a most destructive fire on the enemy, who retired with great loss and abandoned the gun. I beg briefly to add that I cut off the howitzer a ham and some spirits, which I gave to a soldier to take care of and whose name I remember to this day.[344]

Shortly after the last French counterattack began, the fog and rain lifted, and Reynier saw the Allied 3rd and 5th Divisions poised to cross the river. He had already committed 75 per cent of his troops against the Light Division and had only two infantry regiments to oppose almost 10,000 men. If he did not order a retreat, there was a good chance the 2nd Corps would be destroyed. He ordered his troops to break off the fight and retreat towards Alfaiates. As the French were breaking contact, they were hit in the flank by the 5th Foot from the 3rd Division, causing the troops on the right to scatter. The fighting in front of the Light Division tapered off and the French disappeared in the heavy rain.

The division had no orders to pursue the French, and upon arriving on the battlefield Wellington ordered his troops to halt. Because the division had done the most fighting, they would be allowed to occupy Sabugal and spend the night out of the rain. Lieutenant Harry Smith rode into the town and encountered Captain William Gomm, the 5th Division's DAQMG, and they divided the town so both divisions could billet their men there.[345] Rifleman Costello claimed that they 'arrived just in time to prevent the fifth division from supplanting us, and they consequently were obliged to retrace their steps, which they did with much grumbling and discontent. It was dark before we got into the house appropriated to us. Myself and one or two others turned into a small square room, the floor of which was covered with straw. Though wetted through to the skin, I soon fell into a sound sleep.'[346]

Despite the intensity of the fighting, the Light Division's casualties were not heavy, except for the 43rd Foot.

Table 8.1 Light Division Casualties at Sabugal, 3 April 1811

	Killed Officers	Killed OR	Wounded Officers	Wounded OR	Missing OR	Total
43rd Foot	1*	7	5**	67	–	80
1st Bn, 52nd Foot	–	3	2***	18	–	23
2nd Bn, 52nd Foot	–	–	–	–	–	-
1st Bn, 95th Rifles	1****	1	2*****	12	1	17
2nd Bn, 95th Rifles******	–	1	–	2	–	3
1st Caçadores	–	–	–	–	–	–
3rd Caçadores	–	1	–	2	–	3
Total	2	13	9	101	1	126

Sources: (1st Caçadores) PT AHM-DIV-1-14-223-2 ms 43; (3rd Caçadores) PT AHM-DIV-1-14-223-2 ms 45.
* Lieutenant John McDermid. ** Lieutenant John Creighton died of his wounds on 12 May 1811. Major Christopher Patrickson, Captain Robert Dalzell and Lieutenant Thomas Rylance were severely wounded. Lieutenant William Freer was slightly wounded in the hip. *** Captain Patrick Campbell and Lieutenant John Gurwood. **** Lieutenant Duncan Arbuthnott was hit in the head by a cannonball. ***** Lieutenant Colonel Beckwith was slightly wounded in the head, while 2nd Lieutenant William Haggup was also slightly wounded. ****** One company.

French casualties were heavy, especially among the 17th Léger and the 70th Line Regiments that had attacked later in the day.[347] The two regiments lost over 400 men, including 37 officers. This is a testament to how intense the fighting was during the final attack, which lasted no more than an hour.

Sabugal was the worst scrape the Light Division had got into since the fight on the river Côa the previous year. At one point the 1st Brigade was fighting eleven battalions by itself, and the men were outnumbered 3 to 1 before the 2nd Brigade arrived. However, the timely arrival of those 2,000 men was soon offset by the commitment of the 3,000 men of Heudelet's division in the final attack of the day. The many walls in the Light Division's position, the numerous aggressive local counterattacks that often prevented the French from deploying from column into line, and the piecemeal commitment of the French troops, all combined to offset the French numerical superiority.

Chapter 9

THE WAR OF THE OUTPOSTS, APRIL 1811

Wellington's attack at Sabugal forced the French to move beyond the Côa river. Masséna's army was in poor condition and numbered no more than 40,000 men,[348] hungry, and short of ammunition, artillery, waggons and horses. He could have stopped at the Agueda river and tried to rebuild his army there but everything he needed to do so would have to be brought over 100km from his magazines in Salamanca. He initially fed his men from the supplies in Almeida and Ciudad Rodrigo, but then decided he had no recourse but to retreat to Salamanca. As his corps pulled back to Ciudad Rodrigo, they continued eastwards and the 6th Corps was the last to reach Salamanca, arriving there on 11 April.

Although Masséna saved his army, he did so at the expense of the garrisons of Almeida and Ciudad Rodrigo. Their stocks of food were very low and they would not be able to survive an extended siege or blockade unless they were resupplied. Over the next month Masséna had to get food to them or they would be forced to surrender. Wellington's Army was in better shape but it too was having supply problems. Furthermore, he had no siege artillery to press a formal siege of either town. Instead, he chose to blockade both towns, in the hope he could starve them into surrender. Masséna had to choose between letting his garrisons fall through starvation or, after resting, refitting and reorganizing his army, marching back to the border with his army carrying supplies for the garrisons.

On 4 April the Light Division had a late start and did not begin marching until 9am. The division took the road to the southeast instead of the direct road to Alfaiates. They marched along the same route as the 3rd and 5th Divisions, and the road was clogged with troops.

The corpses of men and horses marked the passage of the French. The 1st Brigade led the division column through the mountains via Quadrazais and Val de Espinho and then on to Soito before stopping a few kilometres short of Alfaiates. Simmons claimed that the 95th Rifles marched another 10km to Forcalhos before halting for the night.[349] The 2nd Brigade followed the 1st Brigade but stopped at Quadrazais for the night.[350]

The 95th Rifles marched into Spain on 5 April and spent the night in La Albergueria de Argañán, while the rest of the division stopped at Forcalhos. The next day the division was quartered in La Albergueria, where it remained until 9 April, except for the Right Wing of the 95th Rifles which had moved 30km to Fuentes de Oñoro the day before.[351] Once again the division had outmarched its supply trains and there was little food available. The 3rd Division had the same problem and there were rumours that the 'old rogue Picton had seized the supplies of the Light Division for his 3rd'.[352] The troops were hungry and some decided to take matters into their own hands. Private Garretty of the 43rd Foot and his messmates

> went in search of bread or any other article of sustenance we could procure. After wandering at least ten or twelve miles from the camp ground, we observed a young heifer, to which we immediately gave chase; but the animal was so timid, and withal so swift of foot, that after a weary pursuit the game was lost. The French soldiers had, in fact, laid waste the land. Having spread themselves over the surface of many a league, they had, like a devastating army of locusts, devoured every particle of food within reach; and what in some respects is worse, what they did not eat was destroyed. On ascending an eminence, we saw the smoke of several burning villages. One of the men discovered also, at a moderate distance, what appeared to be two or three huts; we accordingly made for them: on arriving near the spot we found they were tents, pitched apparently for temporary use. Two or three women and some children presently appeared, when we asked if they had any bread and wine to sell; telling them at the same time, to secure their favour, that we were English soldiers. They were inexorable, and declared they had nothing: but one of our party, not disposed to credit the ladies, forced his way into the tent, and dragged out a leathern bottle, containing perhaps twenty or thirty gallons of liquid. We flattered ourselves it was wine, but on inspection it was filled with oil. Several loaves of bread were, however, discovered, with which we made free; but had nearly paid a high price for the liberty taken. All on a sudden the whole party of women and children set up a dismal piercing shout, and almost at the same instant a numerous and armed party of men were observed rapidly coming down the mountain side

upon us. We were few in number, and unfortunately were without our muskets. Sensible that if overtaken, our lives were forfeited,[353] a hasty retreat became necessary. We were chased for several miles; but owing to our superior speed, we at length left our pursuers behind. When out of reach of danger, we halted, almost dead with fatigue, and divided our spoil. It amounted to a small piece of bread for each; but sweet a morsel was, no man can tell, but he who has been driven to desperate acts by the call of biting hunger.[354]

On 9 April the division was sent north to many of the villages it had occupied the previous year. Its mission was to serve as a screen between the French forces east of the Agueda river near Ciudad Rodrigo and the bulk of Wellington's forces. They marched at 8am as the weather turned very cold. By mid-afternoon, when they reached their new billets, it had begun to snow. The 2nd Brigade was responsible for manning the outposts along the Azaba river. The Left Wing of the 95th Rifles and the 1st Battalion, 52nd Foot, occupied Gallegos de Argañán, while the 2nd Battalion, 52nd Foot, was at São Pedro Rio Seco about 25km to the west. The 1st Brigade was in the villages near São Pedro, while its five 95th Rifles companies occupied Fuentes de Oñoro. The division HQ was at Vilar Formoso. The division would occupy these villages until 16 April. The only exception was the 2nd Battalion, 52nd Foot, which moved to La Alameda de Gardon on 11 April.[355]

On 11 April the division was tasked with providing support for the 6th Division, which was blockading the French garrison of Almeida. Each morning the garrison sent a herd of livestock onto the glacis where the animals would graze all day, before being brought back into the fortress at night. The large number of guns on the walls of Almeida prevented the musket-armed men of the 6th Division from getting close enough to capture or kill the animals. As a result, a detachment was formed under the command of Captain Alexander Cameron, consisting of 150 riflemen and Lieutenants John Cox, Edward Coxen[356] and George Simmons. Captain Kenneth Snodgrass's 100-strong company from the 2nd Battalion, 52nd Foot, was also assigned to the detachment. Cameron was to march to Almeida and send out the riflemen in skirmish order to shoot the animals. Snodgrass was to provide support should the garrison make a sortie against them. The riflemen would be in place by dawn each day and would open fire as soon as the animals came out. The herdsmen would then gather up the animals and drive them back into the fortress. The rifles would retire at dusk and return the next day. The detachment did this duty until 16 April, when they were relieved by another detachment. Although the plan appeared to be sound, its results were not and little was accomplished by the detachment during the five days. Sadly, Sergeant M'Donald was killed near the walls of Almeida.[357]

The rest of the division was manning the outposts on the Azaba river. Word had been received that the French convoy of supplies was moving from Salamanca to Ciudad Rodrigo. On 11 April the 1st Battalion, 52nd Foot, was sent with the 1st KGL Hussars to intercept it. They marched 40km to the east, hoping to catch the convoy at Sancti Spiritus. To do this, they had to cross both the Azaba and Agueda rivers without alerting the French garrison in Ciudad Rodrigo. To support them, the 43rd was ordered to march at noon without their knapsacks to Marialba. By the time the 52nd Foot and the cavalry arrived at Sancti Spiritus, the convoy had reached the city.[358]

On 15 April word was received that another French convoy was moving towards Ciudad Rodrigo. At 2am the next day the division formed up and marched to the ford across the Agueda river at Molino dos Flores to try to capture it. The 1st KGL Hussars crossed the river and caught the convoy in the open about 5km from Ciudad Rodrigo. The convoy had a 300-man infantry escort which quickly moved into a walled compound and waited for help from the city. Major Mellish went forward to ask them to surrender but before the division's infantry could reach them, a large French relief force arrived and the convoy made it to safety in the fortress.[359]

The 1st Brigade returned to their quarters in Espeja and Fuentes de Oñoro, but the 2nd Brigade was sent to new billets closer to the Agueda river. The 1st Battalion, 52nd Foot, was now responsible for piquets at Molino dos Flores and Marialba, the 2nd Battalion at Sexmiro, and the 1st Caçadores at Barba del Puerco.[360] For the next six days heavy rains and cold weather kept the French inside the walls of Ciudad Rodrigo. Most of the fords across the Agueda river were flooded.[361]

General Craufurd finally returned to Portugal on 9 April, but it would be many weeks before he was back in command of the division. In the meanwhile, on 22 April Lieutenant General Stapleton Cotton was appointed the new commander of the cavalry and the advanced posts of the army. This included the Light Division.[362] General Erskine, who had commanded it since 9 March, returned to the 5th Division, of which he had been appointed commander on 6 February. The Light Division officers had not much to say about his time in command, but those who did were not impressed. They often described him as short-tempered when things did not go according to his plans. George Napier, 52nd Foot, said that at Casal Novo on 14 March Erskine was blustering and swearing at his captains because he did not believe their

The Arunca river that runs through Pombal. (*Courtesy of Moisés Gaudêncio*)

Pombal bridge, taken from the right bank. (*Courtesy of Moisés Gaudêncio*)

The narrow streets of Pombal. (*Courtesy of Moisés Gaudêncio*)

The narrow streets of Pombal. (*Courtesy of Moisés Gaudêncio*)

The steep climb leading to the castle. (*Courtesy of Moisés Gaudêncio*)

Pombal castle. (*Courtesy of Moisés Gaudêncio*)

The approach to Redinha from Pombal. (*Courtesy of Moisés Gaudêncio*)

A view from the hills where the Light Division waited before the attack. Redinha is in the left centre, on the other side of the open area. (*Courtesy of Moisés Gaudêncio*)

Redinha bridge, taken from the west bank. (*Courtesy of Moisés Gaudêncio*)

The Anços river as it flows through Redinha. (*Courtesy of Moisés Gaudêncio*)

The valley that the Light Division marched across. Notice how flat the terrain is and how narrow the Anços river is. (*Courtesy of Moisés Gaudêncio*)

The old Lisbon–Coimbra road just south of Condeixa-a-Nova. (*Courtesy of Moisés Gaudêncio*)

The road leading to Casal Novo from Condeixa-a-Nova. (*Courtesy of Moisés Gaudêncio*)

Streets of Casal Novo. (*Courtesy of Moisés Gaudêncio*)

The hills to the east that the French crossed after withdrawing from Casal Novo. Mermet's Division defended these hills. (*Courtesy of Moisés Gaudêncio*)

The road through the hills on the east side of Casal Novo. In 1811 these hills would have been covered with olive trees and some light woods. (*Courtesy of Moisés Gaudêncio*)

Foz de Arouce from the Allies' position. The bridge is just to the right of the building near the church. The church, which is not mentioned in any accounts, was there in 1811. (*Courtesy of Moisés Gaudêncio*)

The Ciera river near Foz de Arouce. (*Courtesy of Moisés Gaudêncio*)

The bridge at Foz de Arouce, taken from downstream. This is the side where many Frenchmen fell over and drowned. The photo was taken in October after a very dry year. During a normal year's rainfall, the grassy area in the foreground would be under water. (*Courtesy of Moisés Gaudêncio*)

The road across the bridge at Foz de Arouce. It is wide enough for only one car. Note how close the hill is to the buildings on the east side of the bridge. (*Courtesy of Moisés Gaudêncio*)

View of the valley from which the Allies attacked after moving through the mountains in the distance. (*Courtesy of Moisés Gaudêncio*)

View of the Alva river valley from the Allies' approach. The bridge is in the left centre, just above the star. (*Courtesy of Moisés Gaudêncio*)

The Alva river just upstream of the Ponte de Mucela. (*Courtesy of Moisés Gaudêncio*)

The Ponte de Mucela viewed from the Allies' side. (*Courtesy of Moisés Gaudêncio*)

View of the French positions at Sabugal, taken across the Coa river reservoir. The 1st Brigade attacked on the far right. (*Courtesy of Vic Powell, Portsmouth Napoleonic Society*)

View of the heights where the 1st Brigade of the Light Division initially fought, taken from the far side of the Coa river reservoir. (*Courtesy of Robert Pocock, Campaigns & Culture*)

The slope up which the 1st Brigade initially attacked. The Coa river reservoir is just over the tree line at centre right. (*Courtesy of Robert Pocock, Campaigns & Culture*)

View of the French positions east of Fuentes de Oñoro. (*Authors' Collection*)

The Light Division's position northwest of Fuentes de Oñoro on 3 May before it was ordered north to support the 6th Division. (*Authors' Collection*)

View looking east over the plains south of Fuentes de Oñoro, as seen from the ridge where the 7th Division was located on 5 May. The cavalry actions took place on the open ground in the centre. The 95th Rifles and the 3rd Caçadores fought to clear the wooded area at top centre. (*Authors' Collection*)

View looking northwest from Poço Velho, showing the Light Division's position before it began its withdrawal on 5 May. (*Courtesy of Robert Pocock, Campaigns & Culture*)

View from west of Poço Velho of the terrain over which the Light Division manoeuvred on 5 May. (*Courtesy of Ashley Truluck*)

View of the ridge to which the Light Division moved after its withdrawal across the plain on 5 May. (*Courtesy of Robert Pocock, Campaigns & Culture*)

View from the ridge of the plain over which the Light Division moved during its withdrawal on 5 May. (*Courtesy of Robert Pocock, Campaigns & Culture*)

reports. Napier also accused him of cowardice that day which caused the death of Major John Stewart because 'he never had the character of a brave man while in our division, notwithstanding he said that which caused the death of as fine, enterprising, and gallant a soldier as ever faced the enemy'.[363] Lieutenant Harry Smith, the brigade major of the 2nd Brigade, referred to him as a 'near-sighted old ass',[364] while Lieutenant Kinloch, also of the 52nd Foot, sarcastically called him and General Brent Spencer 'wiseheads' and blamed them for the failed attempt to stop 'the supplies & troops the French were throwing into Ciudad Rodrigo, this (though a very easy matter) they bungled most dreadfully & had no other effect than getting them laughed at by the whole army & knocking up the troops'.[365]

On 23 April a French force of 1,500 infantry and 75 cavalry[366] made a sortie out of the city and pushed back the 1st KGL Hussars' piquet at Carpio. The French then drove towards the bridge at Marialba where the piquets, commanded by Lieutenant Charles Eeles, were waiting to be relieved. Shortly before the French appeared, the relief piquet arrived from Captain Robert Campbell's company from the 1st Battalion, 52nd Foot, led by Lieutenant Henry Dawson. They were in the process of turning over their duties when word of the approaching French reached them. Dawson, the senior of the two officers, immediately took command. He wrote home five days later:

> I was posted with 30 men, fortunately we were just relieving (Lieutenant Eeles with 30 men of the 95th came to relieve the party then on picquet), which increased my party to 60 and another officer. On receiving intelligence of their approach I proceeded with 20 men over the bridge to a small height that commanded the road from the village of Marialva [Marialba], with the intention of covering the cavalry picquet that was in front and of retiring upon the bridge. I succeeded to the best of my wishes, checked their cavalry completely, who were obliged to retire behind a hill till their infantry came up, they soon dislodged me from the height and I retired as fast as I could over the bridge, the remainder of my men were posted on heights commanding the bridge and where I had ordered them to stand as long as possible. On seeing about 3 or 400 men moving down in front of me in skirmishing order, I began to be rather fearful of our safety. Our fire was so well kept up that they came to a check for some little time; at this time some of my men on the right were falling back from the very heavy fire of the French, I was just in the very act of ordering the whole to retire, when to my great joy I saw Captain Dobbs with his company coming to my assistance, and although they had succeeded in gaining the bridge with about 40 men across it, they were obliged to retreat and left us in full possession of our post.[367]

Captain Joseph Dobbs, 1st Battalion, 52nd Foot, was the overall commander of the piquets along the Azaba river. He had sent Dawson to cover the bridge while he stayed with his company at the Marialva ford about 2km south of the bridge. The ford was flooded and impassable to infantry. When he heard the firing coming from the bridge

> he left a corporal and three men to guard it, and dashed off with the remainder to the bridge. He arrived most opportunely, the enemy having forced the passage, and he, having seen the state of affairs whilst coming over the heights above the bridge, charged down on the enemy, who, supposing that he was only the advance of a large force, gave way and re-crossed the bridge; on which my brother established his men amongst the rocks on our side of the bridge, keeping up such a fire that the enemy were unable to force the passage a second time. Their manner of advance was rather singular – a drummer led the company, beating what we had nicknamed 'Old Trowsers'; as long as he survived they continued to advance, but as soon as he fell, they immediately turned tail and ran back, when they had to go over the same process for another attack. This continued for a considerable length of time until we, the 1st and 2nd battalions of the 52nd, were able to come to the relief of the Picquet, when the enemy returned to their main body at Ciudad Rodrigo. It may be supposed how much my brother exposed himself, when I state that he had a shot through his cap, another through his jacket, another cutting the flap of his trowsers across, and another on the blade of his sabre, now in my possession.[368]

The British casualties were light: the 52nd Foot had 1 officer,[369] 1 sergeant and 14 other ranks wounded. In his dispatch covering the action Wellington mentioned both Dobbs and Eeles, but not Dawson. 'The enemy had on the 23rd attacked our pickets on the Azava, but were repulsed. Captains Dobbs and R. Campbell of the 52nd regiment, and Lieutenant Eeles of the 95th regiment, distinguished themselves on this occasion, on which the allied troops defended their posts against very superior numbers of the enemy.'[370]

Reports of the French Army marching towards Ciudad Rodrigo became a daily occurrence. The 3rd Division was ordered to move closer to the Spanish border and on 24 April the 1st Brigade vacated their quarters to make way for them. About 1pm they marched in the rain to Villar de Puerco,[371] Barquilla and Sexmiro, which was occupied by the 43rd Foot.[372] This put the brigade in a good position to block the French from using the fords near San Felices Chico.[373] The 2nd Brigade was displaced by the 1st Brigade, and moved south to cover the main road from Ciudad Rodrigo and the fords across the Azaba river. The 1st Battalion, 52nd Foot, was at Gallegos and remained responsible for picqueting the bridge at Marialba, while its 2nd Battalion went to Espeja, where the men found 'very comfortable quarters, plenty of provisions to be bought, but very dear, and money terribly scarce. The church here, except the altar, at which Mass was performing today, had been lately destroyed by fire, by the Spaniards lighting some straw under which the French had left some ammunition.'[374] The 2nd Battalion provided the piquets at the Carpio fords 3km to the east.

The piquets along the Agueda and Azaba rivers reported increased French activity to the east. On 27 April the division was alerted at 1am to be prepared to march. But someone on the Staff mixed up the locations of the brigades and they were sent marching in opposite directions. The 1st Brigade was assembled behind Gallegos by 5am and then marched 8km south to Espeja, where it waited for the enemy. An hour later word was received that the enemy force had attempted to cross the bridge at Marialba, which was in the opposite direction. The 1st Brigade then 'marched to the same ground we occupied in the morning. Halted for a couple of hours and then returned for Espica [sic] which we reached about 7 in the evening having been 18 hours under arms & having marched about 24 miles.'[375]

The 2nd Brigade received orders about midnight and began marching at 3am north to Gallegos. It remained under arms till 8am, when it was told to go into quarters there. Some 5km to the east, at the Marialba bridge, was Lieutenant James Love, in temporary command of Captain James Reynett's company.[376] When two large columns of infantry approached, Love was reinforced with two companies and skirmished with the French for a few hours. The enemy did not press their attack and retired about 4pm. Ten men from the 1st Battalion, 52nd Foot, were wounded during the fight.[377]

The last three days of April saw little skirmishing but there were many reports of French troops arriving in the vicinity of Ciudad Rodrigo. Deserters came into the lines reporting that Marshal Masséna himself had arrived in Ciudad Rodrigo on 27 April, while by the end of the month a large number of French cavalry had crossed the Agueda river. There were now about 15,000 French soldiers in the vicinity of Ciudad Rodrigo. Wellington anticipated that Masséna would make a move to force the Allies to lift the blockade of Almeida and sent out orders on 29 April what the army was to do in that event. General Cotton 'will give orders to the troops in front to retire, the Light division falling back from Gallegos and Espeja, by the direct roads from these two places to Fuentes de Oñoro.'[378]

On paper at least, the Light Division, despite being in the advance guard of the pursuit of the French from Portugal, was in fairly good shape and by the end of the month could muster about 4,000 officers and men. However, it had started the campaign in March with the same number, and had been reinforced in late March with the arrival of the 2nd Battalion, 52nd Foot, numbering some 650 officers and men. The net gain was negligible, because the reinforcements were offset by casualties, exhaustion and sickness. By 25 April the British battalions had lost 108 other ranks killed and had 642 men too badly wounded or too sick to fight. Additionally, another 93 other ranks were on command and not with the colours. Particularly concerning was the 2nd Battalion, 52nd Foot. On 25 April it could muster with the colours only 449 other ranks. It had 135 men on the sick rolls and had had three men die since landing in Lisbon in early March. This was a loss of 23 per cent. Although the battalion fought at Sabugal, it did not suffer any casualties, nor were any noted among their outposts. All their losses were due to exhaustion and sickness from campaigning. Lieutenant Charles Dawson, who was in the battalion, wrote home on 29 April that 'our poor 2nd Battalion I am afraid cannot remain long in this country, their spirits are sinking from the Walcheren ague,[379] we have about 150 sick to the rear since we came into the country'.[380]

Chapter 10

BATTLE OF FUENTES DE OÑORO, 3–5 MAY 1811

the Light Division near the centre, as a flying corps, ready to be despatched to any point of this extended position most menaced.

Captain Jonathan Leach, 95th Rifles[381]

By the end of April Wellington believed that the French would advance. There were only two questions: when would they move, and in which direction? Would they come down the main road towards Fuentes de Oñoro? Would they move to the north and head directly to Almeida? Would they go south and try to force the Allies back across the Côa river? On 30 April Wellington issued an order to cover every contingency:

> In the event of the enemy passing the Agueda, and moving forward in force, the allied army will oppose his progress by occupying the high country, of which the left is between the Dos Casas and the Turones[382] rivulets, and the right extends by Nave d'Aver behind Almedilla,[383] towards Furcalhos. The body of the army will be drawn towards the right or towards the left of this line of country, or will be concentrated at any particular part of it, according to the direction which the enemy appears to give to the principal part of his force. When it appears that the enemy is decidedly moving forward in force, therefore, Sir S. Cotton[384] will give orders to the troops in front to retire, the Light division falling back from Gallegos and Espeja by the direct roads from these two places to Fuentes de Oñoro, and the cavalry falling back toward the line of position in such direction as circumstances may at the time require.[385]

On 1 May the 1st Brigade was in the vicinity of Espeja and the 2nd Brigade at Gallegos. As per standing orders, the division stood to about

4am and waited for an hour after sunrise before being dismissed. The division's baggage was sent to the rear and would only return to the quarters just before sunset.[386] The division was still responsible for manning the outposts along the Azaba river and for the Agueda river from its confluence with the Azaba river northward. Both rivers were impassable except at the bridges and fords. Major General George Anson's cavalry brigade[387] patrolled the no man's land between the Azaba river and the Agueda river.

About 11am the piquets at the Carpio de Azaba ford saw many French cavalry approaching, their mission not to seize the ford but to see if it was passable. The French commander sent 'one squadron and about three hundred infantry, who crossed and then fell back on their support'.[388] After determining that the ford was passable, the French commander ordered his men to withdraw to Ciudad Rodrigo. Along the Agueda river at the Molinos dos Flores ford Lieutenant Kincaid, who commanded the piquets there, saw that the French who had occupied the outposts on the opposite bank the day before were no longer there:

> The French held a post on the opposite side – but at daylight in the morning I found they had disappeared. Seeing a Spanish peasant descending on the opposite bank – and the river not being fordable to a person on foot, while its continuous roaring through its rugged course drowned every other voice I detached one of the dragoons, who brought him over behind him, and as he told me that the French were, at that moment, on the move to the left, I immediately transmitted the information to head quarters. I was soon after ordered to join my battalion, which I found lodged in a stubble field about half way between Gallegos and Alameda.[389]

The division waited in the field under arms for many hours. Once it was certain that the French had retired, the division returned to its billets and those on piquet duty returned to their outposts.

The next day the division stood to and at 10am the piquet at the Marialva Bridge signalled that a French column was approaching.[390] Before long, the piquets along the Azaba river saw 'the cavalry picquet of Carpio [de Azaba] . . . riding about,[391] when they fell back and immediately the columns of the enemy came down to the woods nigh the Azava [Azaba], where they halted for some time'.[392] A third column was seen moving to the right of the enemy column at Carpio. About noon the 1st Brigade received orders to withdraw down the road and stopped in the woods about 3km behind Espeja.[393] The 2nd Brigade left Gallegos about 1pm and marched 6km to Alameida, where they halted.

From their positions they could see the Allied cavalry skirmishing with French cavalry as they withdrew.

About 6pm the French halted for the night and the Allied Quartermaster General wrote an order at 6:30pm:

> Col. Beckwith's brigade of the Light division is to be in the woods on the right of the cavalry, and the remainder of the division in the woods on the left of the cavalry. Col. Beckwith will endeavour to keep a piquet on the hill of San Cristoval;[394] and he will have a post at Quinta da Aguila, to enable him to communicate with Nave d'Aver and with Pozo Velho.[395] The left of the Light division will in like manner put itself in communication with the infantry of the 5th division, which occupies the village of Alameda; and also with the troops at Fuentes de Oñoro.[396]

The orders took about an hour to reach the 2nd Brigade in Alameida, 12km away. It began marching at 8pm and bivouacked 'in a wood, 1st brigade about one mile on our right. Slept close to our arms from 11 till 2am.'[397] French cavalry was spotted moving into Espeja at dusk and Beckwith ordered the brigade into squares, which they remained in all night because it was quite dark, with a waning moon. The darkness caused problems for Captain Duffy, who was sent to the army headquarters for new orders and on his way back was nearly taken prisoner when he rode into a French outpost by mistake.[398]

The following morning the division was up before first light and at about 7am began moving towards Fuentes de Oñoro. The 2nd Brigade marched just south of the main road, while the 1st Brigade moved through the Quinta da Aguila,[399] and then angled northwest to Fuentes de Oñoro.[400] Beckwith decided not to leave the outpost on San Cristoval Hill. According to Kincaid, Lieutenant Colonel Arentschildt, the commander of the light cavalry screen,

> looked rather blank when he found, next morning, that the infantry were in the act of withdrawing, and tried hard to persuade Beckwith to leave two companies of riflemen as a support, assuring him that all the cavalry in the world were unable to harm them in such a cover; but as the cover was, in reality, but a sprinkling of the Spanish oaks, our chief found it prudent to lend his deaf ear to the request. However, we all eventually reached the position of Fuentes unmolested, a piece of good luck which we had no right to expect, considering the military character of our adversaries, and the nature of the ground we had to pass over.[401]

Upon reaching Fuentes de Oñoro, the division marched through the town and took a position on a hill beyond. For the first time in

15 months it was not in the front lines. Later that morning orders were received for the men to stay 'formed in close column where the ground admits of it, that they may be the better prepared to make any movement which may be directed'.[402]

Until Wellington could determine which way the French would attack, he had to cover all options. This forced him to deploy along a 25km front. To do this he had 34,000 men in seven infantry divisions. He also had three brigades of cavalry which could field about 1,800 sabres.[403] In the north near Fort Concepcion was the 5th Division, the closest division to Almeida, where Masséna intended to supply. About 4km south of the 5th Division was the 6th Division, located on high ground about a kilometre to the west of the village of Alameda. Wellington placed the bulk of his army 10km further south in Fuentes de Oñoro. In the hills behind the town were the 3rd Division on the left flank and the 1st Division on the right flank. The Light Division was positioned behind the 3rd Division, while the 7th Division was behind the 1st Division. On the far right flank of the army, 8km away, were Spanish guerrillas occupying Nave de Haver.

The front line of the army was located along the Dos Casas river. It appeared to be a strong position, but there were several weaknesses. The French approach to the town had to cross the river, which was less than a foot deep, while the terrain on the opposite side of it 'is in general wood which afforded the enemy shelter & gave him the advantage of moving without our being able to ascertain his numbers'.[404] The second weakness was that the army had the Turones river to its rear, which could be impassable in places if there were heavy rains. The biggest weakness, however, was there was only the bridge at Castelo Bom across the Côa river 10km to the west of Fuentes de Oñoro. The next closest bridge was at Sabugal, 30km to the southwest. If the French were able to break through and capture the bridge at Castelo Bom, the army would be split and there was a danger that the 5th and 6th Divisions would be cut off.

Aware of this threat, on the morning of 3 May Wellington gave detailed orders for what the divisions were to do if this happened. The Light and 3rd Divisions were to move south 'by the Caril [sic] road[405] to the turn near where the road to Villar Maior branches off from the Caril road; and if necessary to retire farther, these divisions will pass the rivulet behind them by the fords between Aldea da Ribeira and Villar Maior'.[406]

Masséna had spent the previous month rebuilding his army and on the morning of 1 March he had about 48,500 men. There were 44,000 infantry organized into four infantry corps and 4,500 cavalry troopers

BATTLE OF FUENTES DE OÑORO, 3–5 MAY 1811

in eight brigades.[407] As they advanced towards Fuentes de Oñoro, the 2nd Corps, with its two divisions, was just to the north of Alameda.[408] To the south of Alameda was the single division of the 8th Corps.[409] In front of Fuentes de Oñoro were the 17,000 men of the 6th Corps in three divisions. In reserve, behind the 6th Corps, were the two divisions of the 9th Corps, with another 11,000 men.

Wellington observed the French deployment and decided to reinforce his left flank. About noon, the Light Division was ordered to march north and position itself behind the 6th Division in the hills above Alameda. Captain Duffy of the 43rd Foot noted in his diary that 'the ground is commanding and inaccessible for artillery or cavalry, covered with pieces of detached rock. From there on to Fort Conception it is impassable for any arm. In these were the only passes in the neighbourhood by which the enemy could possibly reach Almeida, which was understood to be his principal object.'[410] As the Light Division marched north, the French 6th Corps attacked Fuentes de Oñoro. Defending the town were the 24 light companies of the 1st and 3rd Divisions. The attack was preceded by a cannonade that began at 3pm. The fighting ebbed and flowed, with the French initially taking most of the village, but then being pushed back by a counterattack. The fighting ended at dark[411] with the French occupying the southern edge of the town and the Allies in control of the rest.

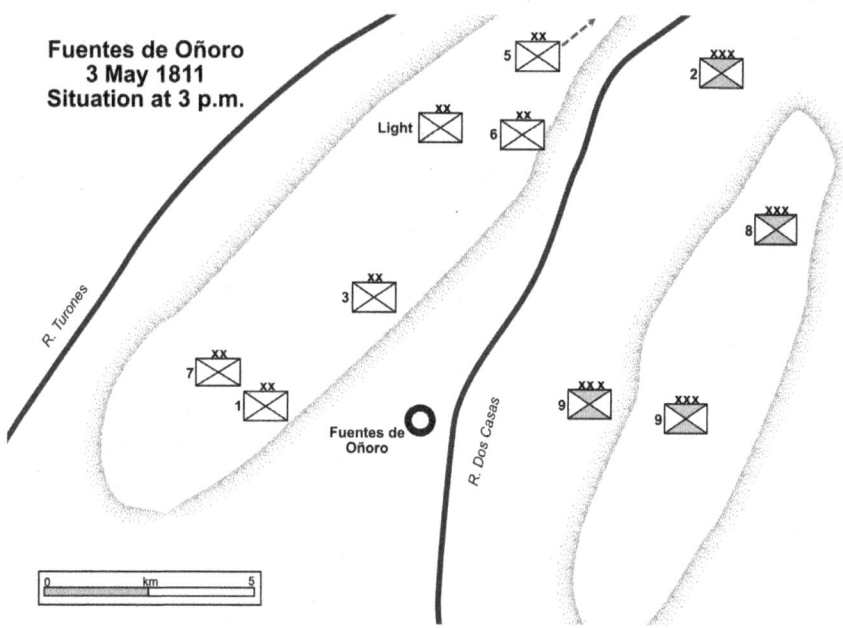

The heavy fighting in the town was of great concern to the officers and men of the Light Division, which had occupied it for many months in 1810. They had made friends among the local population and feared for their safety. While the division was marching away, Simmons' 'old patron (landlord), happening to single me out as he passed through our martial band, came and caught hold of me, the tears running down his aged cheeks. "Oh, sir, I hope God will guard and protect you. If you beat these monsters, I do not care though my house and everything I have left is destroyed."'[412]

Captain Fergusson wrote in his diary:

> the people were well known to us. It was a beautiful & retired village, its inhabitants perfectly primitive, good, kind & hospitable, appeared to enjoy all the happiness of a quiet, simple & retired life, until that dreadful scourge war suddenly drove them from their homes & property to poverty & misery. Poor Camillo's family we greatly pitied; a good Spaniard who possessed large flocks and great property as a farmer, his daughter Josepha beautiful & lovely with some fine young men [as] sons, were all driven from the shelter of their homes.[413]

The fighting in the town was fierce and much damage was done. Private Garretty wrote later that 'it had escaped all injury during the previous warfare, though occupied alternately for above a year by both sides. Every family in it was known to our division; and it was therefore a subject of deep regret to find that the preceding troops had pillaged it, leaving only the shells of houses where, three days before, a friendly population had been living in comfort.'[414] After the battle the officers and men donated money to help alleviate the sufferings of their friends there.[415] Garretty states that 8,000 dollars, the equivalent of £1,800 pounds,[416] was raised but 'the injury sunk deeper than the remedy'.[417]

The Light Division was standing to when dawn broke on 4 May. Little had changed from the night before, including their orders. The men remained in their positions and could hear scattered firing coming from Fuentes de Oñoro but nothing to indicate an attack was happening. The division was formed up in columns waiting for orders when General Craufurd arrived. He was greeted with three cheers from each regiment as he rode by[418] and when he passed the 'Caçadores, particularly, caused much laughter among us, by shouting out in Portuguese the moment they caught sight of him, "Long live General Crauford, who takes care of our bellies!", meaning by this exclamation they got their rations regularly, while under his command; the General seemed highly pleased, and bowed repeatedly with his hat off as he rode down the ranks.'[419] Things remained quiet for the rest of the afternoon and shortly before sunset orders arrived for the division to return to Fuentes de Oñoro and take up their old positions behind the 1st Division.[420] These orders also attached four companies of the 1st Caçadores under the command of Major John Algeo to the 5th Division.[421] They would remain with the 5th Division for the rest of the battle.[422] Lieutenant Colonel Jorge Avilez and the two other companies of the battalion stayed with the 2nd Brigade.

The French were not sitting idle on 4 May. Masséna realized that it would be too costly to continue to try to take Fuentes de Oñoro, so he ordered his cavalry to make a reconnaissance to the south to see if he could by-pass the town and force Wellington to retreat. The cavalry found the left flank of the Allies lightly defended at Poço Velho and reported that it was possible to get around the position centred on the town. Wellington received word of this reconnaissance and that night ordered Major General William Houston's 7th Division to move to Poço Velho. This was also what prompted the orders for the Light Division to return to their former positions overlooking Fuentes de Oñoro. Also on the left flank were two brigades of light cavalry, manning piquets.

Masséna's plan was for a two-pronged attack. Three divisions would attack Fuentes de Oñoro, while three divisions totalling 17,500 men would attack on the left to turn the Allies' flank. This attack would be supported by four brigades of cavalry totalling about 2,500 troopers.

The French moved under the cover of darkness and hit the right flank of the Allied line at first light.[423] The 7th Division and the light cavalry were caught by surprise and withdrew to the ridge in the west. The light cavalry covered its withdrawal in a series of attacks and counterattacks.

Shortly after the attack began, Wellington pivoted his line through 90 degrees. Colonel Henry Mackinnon's brigade of the 3rd Division would defend Fuentes de Oñoro, while General Charles Colville's brigade formed in a line facing south. Its Portuguese Brigade was in reserve behind Colville. The 1st Division was to the right of the 3rd Division, with General Edward Stopford's Guards Brigade on the far right. On the flanks of both divisions was artillery.

Wellington ordered the Light Division to move south to support the 7th Division. The 1st Brigade led the march, and Beckwith sent his five companies of rifles and the 3rd Caçadores into the woods just south of Fuentes de Oñoro, while the 43rd Foot marched on the reverse slope of the ridgeline and formed on the left of the 7th Division.[424] The 2nd Brigade followed the 43rd Foot below the ridgeline and formed on the left of the 43rd Foot. Drummond sent the Left Wing of the 95th Foot, now commanded by Major Peter O'Hare, to reinforce the men from the 1st Brigade in the woods.

The fifteen companies of British and Portuguese riflemen quickly engaged the advancing French light infantry, who soon began to retreat. A running fight ensued, and the French were pushed to the southern edge of the woods close to Poço Velho. Kincaid of the Rifles was in this fight and came close to being killed:

> Our battalion was thrown into a wood, a little to the left and front of the division engaged, and was instantly warmly opposed to the French skirmishers; in the course of which I was struck with a musket-ball on the left breast, which made me stagger a yard or two backward, and, as I felt no pain, I concluded that I was dangerously wounded; but it turned out to be owing to my not being hurt. While our operations here were confined to a tame skirmish, and our view [confined] to the oaks with which we were mingled, we found, by the evidence of our ears, that the division which we had come to support was involved in a more serious onset, for there was the successive rattle of artillery, the wild hurrah of charging squadrons, and the repulsing volley of musketry.[425]

At about this time the 1st Royal Dragoons made a counterattack to check the advancing French cavalry. Rifleman Costello witnessed their charge:

> We had no sooner beaten back the enemy than a loud cheering to the right attracted our attention, and we perceived our 1st heavy dragoons charge a French cavalry regiment. As this was the first charge of cavalry most of us had ever seen, we were all naturally much interested on the occasion. The French skirmishers who were extended against us seemed to participate in the same feeling, and by general consent, both parties agreed to suspend firing while the affair of dragoons was going on. The English and French cavalry met in the most gallant manner, and with the greatest show of resolution. The first shock, when they came in collision, seemed terrific, and many men and horses fell on both sides. They had ridden through and past each other, and now they wheeled round again. This was followed by a second charge, accompanied by some very pretty sabre-practice, by which many saddles were emptied, and English and French chargers were soon seen galloping about the field without riders. These immediately occupied the attention of the French skirmishers and ourselves, and we were soon engaged in pursuing them, the men of each nation endeavouring to secure the chargers of the opposite one as legal spoil. While engaged in this chase we frequently became intermixed, when much laughter was indulged in by both parties at the different accidents that occurred in our pursuit.[426]

The Light Division was in a good place to observe the action. Lieutenant Charles Dawson, 52nd Foot, saw much of it and wrote home a week later:

> We halted upon a plain opposite to a large wood where the French were and had the pleasure of seeing our artillery upon some heights on our right, playing in upon them in grand style, they were however shortly after obliged to retire, as the enemy's cavalry & artillery were quickly advancing; then commenced the engagement. We had an opportunity of seeing the enemy's cavalry charge the Chasseurs Britanniques who were in line, they gave them a pretty warm reception &c as to make them turn tail, after firing the front rank came down to the kneel and the rear rank to the charge. They did not try them a second time, the 16th Light Dragoons afterwards charged them, supported by the 14th and Royals. As soon as the 16th came up to the first squadron of the enemy, they opened out and let them in and then closed again, which threw the 16th rather into confusion, but being well supported by the 14th and Royals, they cut their way out without much loss. The Royals made three very pretty charges indeed & have been fortunate in not losing many men & not an officer. We certainly were not able to cope with them in cavalry, they were at least 5 to 1 & the greatest part fresh horses, whilst our horses have been harassed about with little or no corn to eat.[427]

The French commander saw that he could not overrun the 7th Division without infantry and temporarily halted the attacks. He then ordered Marchand's division from the 6th Corps to move up and clear the woods occupied by the Allied riflemen. Wellington took advantage of the halt in the fighting and ordered the 7th Division to retreat west to the ridgeline towards the Turones river. Once there it was to form a line facing south. Its right flank would be anchored on the Turones river, while its left would be close to the 1st Division.

This put the Light Division in a very dangerous position. It was 5km from the new Allied line and would have to withdraw while threatened by cavalry to its front and infantry to its left flank, all the while under fire from French horse artillery. If Craufurd ordered the battalions into squares to protect them from the cavalry, they would be vulnerable to attacks by the infantry and artillery fire. If he kept them in line or column they might be ridden down by the cavalry. It was a tough decision, because the division needed to return to the Allied lines as quickly as possible or be cut off and possibly destroyed. Craufurd had no choice but to order his men into columns and to begin marching away. The plan was to march fast and when the cavalry appeared ready to charge, each battalion would form into a square.

In theory this should work, but what about the 95th Rifles? They had not acted together since August 1810, when their battalion was split into two wings and each wing was assigned to a different brigade. Additionally, there was the company from the 2nd Battalion, 95th Rifles. Where would it go? And then there was the matter of the two 1st Caçadores companies. How would they form a square?

None of the primary sources tell us what the Rifles or the caçadores did. Charles Dawson wrote home that 'we expected they would have come down upon us, so we formed into 3 hollow squares and waited for them'. These three squares were likely those of the 43rd Foot and the 1st and 2nd Battalions of the 52nd Foot. Captain William Napier of the 43rd Foot, who had been severely wounded at Casal Novo on 14 March, was back with the brigade in time for the battle. In his history of the war, he wrote only that the Light Division 'retired slowly over the plain in square, having the British cavalry principally on his right'.[428]

Lieutenant Dawson referred only to the three British light infantry battalions forming squares; he failed to mention the 1st Caçadores, who were on the plain with the rest of the 2nd Brigade. When the order was given to form close columns, the 3rd Caçadores and the 95th Rifles were still in the woods. The 3rd Caçadores left the woods first and formed into a column, while the 95th Rifles slowly fought their way out of the woods and also formed into a column 'ready to form square at any moment if charged by cavalry'.[429] Rifleman Costello was in the last company to leave the woods, and remarked that they 'had to run for their lives into a square formed by the 52nd'.[430] Whether the 95th Rifles ever attempted to go into a square is not known. They did form a square three days before, but none of the accounts written by the Rifles mention doing so. It is likely they marched in column ready to form a square, but never did so.

The division began its long march to the safety of their lines 5km to the north. The battalions marched in a checkerboard fashion. When the French cavalry approached, the lead battalions would form squares while the rear battalions moved past them for a short distance and then formed their own square. Occasionally the battalions marched in square, but this was very slow going because of the need to keep the formation together. While they marched, they were threatened by the enemy cavalry, but none tried to charge them. 'The execution of our movement presented a magnificent military spectacle, as the plain, between us and the right of the army, was by this time in possession of the French cavalry, and, while we were retiring through it with the order and precision of a common field-day, they kept dancing around us, and every instant threatening a charge, without daring to execute it.'[431]

BATTLE OF FUENTES DE OÑORO, 3–5 MAY 1811

The real danger was that the squares were under artillery fire for most of the way. Lieutenant Dobbs of the 2nd Battalion, 52nd Foot, wrote that 'the balls sometimes hopping in and out of the square, at others striking a face, killing and wounding all in the way; in which case the ranks would close in and continue the operation, as if nothing had happened'.[432] For his fellow officer, Lieutenant Charles Dawson, it was not a pleasant experience: 'All this time their cannon were playing upon our squares, but were not able to hit the exact place where we were, as there was a small elevation of ground that covered us; their shot went rather close over our heads. This having been the first time I had stood to be shot at by cannon, I must confess that I did not much relish it, but after a few shots had passed, it became more familiar to me.'[433]

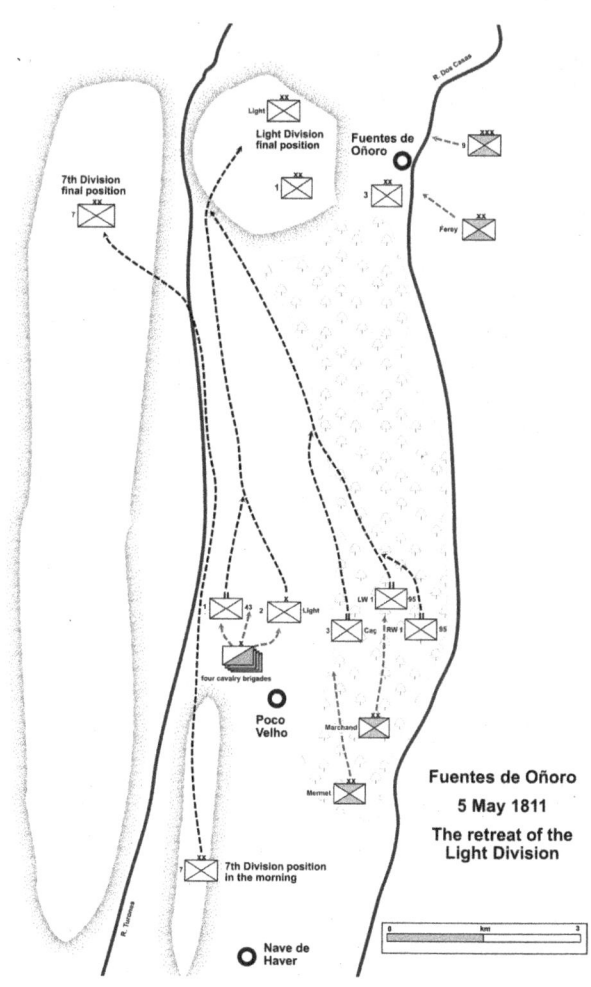

The division's withdrawal was somewhat stop-and-go, and it took several hours.[434] They arrived on the right of the Allied lines west of Fuentes de Oñoro about 10am and 'a company of Guards wheeled back, their battalion being in line; we passed through and then halted in column and became a support to that part of our line'.[435] The division was stationed in columns behind the 1st Division for the rest of the day. Shortly after the division reached its new positions, the French moved up several companies of artillery and began bombarding the lines. To protect his men from this fire Craufurd ordered them to lie down.

For most of the soldiers, this was the end of the fight. However, to the right front of the line was an area of rocky ground that would provide excellent cover for the enemy's skirmishers. The 3rd Caçadores were sent there to prevent the French from seizing it.[436] There they fired at any French who came near and their efforts were so effective that 'even a rat could scarcely have hoped to advance alive'.[437] To screen the right flank of the line, Major O'Hare was sent down to the Turones river valley with the Left Wing of the 95th Rifles to discourage any French attempts to get into the rear area.[438]

Having failed to overcome the Allies' right flank, the French turned their attention back to Fuentes de Oñoro. The fighting there continued until late in the afternoon. Although the French did take much of the town, they were forced back by late afternoon. The Light Division was not involved in this fighting, but at nightfall the division's 1st Brigade was ordered to relieve the defenders of the town and take over the outposts. The 2nd Brigade was moved into a hollow on the west side of the town.[439]

Despite the fierce fighting that engulfed the town during the day, once it died down the two armies' outposts treated each other with respect and courtesy. Captain Leach of the 95th Rifles was on duty that night when

> a flag of truce came in, requesting permission to send into the village unarmed parties to bring away their wounded, who filled the streets and houses. During this truce, several French officers came down to the little bridge over the Duas Casas, at the foot of the village, on which happened to be posted a file of men of my own company, whilst two French grenadiers were on sentry at the other end of it. On the centre of the bridge three French officers met and conversed a considerable time with the officers of my company, and were politeness itself. After offering us a pinch of snuff, by way of prelude, the events which had taken place during the day were discussed. They paid many compliments to the gallant conduct of our army, and declared that to-morrow would be a great and decisive day, and full of glory for one of the two armies. The captain of the 9th Light Infantry was a remarkably smart, talkative, Frenchman-like, little fellow. He had two musket-shots through his cap,

one of which had grazed his head, and the blood was trickling down his face at the moment. He treated it very lightly, saying it was a mere nothing – the fortune of war!⁴⁴⁰

Simmons had piquet duty that night and

> was on piquet in the lower part of the village, near a little stream of water which passed through part of the town. The enemy had a captain's piquet on the opposite side of the little hill, and a heavy column of infantry was formed behind a small church, either waiting for orders or fearing an attack. We gave some badly-wounded Frenchmen to the piquet, and the officer allowed some of ours to be given up. A French officer said to me, 'This place is appropriately named the Fountain of Honour; God knows how many of our friends on both sides have drunk deep of its waters, and with to-morrow's dawn most likely many more will do so.' My only reply to this was, 'The fortune of war will decide that, and we are ready to try its chances when our illustrious chief gives the order to advance.' The remainder of the night was occupied in knocking down many an honest man's garden wall and making a strong breastwork to fire over as soon as the day dawned. Only a few random shots were fired during the night. Before day every man stood to his arms and carefully watched its dawning.⁴⁴¹

Those not on piquet duty helped to recover the dead and wounded from both armies. The French had requested permission to 'remove some of their wounded & dead from the streets which was granted, in consequence of which soldiers of both parties were mixed together in the streets for near an hour'.⁴⁴² Once the French left with their wounded, the rest of the night was spent 'strengthening part of the walls near the church & demolishing others that gave the enemy cover in advancing'. Kincaid

> was sent, with a section of men, in charge of one of the streets for the night. There was a wounded serjeant of highlanders lying on my post. A ball had passed through the back part of his head, from which the brain was oozing, and his only sign of life was a convulsive hiccough every two or three seconds. I sent for a medical friend to look at him, who told me that he could not survive; I then got a mattress from the nearest house, placed the poor fellow on it, and made use of one corner as a pillow for myself, on which, after the fatigues of the day, and though called occasionally to visit my sentries, I slept most soundly. The highlander died in the course of the night.⁴⁴³

That night Rifleman Costello's company was responsible for the outposts near an old mill on the river when General Craufurd came by to inspect the piquets:

> The opposing lines of sentries were very close to each other: the French being divided from us only by a narrow plank thrown across the milldam, which was occupied on one side by our company, who were now on picquet. A blacksmith of ours of the name of Tidy, who had erected his forge in the old mill, was at work close by, shoeing the officers' horses. The French sentry had crossed the plank to light his pipe, and was standing carelessly chatting with me, when who should I see approaching, but General Crauford inquiring if Tidy had shod his horse. The Frenchman's red wings soon attracted the General's notice, and he suddenly with his well known stern glance, inquired, 'Who the devil's that you're talking with, rifleman?' I informed him the French sentry, who had come over for a light for his pipe. 'Indeed,' replied Crauford, 'let him go about his business, he has no right here, nor we either,' said he, in a low whisper to his aide-de-camp, and away he walked.[444]

The next day the two armies waited in their positions, but no action was taken by either side. The 2nd Brigade relieved the 1st Brigade in the town and 'by working during the whole night in making temporary fortifications with the stone walls, they succeeded in strengthening the place very much against a future attack. 2nd Battalion 52nd had four companies alternately on picquet among some rocks on the right of the village; the whole range of sentries within musket shot of each other and our whole army bivouacked, ready to stand to their arms along the position.'[445] Lieutenant Dobbs was on piquet duty and confirmed the unspoken truce between the outposts: 'Our side of the stream was so steep that we could not get at the water, while theirs was easy of access; on making friendly signals to them, they filled wooden canteens for us – we throwing them over, and they returning them filled.'[446]

In their free time the officers and soldiers looked to see what had happened to their Spanish friends. Kincaid was worried about the town's priest and went to his house

> at the top of the town. He was an old friend of ours, and an old fool, for he would not leave his house until it was too late to take anything with him; but, curious enough, although it had been repeatedly in the possession of both sides, and plundered, no doubt, by many expert artists, yet none of them thought of looking so high as the garret, which happened to be the repository of his money and provisions. He came to us the day after the battle, weeping over his supposed loss, like a sensitive Christian, and I accompanied him to the house, to see whether there was not some consolation remaining for him; but, when he found his treasure safe, he could scarcely bear its restoration with becoming gravity. I helped him to carry off his bag of dollars, and he returned the compliment with a leg of mutton.[447]

The cease-fire continued over the next three days. Deserters came into the lines and reported that Masséna had given up on resupplying Almeida and preparations were being made to withdraw. Dobbs was on piquet duty on the night of 9 May and the next day a 'few hours before daylight I heard the rolling of wheels, but could not tell whether the enemy was retiring or bringing up more artillery. As our sentries were on one side of a narrow stream, and the enemy's on the other, it was not easy for them to get off without being perceived, but they managed it thus: when relieving sentries, they placed a straw figure, with a French cap on its head, and a pole like the barrel of a musket standing at its side. Not wishing to create a false alarm, it was some time before I could ascertain the truth, but at once reported my suspicions to Head Quarters.'[448]

The battle was over and for once the Light Division had escaped with relatively few casualties (see Table 10.1).

Table 10.1 Light Division Casualties at Fuentes de Oñoro, 3–5 May 1811

	Killed Officers	Killed OR	Wounded Officers	Wounded OR	Missing OR	Total
43rd Foot	–	–	–	9	–	9
1st Bn, 52nd Foot	–	1	–	6	–	7
2nd Bn, 52nd Foot	–	–	–	7	–	7
1st Bn, 95th Rifles	–	–	–	7	–	7
2nd Bn, 95th Rifles*	–	2	–	4	–	6
1st Caçadores	–	–	–	15**	–	15
3rd Caçadores	–	1	1***	6****	–	8
Total	–	4	1	54	–	59

Sources: Oman, vol. 4, p. 624; (2nd Bn, 95th Rifles) Verner, vol. 2, p. 278; (1st Caçadores) PT-DIV-1-14-223-2 ms 45 and PT-DIV-1-14-270-01_m0178; (3rd Caçadores) PT AHM-DIV-1-14-270-01_m0171.
* One company. ** Four other ranks were wounded on 3 May, while two sergeants and nine other ranks were wounded on 5 May. *** Lieutenant Anthony Francis de Breunig, 60th Foot. **** Two sergeants and four other ranks were wounded on 5 May.

Chapter 11

THE MARCH TO BADAJOZ, MAY–JUNE 1811

Lieutenant Dobbs's report of the French withdrawing from Fuentes de Oñoro was supported by others. One common thread to the reports was the sound of drumming coming from the French lines throughout much of the night. At daybreak infantry and cavalry patrols were sent out and confirmed that the French were retreating towards Ciudad Rodrigo. General Craufurd had accompanied one of the patrols and once he was convinced that the French were withdrawing, he gave the order for the division to advance. The 1st Brigade marched the 14km to their old quarters in Espeja, which they found had been ransacked by the French. The 2nd Brigade began moving about 11am and marched 15km to Gallegos. Because the enemy had moved close to Ciudad Rodrigo, the division set up outposts along the Azaba river. Ewart's company of the 2nd Battalion, 52nd Foot, manned the position at the Carpio ford. About 11pm a loud explosion was heard from Almeida.[449]

On 11 May the division stood to at daybreak. As on the previous day, the weather was fine. No contact was reported with the enemy. Reports were received that the French Army was retreating to Salamanca, harassed the whole way by Spanish guerrillas. Once again, the Light Division was working closely with its old friends the 1st KGL Hussars, who shared quarters and outpost duties with the 1st Brigade, while the 2nd Brigade did so with the 16th Light Dragoons. The cavalry was withdrawn from the outpost at dusk, leaving the infantry to themselves.[450]

The division stood to at dawn,[451] and after waiting for an hour returned to its quarters. About 7am the cavalry piquets on the far side of the Azaba river reported that many cavalry were seen in the distance. The brigades formed up in front of their villages and soon the 1st KGL Hussars' screen of 50 men was forced back across the river by two squadrons of French cavalry. Rather than stopping at the Carpio ford, the French continued over the river and southwest towards Espeja. Beckwith ordered his two battalions into square and the five companies of the Rifles into some woods on their flank. One of the French squadrons approached within 400m of the squares and was brought under rifle fire.[452] After losing several horses, the French withdrew and returned to Ciudad Rodrigo via the Carpio ford. Once it was certain that the French were gone, the piquets returned to their posts on the river. Later that day word was received that the loud explosion they heard two nights before was the French blowing up the guns and walls of Almeida, prior to evacuating the city and escaping across the Agueda river at Barba del Puerco.

The French continued to pull back to their cantonments at Salamanca and it was quiet for the next twelve days. For the first time in two months the division was able to relax a bit and on 13 May the outposts were reduced from company size to section size.[453] About this time word reached the army that the French in southern Spain were marching to relieve Badajoz, which had been under siege by the Allies since mid-April. On 14 May Wellington ordered the 3rd and 7th Divisions to march south to reinforce the Allied army.[454] Three days later Wellington left with his personal staff to see the situation for himself. Prior to heading south, he left instructions for Lieutenant General Brent Spencer on what to do should the French advance in force from Salamanca. Spencer was to withdraw his four divisions[455] across the Côa river, leaving only a screen near Ciudad Rodrigo. He was then to march south with the rest of his force and defend the river from Sabugal to Penamacor.

The sunny weather that the division had been enjoying worsened on 16 May and it rained for several days.[456] During this down-time, many officers took the opportunity to ride to Almeida to see the destruction done by the French when they evacuated the town. What they saw shocked them. Almeida

> was nearly a heap of ruins, many of the houses destroyed and the fortifications blown into the ditch in a most surprising manner; few of the inhabitants to be seen, and these in a miserable condition. They stated that the French had kept them all shut up in their houses for the three days prior to their going away, during which time they had suffered much for want of provisions. A large quantity of stores and ammunition still remained in the place, and many of our artillery were employed in clearing the ditch and in trying to drill the spikes out of the guns, some of which were left double shotted.[457]

THE MARCH TO BADAJOZ, MAY–JUNE 1811

On 22 May word came of the Allied victory at Albuera on 16 May. It was a hard-fought battle and the three Allied divisions involved lost over 6,000 men. Around 24 May intelligence was received that Marshal Auguste de Marmont, the new commander of the French Army of Portugal, was advancing from Salamanca. Spencer, in compliance with Wellington's instructions, began preparing to move his 20,000 men away from Ciudad Rodrigo. The next day the Light Division received orders to be ready 'to march at an hour's notice. It was generally expected that the division (a similar order was given both to the 1st Division & also a brigade of Portuguese) would move immediately, it did not arrive till the evening & directed our march by daylight tomorrow.'[458] The 5th Division would take over their outpost duties.

The Light Division was on the road at 5am on 26 May, with the 2nd Brigade following the 1st Brigade. The original orders were for the 1st Brigade to march to Alfaiates via Nave de Haver, but the destination was changed to Aldeia da Ponte before they set out. The 2nd Brigade was to halt at Nave de Haver. After arriving at Aldeia da Ponte, orders arrived cancelling the march; instead they were to return to their recently vacated cantonments. The next morning the 1st Brigade marched back to Espeja, but this time through La Alamedilla. Upon arriving at their old billets, the division took up outpost duty again. The information that Marmont was advancing was wrong, so Spencer ordered his men back to their positions near Ciudad Rodrigo. Marmont was indeed planning to move south to support Marshal Soult in his attempt to relieve the French garrison in Badajoz, but he needed time to collect the necessary supplies to feed his men.

For the rest of May and the first four days of June the outposts had little to report. However, in the evening of 4 June Spencer received word that Marmont was near Ciudad Rodrigo and passed orders to his men to be ready to move early the next day. Later that night Craufurd ordered his troops to 'have everything clear of the cantonments by 2 o'clock in the morning'.[459] These orders were not well received by the officers of the Right Wing of the 95th Rifles, for when the orders arrived, they

> were celebrating the birth-day of George the Third, in the village of Espeja, with wine, cigars, and a dance with the Spanish fair ones . . . I will be sworn that our fair partners would have been fully as well pleased, as we should also, if the order had arrived some twelve hours later, for it broke up a merry party, and obliged us to retire to our hovels, to order our baggage-mules to be saddled, and to march without a wink of sleep; no not even enough to give us a chance of dreaming of our black-eyed signoras.[460]

Once up, they 'marched out on the road to Nave de Haver about a mile and waited till after sunrise, when the reports from the front announced all quiet'. More information came in during the day and it was confirmed that the French were advancing. Captain Duffy wrote in his diary for the day that 'the enemy's cavalry in the amount of 3 thousand reports state arrived this evening at Rodrigo. 4 pieces of artillery & 3,500 infantry in addition stated as the advance guard. These reports mention that the principal force is moving by the Puerto de Banos to the south.'[461]

That night, Spencer issued the order to withdraw south the next day. The Light Division was up well before dawn on 6 June and moved towards the rear. The men were surprised at how disorganized the other divisions were. Lieutenant Freer of the 43rd Foot wrote:

> instead of returning to Espeja the division was ordered to collect at Nave de Haver. We had not reached it before the report of the enemies advancing was sent in. Remained until the enemy appeared on this side [of] Espeja in [a] considerable force of cavalry. When we fell back on the Aldea de Ponte [Aldeia da Ponte] road, but instead of finding everything well off, as it was natural to expect from the degree of alertness in which we had been kept the preceding day, sick, baggage &c filled the road belonging to the other divisions. The skirmishing in our rear became brisk and the enemy observing our mingled line of march, attempted to push our cavalry & obliged them to charge very superior numbers, which checked the ardour of the enemy and enabled the sick and baggage in the rear to get off.[462]

The 1st Brigade marched 45km from Espeja to Nave de Haver and on to Aldeia da Ponte, stopping for the night in woods near Alfaiates.[463] The 2nd Brigade, billeted in Gallegos, moved out at 3am and marched through Fuentes de Oñoro to Nave de Haver, and then followed the same route as the 1st Brigade. The other divisions took different routes. The 2nd Brigade was ordered to leave piquets along the road to Aldeia da Ponte to provide warning should the French follow them.[464]

The division was up well before dawn on 7 June and instead of standing to moved off at about 3.30am. They marched about 10km to Soito and set up in defensive positions in expectation of a French advance. After waiting two hours they marched to Sabugal.[465] They crossed the Côa river at the same ford they had used during the battle two months before, and bivouacked in woods filled with chestnut trees. There they met a gruesome sight. Simmons, with the Right Wing of the 95th Rifles, deliberately entering a river after marching some distance with a burning sun over one's head, the perspiration running in streams from every pore. Although I was well used to such movements it was not pleasant, but on the former occasion I took the water as kindly as a water dog, for the French skirmishers were firing in our faces. We bivouacked in a wood of chestnut-trees, where several of our brave fellows had been buried, and whose bones had been dug up by wolves and were strewn above their graves. A gallant young fellow, Lieutenant and Adjutant M'Diarmid,[466] 43rd Light Infantry, who was wounded with myself at Almeida, and who joined again when I did, had fallen in fight here. I went to see if his grave had escaped the general disturbance. I found his skull lying at some distance; I was convinced that it must be so, as the hair was still in patches on it. There was no mistaking it; his hair, when alive, was auburn and very curly. His bones were partly eaten and thrown about in the same way. This appearance of a friend whom I had esteemed and had so often associated with, and so recently too, produced many gloomy reflections. I collected the straggling relics and replaced them and covered them over as the last tribute I could pay him.[467]

It was not a restful night:

We experienced, in the course of this very dark night, one of those ridiculous false alarms which will sometimes happen in the best organized body. Some bullocks strayed, by accident, amongst the piles of arms, the falling clatter of which, frightened them so much that they went galloping over the sleeping soldiers. The officers' baggage-horses broke from their moorings, and joined in the general charge; and a cry immediately arose, that it was the French cavalry. The different regiments stood to their arms, and formed squares, looking as sharp as thunder for something to fire at; and it was a considerable time before the cause of the row could be traced. The different followers of the army, in the mean time, were scampering off to the rear, spreading the most frightful reports. One woman of the 52d succeeded in getting three leagues off before day-light, and swore, 'that, as God was her judge, she did not leave her regiment until she saw the last man of them cut to pieces!!!'[468]

Even the chain of command was affected, according to Lieutenant Harry Smith, the 2nd Brigade's brigade major:

A drove of bullocks galloped over our men asleep in the bivouac, and for some time the officers could hardly persuade our best soldiers they were not French cavalry. My Brigadier, Drummond, was sleeping under a tree on his little portable iron bedstead. The light of a fire showed him, to my amusement, in his shirt (not a very long one), endeavouring to climb into the tree. I fell in his guard, and manfully charged nothing up a road leading to our camp, while General Craufurd lay on his back laughing to hysterics, poor fellow.[469]

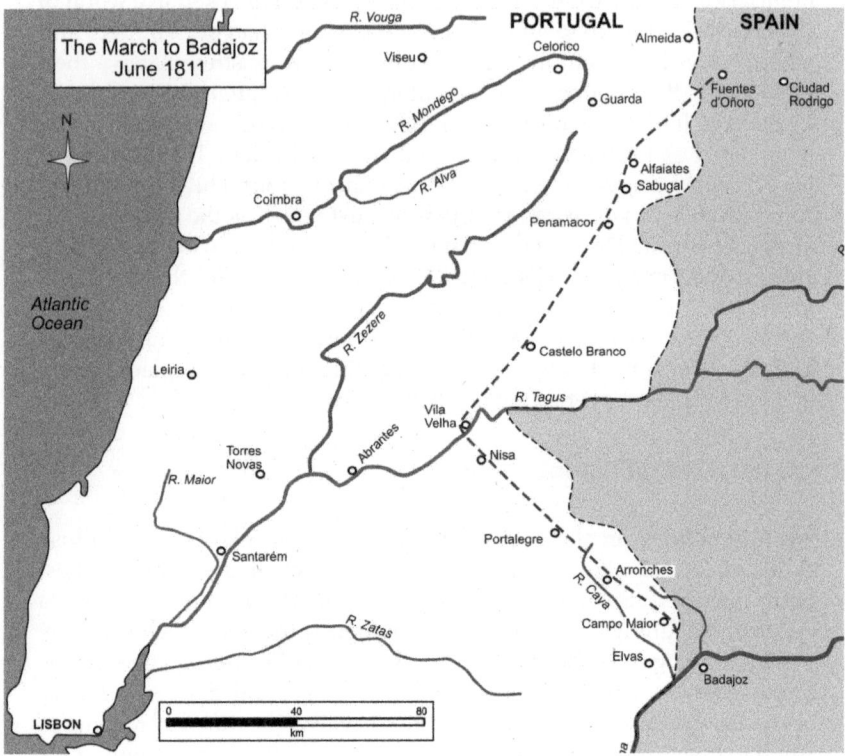

Spencer had received word the previous night that the French advance was just a feint to secure its flank, while the main part of the army marched south via another route 50km to the east. Knowing that Marmont did not threaten Portugal, Spencer, following his original orders from Wellington, commanded his men to march south to Badajoz.

For the next two days the division marched through the mountainous Serra de Estrella and halted for the day on 10 June.

Table 11.1 *Route of the Light Division, 8–9 June 1811*

Date	Route	Distance Travelled
8 June	Meimoa–Penamacor	45km
9 June	Pedrogao de Sao Pedro–Sao Miguel de Acha	23km

Marching 65km over two days does not sound like much of a march for the division, but they were travelling through very rugged country and if the weather had been bad, the march would have been slower. Lieutenant Henry Oglander of the 43rd Foot recorded in his diary how strenuous the first day's march was:

> The road at first past [sic] along the top of a ridge of mountains, partly covered with wood & underwood and some part with the gum cistus; it was narrow and bad; in wet weather it can hardly be passable. Towards the termination of the ridge, a very fine view of the valley of Meimoa opened itself suddenly, bounded by part of the majestic [sic] Serra de Estrella. On descending the mountains into the valley, the road nearly followed the course of the river Meimoa as far as that village, where it passes the river by a bridge of several arches. We halted to cook near the village and continued our march in the evening to Penamacor. The road for a short distance crosses the valley and then ascends the mountains which divide it from the vast plain in which the lofty mountain of Penamacor is placed. The ascent up this mountain is very steep and laborious, as is also the descent on the other side; forming on both parts a path of such strength that it would be scarcely possible to force it with any superiority of numbers. On reaching the summit, a most magnificent view bursts into sight. Penamacor on the edge of a high & rugged mountain bounds it on one side, but on the other it extends along the plain to Castelo Branco & the vast circle of the Estrella. Having descended this chain, we mounted the height of Penamacor, in which town we took up our quarters for the night.[470]

Unfortunately for the men, the weather turned extremely hot and would continue to be so for many days. The division awaited orders to march on 11 June, but the staff officer carrying them got lost and it did not set out until after 1pm. The heat became so oppressive that many men fell out of the march, no longer able to move on.[471] Craufurd finally called a halt at Escalos de Cima, having marched only 15km.[472] The following day the division returned to its old routine of marching early in the morning. On 12 June they marched for 10km but then halted in some woods until 4pm, when they marched another 23km to Vila Velha.[473] The large numbers of men moving on the roads caused traffic jams, the worst of which happened when they reached the Tagus river, where the only way across was by a flying bridge that could hold only so many men or vehicles, so that it could take an hour to pass an infantry battalion over to the other bank.[474] The division was ready to march at 2am on 13 June, but were preceded by a troop of horse artillery and a cavalry brigade. Thus the men were not able to begin crossing the Tagus bridge until noon. The 2nd Brigade had the honour of going first,[475] and it was after 3pm before the 1st Brigade finished crossing.[476]

The division then continued to Nisa, but once again found the going tough:

> After passing the Tagus, the road immediately begins to ascend a very steep mountain, it runs along its summit for near a league & then descends into a very deep ravine, in the bottom of which runs a considerable river, over which is a small bridge on buttresses. Thence it ascends the opposite side of the ravine, which is by far the steepest and most difficult; from the summit it runs on a level to Niza. The whole of this tract is quite barren and consists of various chains of considerable hills, which fall in height as they become remote from the Tagus; were it not for their excessive steepness, the road would be good. The distance is only reckoned to be 2 leagues, though they certainly seem to the traveller [sic], whether from their being really more, or from the badness of the road, to be at least three.[477]

After spending the night in the vicinity of Nisa, the division marched to Alpalhão the following day and arrived in Portalegre on 15 June. There it halted for three days and then marched to Arronches, where it stopped for four days. It was ordered to march on 23 June, but only moved 25km before halting 5km short of Campo Maior. The men went into encampments for the rest of the month at Monte Reguengo. Although located close to the Caya river, it was described by one Rifles officer as 'the hottest and most parched piece of ground in the Peninsula'.[478] The men were ordered to build huts for shelter because they would probably be there a long time. Two days after arriving, the 'scorching sun had dried up the herbage, and some of the campfires communicated with the long grass on which we were lodged; the fresh summer-breeze wafted the ground flame so rapidly through the bivouac that before all the arms and accoutrements could be removed, many of the men's pouches were blown-up, and caused some accidents'.[479] The weather continued to be hot and when not on duty, the officers and men would spend time cooling off in the river. One officer claimed that they were 'living three parts of the day up to the neck in a pool of water'.[480] The division had little to do except serve as a reserve should the French move on Badajoz, 20km to the southeast. It was called out on both 24 and 28 June because HQ had received word of the French advancing, but both times the men had returned to their bivouacs by the end of the day.

Table 11.2 Route of the Light Division, 11–23 June 1811

Date	Route	Distance Travelled
11 June	Escalos de Cima	15km
12 June	Castelo Branco–Sarnadas–Vila Velha	33km
13 June	Nisa	32km
14 June	Alpalhão	30km
15 June	Portalegre	25km
19 June	Arronches	25km
23 June	Monte Reguengo near Campo Maior	16km

On 4 June General Craufurd was promoted to major general, and word of his promotion reached Wellington by 13 June.[481] This lessened any pressure on Wellington to replace him at the head of the Light Division because he was too junior.

Chapter 12

MISERY IN THE SOUTH AND HUNGER IN THE NORTH, JUNE–AUGUST 1811

> The heat is so great that it is quite impossible to stir out of our huts except in the evening, so that our time does not pass very happily, no books or possibility of amusement or exercise of any kind, in fact it is the only unpleasant time I have passed since I came to the country.
>
> Lieutenant Charles Kinloch, 52nd Foot[482]

The purpose of moving a significant part of Wellington's Army south to the vicinity of Badajoz was to provide support to their comrades besieging the city. The siege had begun on 22 April but was lifted on 12 May when French forces approached to relieve it. The resulting battle at Albuera on 16 May forced the French to retreat, and the siege recommenced on 18 May. Albuera showed that although the Allied force was strong enough to conduct the siege, it was too weak to do so at the same time as providing a covering force to prevent a French force from relieving the city. Thus, the Light Division and three other divisions were ordered south to protect the siege operations. The French in southern Spain continued to threaten the besiegers and were strengthened in mid-June when Marmont marched south to reinforce them.

The constant threat of a French relief column was not the only problem facing the Allied forces besieging the city. They also suffered from a lack of siege guns and engineers, so little progress was made. Shortly before the Light Division arrived, Wellington decided to abandon the siege, although he would keep his army in the vicinity of Badajoz for the next six weeks.

With the move south came a change in how the Light Division operated. For the first time in two years the men bivouacked in the field for an extensive amount of time, rather than being quartered in houses and barns. The living conditions were rough. The weather was extremely hot and except for a 16-minute shower no rain fell the whole time they were bivouacked at Monte Reguengo.[483] Most of the soldiers built huts out of tree branches, but some slept under the stars. The area was infested with snakes and scorpions, which added to their discomfort. Kincaid discovered that

> a decayed tree full of holes, against which the officers of our company had built their straw hut, was quite filled with snakes, and I have often seen fellows three feet long winding their way through the thatch, and voting themselves our companions at all hours, but the only inconvenience we experienced was in a sort of feeling that we would rather have had the hut to ourselves. One morning in turning over a stone on which my head had rested all night, I saw a scorpion with the tail curled over his back looking me fiercely in the face; and though not of much use, I made it a rule thereafter to take a look at the other side of my pillow before I went to sleep, whenever I used a stone one. An officer in putting on his shoe one morning, found that he had squeezed a scorpion to death in the toe of it. That fellow must have been caught napping, or he certainly would have resisted the intruder.[484]

The division's bivouac area was near the Caya river and the excessive heat and lack of rain caused it to dry up and form into stagnant pools, which became prime breeding grounds for mosquitos. The Caya river is a tributary of the Guadiana river, where Wellington bivouacked his army in 1809. There the army was wracked by Guadiana Fever, a form of tertian malaria that is endemic to the area. It is rarely fatal, but its victims are weakened by cycles of high fever followed by no fever. It can last for months.[485] Now, the Light Division was hit hard by the fever and by mid-July the division reported that 580 of its 3,367 British strength were sick (see Table 12.1).[486] The problem was so severe that Craufurd set up a division hospital in Costelo de Vide rather than sending them on to the army level hospital.[487]

Table 12.1 Light Division, Other Ranks Sick, 24 July 1811

Unit	Strength	Sick	% of Effectives
43rd Foot	1,243	185	15
1st Bn, 52nd Foot	889	150	17
2nd Bn, 52nd Foot	402	150	27
1st Bn, 95th Rifles	744	88	12
Company 2nd Bn, 95th Rifles	89	7	8
Total	3,367	580	17

Humans were not the only ones suffering. The weather and lack of suitable forage impacted the numerous horses and mules owned by the division's officers. Captain Leach remarked:

> Had Don Quixote lived at this time, he might have gone blindfold through our camp, quite certain to have found a Rosinante in any horse on which he first laid his hands. Chopped straw and stagnant water, with constant exposure to a broiling sun, and being picketed under a shadeless tree, reduced them to a pitiable state, and established the well-known furrows down the hind quarters, so strongly indicating poverty and starvation . . . the horses of infantry officers resembled scarecrows, and were fit subjects only for the fox-hound kennel, the infinite amusement we often derived from witnessing the glance of sovereign contempt which some of the young aides-de-camp deigned to throw on us and on our Rosinantes.[488]

Providing food for the officers and men was also becoming an issue. By the end of May Wellington's commissary officers were able to procure enough rations for the divisions around Ciudad Rodrigo. However, the shifting of four divisions of troops to the south played havoc with the supply lines and by mid-July the Light Division was on short rations. Compounding the problem was the fact that no one had been paid for a while and it was difficult to supplement the meagre rations if there was no money to pay for it. Lieutenant Dobbs remembered draught animals being killed to feed the men, which would cause problems later on. 'We were frequently days without bread or salt; and the draught bullocks, which appeared likely to die, were killed and served out for rations.'[489] He also noted that being 'unable to procure cows' milk, and goats' milk being very scarce, we found it a great comfort to have our own goats. We had several to each company, and they became so tame, that we found them very trouble some; they would occupy our beds, and follow us about when we did not want them. The officers of each company messed together, and had a boy to drive the goats.'[490]

Since they were no longer in the front lines and manning outposts, the men had little to do. Idle soldiers can think of all kinds of ways to get into mischief in order to alleviate their boredom. To prevent too many incidents Craufurd had the division conduct field exercises every other day from 4 to 7am starting on 16 July. Pack's Portuguese Brigade also joined them.[491] On 20 July the Light Division was ordered into cantonments in the vicinity of Castelo de Vide. The next day it was on the road before sunrise[492] and marched 16km to Arronches, where the men stopped in some woods to wait out the heat of the day and to cook their rations. While there, the 43rd Foot was joined by 16 officers and 330 men who had come out as replacements from England.[493] Among the new officers was Lieutenant John Cooke, who recalled seeing the division for the first time:

> We descended into the valley, and, at the edge of a wood, awaited the coming of the division, from an advanced camp on their way to Castello de Vida. Every eye was on the stretch, and in the distance we descried a cloud of dust rolling towards us, the bright sparkling rays of the sunbeams playing on the soldiers' breast plates, when suddenly the leading regiment of the light division burst forth; their bronzed countenances and light knapsacks, and their order of march, all united to inspire a conviction that their early discipline had not only been maintained amidst privations, battles and camps, but had become matured by experience. They had traversed mountains, and forded rivers; the grim and icy hand of death had grasped many in the unhealthy marshes of the Alentejo, and with sure effect had scattered balls amidst their ranks without distinction: yet the remainder of these veterans were still bent onwards, to gather fresh laurels in the rugged and uncertain paths of fortune ... A cloud of dust alone marked their further progress as they receded from our view. Following in succession, we brought up the rear. At the expiration of an hour's march, we entered a wood, formed column, called the roll, and the whole division was then dismissed. The assembled multitude of voices, the tearing and cutting down of branches of trees, crackling of fires, rattling of canteens, shooting of bullocks through the head, and the hurrying of parties of soldiers for rum and biscuit for rations, the neighing of horses, braying asses and rampant mules, all resounded throughout the forest, giving new life and merry echoes to its most intimate recesses. Groups of officers stood in circles; every countenance seemed decked in smiles, and a hearty welcome

greeted us from all hands. Under the wide-spreading branches of a venerable cork-tree, decorated with pack-saddles, accoutrements, and other military trappings, dinner was served up and laid out on a pair of hampers, which served us instead of a table. Beef, biscuit, tea, rum, and wine, composed our fare, it being a usual custom to join breakfast and dinner, so as to make one meal serve for the twenty-four hours, the troops merely halting to cook and refresh themselves during the heat of the day. A more happy meal, I can safely say, I never partook of; and with infinite admiration did I regard the purple jackets and battered epaulettes of my companions.[494]

In the late afternoon the division formed up and marched another 25km to Portalegre. The next morning it marched another 22km to Castelo de Vide. All the battalions found quarters in the town except for the Rifles, who were in billets in farms in the area. The riflemen found the buildings and grounds very comfortable but the beds were flea-ridden:

The latter place is surrounded by extensive gardens, belonging to the richer citizen; in each of which there is a small summer-house, containing one or two apartments, in which the proprietor, as I can testify, may have the enjoyment of being fed upon by a more healthy and better appetized flea, than is to be met with in town houses in general . . . and though their beds, on that account, had not much sleep in them, yet, as those who preferred the voice of the nightingale in a bed of cabbages, to the pinch of a flea in a bed of feathers, had the alternative at their option; I enjoyed my sojourn there very much. Each garden had a bathing tank, with a plentiful supply of water, which at that season was really a luxury; and they abounded in choice fruits. I there formed an attachment to a mulberry-tree, which is still fondly cherished in my remembrance.[495]

The division remained at Castelo de Vide until 29 July, when it marched 25km to Nisa and bivouacked in the same woods it had occupied the previous month. It halted there for two days and then crossed the Tagus river at Vila Velha and marched 48km to Costelo Branco via Sarnadas. While at Nisa, several Rifles officers were able to supplement their rations when they went exploring and found 'some bee-hives, which the Spaniards and Portuguese make of the outer bark of the corktree. We laid an embargo on one of them, and marched triumphantly into camp, smothered the bees with gunpowder, and voted the honey a capital substitute for sugar, of which we had none in our canteens, nor money to purchase any'.[496]

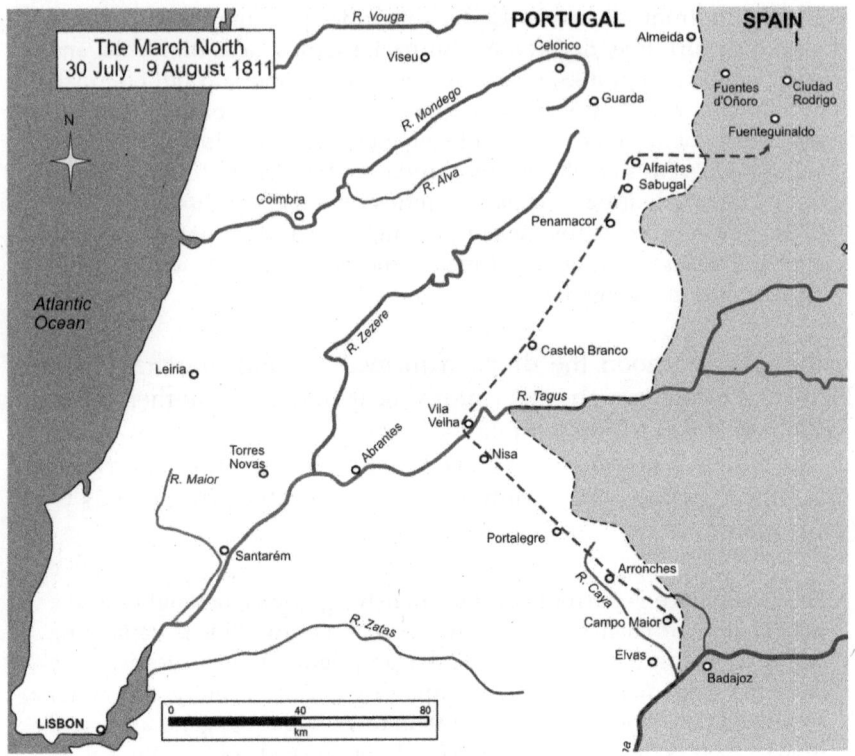

August

On 1 August the division continued its march north. The weather was generally sunny but the road was bad for the first three days of the march:

> The narrow road running at the base of the adjacent mountains was filled with loose stones; woe, therefore, to the sore-footed soldier who happened to stumble amongst them! Woe to the sick or wounded to whose lot it fell to be placed in those Portuguese cars, rudely constructed, with small solid wooden wheels, revolving on an unoiled axletree, and causing an indescribable creeking [sic] noise to be heard at a very considerable distance; sounds so horrible, that the bigotted [sic] peasantry declare they frighten away the evil spirit of Old Nick himself![497]

The road got better after the division passed through Bemposta.

Craufurd, concerned about disease, prohibited billeting in the villages. Most nights the men bivouacked in chestnut groves or woods.

The division halted for three nights at Meimoa. On 5 August Craufurd ordered them to break up their bivouacs around the town and move to higher ground:

> This evening at six o'clock the division moved up to the hill above the town, where it remained during the night. This was done because General C fancied the low grounds were unhealthy; but Mr Gilchrist,[498] who is now the senior surgeon of the division says that if they are unhealthy, they are much more so by day when the sun exerts its whole force to draw the exhalations from the earth, than by night. Yet it is by night he removes us & during the whole day we remain below. The river which flows through this valley is now very low.[499]

On 7 August the division was on the road at 2am and marched 30km to Quadrazais. Craufurd was not happy with how the division conducted the march and ordered that as from the next day, only field grade officers would be allowed to ride. All other officers had to march with their companies, much to their displeasure.[500] Lieutenant Cooke left a description of how the division usually marched but failed to say whether Craufurd's complaint was justified in its last march:

> As the division threaded its march over winding and difficult roads, its horse-artillery might be heard rumbling in the rear, while the winding notes of the bugle horns echoed in the distant valleys. Major-General R. Craufurd commanded the light division. His arrangements and regulations of march stood unrivalled: at the expiration of every hour, the division formed close columns of regiments, and halted for about ten minutes; the leading corps were generally again marching off by the time the rear came up. When any obstacles came across the line of route, each officer, commanding a company, saw that they were closed up before he put them into the regular marching pace, and that even if a break in the column happened of fifty yards between each company. I have frequently witnessed the whole division marching in this manner through a difficult country, by which means they were always in hand, ready to engage by companies . . . The followers of the division (and of the army) were composed of lank Barbary bulls and bullocks; mules loaded with bags of biscuit, kegs of rum, kegs of ball cartridge, reserve ammunition; a few hardy women (mistresses, or wives of soldiers) mounted on strong and weak asses; Portuguese boys, drivers; officers' milch goats; purveyors and medicine chests; and sometimes a few suttlers [sic], headed by a man better known by the name of *Tick*, owing to his giving credit to officers in precarious times.

Compounding the problem was the fact that Craufurd had to evacuate the division's hospital at Costelo de Vide when the order came to move on 1 August. If he had sent his sick to the army hospital, it would not have been his responsibility to move them. However, by setting up an unauthorized hospital, he had to bring the sick with him. He had few carts and the only mules available were those carrying the division's food. This caused problems during the move north, for 'when we marched, he left no less than 107 sick to be moved; to transport which he was obliged to send away his provision mules, which have not yet joined, and we have in consequence been very ill supplied during our march frequently without bread, when the rest of the army had plenty.'[501] By 5 August no bread was available and any food that might have been bought from the local farmers had long been sold.[502]

On 8 August, just outside Soito, the local guide got lost and they ended up taking the wrong road. Just past the town

> instead of continuing along the high road, the division, I presume by the mistake of the guide, turned off to the right by a road which in parts was no more than a pathway, whereby the whole division was obliged to pass in single rank. This circumstance occasioned a delay of at least one hour; besides which it took us a mile out of the way. In such cases the guide ought to be punished, as a warning to himself and others, of the importance of the trust reposed in him. In addition to the verbal order of yesterday, General C thought fit to pen a Divisional Order, stating the cause, as above mentioned & declaring his intention of continuing the measure, till he should be satisfied that the officers from the inconvenience of marching had been brought to a proper sense of their duty.[503]

The next day the division marched into Spain and stopped after 20km at Fuenteguinaldo (see Table 12.2). The 2nd Brigade was billeted in the town, while the 1st Brigade bivouacked in nearby woods.[504]

Table 12.2 Route of the Light Division, 1–9 August 1811

Date	Route	Distance Travelled
1 August	Castelo Branco–Escalos de Cima–Lousa	20km
2 August	Lousa–Sao Miguel de Acha–Bemposta	27km
3 August	Bemposta–Aguas–Meimoa	27km
4 August	Meimoa	

Date	Route	Distance Travelled
7 August	Meimoa–Quadrazais	30km
8 August	Quadrazais–Soito–Alfaiates–Aldeia da Ponte	22km
9 August	Aldeia da Ponte–La Alberguería de Argañán–Fuenteguinaldo	20km
Total		146km

The division stayed at Fuenteguinaldo for only one night, then marched to El Sahugo and on to Martiago, a distance of 23km. Although this was a fairly short distance, they had to cross the Agueda river at a ford; the water was only 60cm deep but the banks of the river were very steep and the road bad. For the first time in over a month it began to rain, which lasted for many hours.[505] The division would remain in billets near these two towns for the rest of the month (see Table 12.3).

Table 12.3 Location of the Light Division, 10–20 August 1811

Division HQ		Martiago
1st Brigade HQ		Martiago
	43rd Foot	Martiago
	Right Wing, 1st Bn, 95th Rifles	Martiago
	Mitchell's company, 2nd Bn, 95th Rifles	Martiago
	3rd Caçadores	Villarejo
2nd Brigade HQ		El Sahugo
	1st Bn, 52nd Foot	El Sahugo
	2nd Bn, 52nd Foot	El Sahugo
	Left Wing, 1st Bn, 95th Rifles	Lariquella
	1st Caçadores	Serradella de Llano

Sources: Ewart, p. 37; Simmons, p. 192.

After settling into their new quarters, the division received orders to make a reconnaissance-in-force towards Ciudad Rodrigo. Wellington would accompany them, as well as squadrons from the 1st Dragoons and the 12th Light Dragoons. The men were on the road at 2am and marched towards Zamarra. The terrain was rough and the road took them through steep canyons. They crossed the Badillo river on the old Roman bridge at Puente de Larilla, just north of Castro de Lerilla, and reached the outskirts of Zamarra about 7am, having travelled about 10km. From there Wellington rode 10km north and stopped at the Monasterio de La Caridad,[506] about 5km south of Ciudad Rodrigo. Escorting him were the Right Wing of the 95th Rifles, several companies of the 3rd Caçadores and the cavalry. Wellington stayed in the vicinity of the monastery until 1pm. Upon his return to Zamarra, the division withdrew and reached its quarters around 5pm.[507]

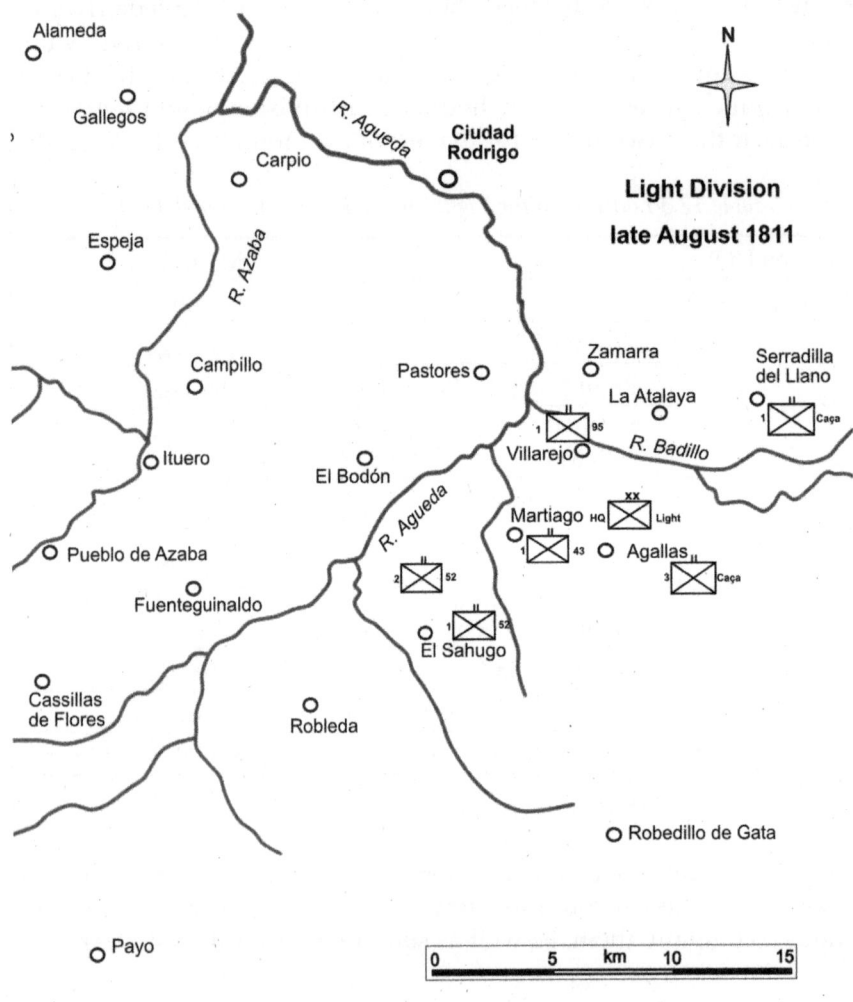

For the next fifteen days life was good for the Light Division. It was not responsible for providing outposts so except for the morning drill that lasted from 6 to 8am, the duties were light. Rations, however, were still short. Foraging from the local countryside was forbidden but officers took to confiscating what food they could find from the farmers and giving them a receipt that they could turn in to the commissary to be reimbursed. That, of course, assumed the farmers could find a commissary; if they could not, the practice was little better than outright theft. Kincaid described some of the tricks they used to obtain bread:

> This neighbourhood had been so long the theatre of war, and alternately forced to supply both armies, that the inhabitants, at length, began to dread starvation themselves, and concealed, for their private use, all that remained to them; so that, although they were bountiful in their assurances of good wishes, it was impossible to extract a loaf of their good bread, of which we were so wildly in want that we were obliged to conceal patroles [sic] on the different roads and footpaths, for many miles around, to search the peasants passing between the different villages, giving them an order on the commissary for whatever we took from them; and we were not too proud to take even a few potatoes out of an old woman's basket.[508]

The weather was generally fine but marked with an occasional thunderstorm. Hunting was a popular way to pass the time for the officers. The riflemen were recruited to help:

> Lord Wellington's Staff frequently went out hunting. On these occasions they generally had five or six men of the Rifles to assist. The place abounded in wolves and wild boars, so that a great deal of amusement was experienced in this sport. I generally had the good fortune to be selected, with others of our battalion, to attend his Lordship's Staff in these excursions. The chase was very exciting, particularly from the ferocious nature of the game we sought. I well remember the first wild boar I saw in one of these hunts: he was a huge fellow, with tusks of a most alarming size, but although we fired several shots, and the hounds pursued him, he escaped.[509]

During this period the Light Division was reinforced. On 21 August Lieutenant Colonel Andrew Barnard arrived with four companies from the 3rd Battalion, 95th Rifles, which had been stationed in Cadiz. The next day Wellington ordered the 1st Division to release Captain James Travers' company of the 3rd Battalion, which had been with the 1st Division since the previous autumn, and send it to the Light Division, where it joined the other four companies of the 3rd Battalion in the 1st Brigade (see Table 12.4).

Table 12.4 Location of the Light Division, 21–28 August 1811

Division HQ		Martiago
1st Brigade HQ		Martiago
	43rd Foot	Martiago
	Right Wing, 1st Bn, 95th Rifles (Four Companies)	Villarejo
	2nd Bn, 95th Rifles (One Company)	Villarejo
	Right Wing, 3rd Bn, 95th Rifles (Five Companies)	Villarejo
	3rd Caçadores	La Agallas
2nd Brigade HQ		El Sahugo
	1st Bn, 52nd Foot	El Sahugo
	2nd Bn, 52nd Foot	El Sahugo
	Left Wing, 1st Bn, 95th Rifles (Four Companies)	Lariquella
	1st Caçadores	Serradilla de Llano

Source: Simmons, p. 192.

Their days of leisure ended on 27 August when word was received that French foragers from Ciudad Rodrigo had been spotted in Pastores and Zamarra. Barnard, with his five rifle companies and the Right Wing of the 1st Battalion, was ordered to march to Zamarra. Captain Wells and three companies of the 43rd Foot were sent to Villarejo. By the time the Rifles had reached Zamarra, the French had returned to Ciudad Rodrigo. Barnard withdrew his troops to Atayala. The next day the three companies of the 43rd Foot at Villarejo returned to Martiago and were replaced by the Left Wing of the 1st Battalion, 95th Rifles. It was quiet for the rest of the month.

The health of the division continued to decline, with a 50 per cent increase in the number of sick in August (see Table 12.5). The vast majority of those hospitalized were suffering from the lingering effects of malaria. Among those who died was Major Richard Elers of the 43rd

Foot. Fortunately, only twenty soldiers had died in the previous month from non-combat deaths.

Table 12.5 Light Division, Other Ranks Sick, 24 August 1811

Unit	Strength	Sick	% Sick
43rd Foot	1,234	269	22
1st Bn, 52nd Foot	883	179	20
2nd Bn, 52nd Foot	562	169	31
1st Bn, 95th Rifles	741	136	19
Company, 2nd Bn, 95th Rifles	89	9	10
Right Wing, 3rd Bn, 95th Rifles	414	80	19
Total	3,923	842	21

Source: Bamford.

There were several major changes to the chain of command within the division during August. Wellington had been concerned for some time with the shortage of British battalion commanders. On paper, three of the four battalions were commanded by lieutenant colonels, but in reality the situation had reached breaking point. The 1st Battalion, 95th Rifles, was technically commanded by Brevet Colonel Beckwith, but he was also serving as the commander of the 1st Brigade. The 1st Battalion, 52nd Foot, had been commanded since December 1810 by Lieutenant Colonel Ross, but he wanted to return to England because he had been offered a job as the Deputy Adjutant General in Ceylon. Compounding the problem, Wellington also knew that Beckwith was worn out after two years of campaigning and was going before a medical board so he could be invalided home.[510] By the end of the month the Light Division would be short of a brigade commander and three of its battalions would be commanded by majors.

Wellington had no suitable general or colonel available to fill Beckwith's place as a brigade commander. The arrival of Lieutenant Colonel Barnard helped to alleviate some of the problems. As early as 6 October 1810 Barnard, who was serving in Cadiz at the time, had been brought to Wellington's attention by Lieutenant Colonel Henry Torrens, the Military Secretary of the Commander-in-Chief of the Army: 'Colonel Barnard is as enterprising and as intelligent a young Man as ever Commanded a Light Corps, and if you want a truly efficient Field Officer with the 95th you cannot do better than to call Colonel Barnard to your army, even if you should not be inclined to draw more of that Force from General Graham.'[511] Barnard's arrival was fortuitous. Wellington's plan was to have Barnard command the 1st Brigade until Beckwith returned from sick leave.[512] Captain Charles Gray, the senior captain in the 3rd Battalion, would temporarily command the five companies while Barnard commanded the brigade. In the 2nd Brigade, meanwhile, Ross, exchanged into the 66th Foot with Lieutenant Colonel John Colborne and left the battalion sometime in mid-August.[513] Unfortunately Colborne had left the Peninsula in early August on home leave and would not return until November.[514] On the morning of his leaving, Ross gave his watch, chain and seals to his friends. George Napier was given the watch and wore it for many years.[515] Major Edward Gibbs assumed command of the 1st Battalion, 52nd Foot, in Ross's place. Commanding the Left Wing of the 1st Battalion, 95th Rifles, was Major Peter O'Hare.

Chapter 13

BORDER ALARMS AND SICKNESS, SEPTEMBER–OCTOBER 1811

At the beginning of September the Light Division was once again short of senior officers, and the situation would only get worse before the month ended (see Table 13.1).

Table 13.1 Organization of the Light Division, 1 September 1811

Division HQ	Major General Robert Craufurd	Commander
	Lieutenant Charles Wood, 52nd Foot	ADC
	Lieutenant James Shaw, 43rd Foot	ADC
	Lieutenant John Bell, 52nd Foot	DAQMG
	Major Charles Rowan, 52nd Foot	AAG
	Charles Purcell	ACG
	Wentworth Parker	Chaplain
1st Brigade	Lieutenant Colonel Andrew Barnard, 95th Rifles	Acting Commander
	Captain Charles Beckwith, 95th Rifles	Brigade Major
1st Bn, 43rd Foot	Lieutenant Colonel Charles McLeod	Commander
Right Wing, 1st Bn, 95th Rifles	Brevet Lieutenant Colonel Dugald Gilmour	Commander
Company, 2nd Bn, 95th Rifles	Captain Samuel Mitchell	Commander

(*Continued*)

Right Wing, 3rd Bn, 95th Rifles*	Captain Charles Gray	Acting Commander
3rd Caçadores Bn	Lieutenant Colonel George Elder	Commander
2nd Brigade	Brigadier General George Drummond	Commander
	Lieutenant Harry Smith, 95th Rifles	Brigade Major
	Lieutenant Thomas Powell, 24th Foot	ADC
1st Bn, 52nd Foot	Major Edward Gibbs	Commander
2nd Bn, 52nd Foot	Major John Hunt	Commander
Left Wing, 1st Bn, 95th Rifles	Major Peter O'Hare	Commander
1st Caçadores Bn	Lieutenant Colonel Jorge Avilez	Commander

* Five companies.

The first seven days of September were quiet. The weather was good, but because of an increase in the number of French foraging parties, the division began to man outposts. The division was also concerned that the French might advance through the mountains to the south, so on 7 September the 1st Brigade was ordered to place outposts at the passes of Robledillo de Gata, Las Erias and Aldehuela. A rifle company was sent to the first place, while a detachment led by Captain Leach, consisting of his company from the 1st Battalion, 95th Rifles, and a company from the 3rd Caçadores, occupied the latter two villages. Leach was not impressed with the two villages. They were

> of the worst possible description, buried in the heart of mountains, as awfully grand and terrific as I ever beheld in Spain, Switzerland, or elsewhere. The inhabitants of those wretched hovels, which I have dignified with the name of villages, were all dressed in the skins of goats, sheep, and wolves, looking more like demons than any thing human. Although no Patagonian in height, I was obliged to stoop double, in order to go in and out of the shed, which, as commandant, I took care should not be the worst in the colony. Some dried fern in a dark corner, which looked as if the devil should have been its inmate, where myriads of fleas had established themselves as 'lords and masters', was my bed, and my pillow a knapsack. Although only a few leagues distant from the villages of Martiago, &c. &c. on the north side of the mountains, from which we

came, where the Spanish language is spoken with tolerable purity, it was quite a hopeless case to endeavour to understand those goatherds, or to make them comprehend us. Their lingo resembled Hebrew or Arabic quite as much as Castilian. During the fortnight which was spent amongst those uncouth goatherds, we were constantly accoutred night and day, and ready to stand to our arms at a moment's notice. The days were passed in patrolling, reconnoitring, and endeavouring to collect information from the mountaineers, who either could not or would not enlighten us as to Marmont's movements. I believe our colonists were not a little nettled because we took possession, by General Crawford's orders, of such goats and sheep as were requisite to ration the troops. Bread and wine were sent to us from the head-quarters of the division every fourth day, across the mountains on mules.[516]

Barnard and the five companies at La Atalaya were withdrawn to Villarejo on 8 September and were replaced by cavalry. More reinforcements trickled in when Captain John Hart's company of the 2nd Battalion, 95th Rifles, arrived from England and joined Mitchell's company in the 1st Brigade on 7 September.[517]

About this time General Drummond was having trouble with his health. First it was gout, 'such a pleasant little fit in his foot which for one day was swelled as big as two larger feet and he could not put it to the ground'.[518] Then he had other health issues and went to Fuenteguinaldo to recuperate. Sadly, the change of scene did not help, and he died in Harry Smith's arms of a putrid sore throat[519] on 8 September.[520] He was buried in the village the next day[521] and his funeral was attended by most of the division's officers who were not on duty.[522]

Some of the problems with feeding the troops were solved, but not in all cases. The riflemen were spread out in many locations, and they were hard to supply. According to Costello, the lack of bread forced them to forage for a substitute, a practice forbidden by Wellington, but the hungry soldiers did not care. They raided the chestnut groves and 'roasted or boiled chesnuts [sic], of which we were allowed a quart a day each. At length we found it necessary to make an incursion into the mountains, to press the Alcaldes of the different villages to supply us.'[523] The division hospital was also short of rations and Lieutenant Charles Dawson, who was a patient there, wrote home that there was no 'commissariat to assist us in provisions & I was obliged to get the sanction of the Juiz de Forno to go into the country to press what sheep & bread we could get, the men were without provisions for 2 days'.[524]

The weather was fine until the night of 11 September, when 'there was a heavy thunder storm, which commenced about 9 pm on the 11th & lasted with little intermission till 7 this morning. The rain was at times very heavy; the thunder exceedingly tremendous. The claps were often very quick in succession & from the reverberation of the sound through the whole chain of mountains, they were so intermingled as to appear but one. The crack then lasted often a quarter of an hour. The weather continued during the day showery & from 8 to midnight the rain fell in torrents.'[525] It would rain for the next ten days.

Reports began to come in that the French were assembling a convoy in Salamanca to bring supplies to Ciudad Rodrigo.[526] At around 3pm on 14 September the division was placed on alert 'to hold itself in readiness to march immediately. The cause of this order is not known, I suppose it is either on account of a convoy having departed from Salamanca for [Ciudad] Rodrigo, which we should of course endeavour to interrupt; or of the movement of Marmont's army, which is said to be on its march for Salamanca.'[527]

Soon word reached the division that Marmont was marching towards Ciudad Rodrigo with 60,000 infantry and 20,000 cavalry. On 23 September Wellington ordered the army out of its cantonments. The 3rd Division was sent to the vicinity of El Bodón, with the Agueda river on its right flank. The Light Division was responsible for the area from the right bank of the Agueda river south to the El Gata mountains. Craufurd ordered the division forward to occupy positions along the Badilla/Agadón river.[528] The 1st Brigade was placed on the right, with the 3rd Caçadores, who had been billeted in Agallas, sent to positions in the mountains on the far right, the Right Wing of the 95th Rifles, which had been in Villarejo, in the centre, and the 43rd Foot on the left between La Atalaya and Agallas.[529] The 43rd Foot marched from its cantonments in Martiago about 11am. As it approached Agallas, word was received that 'the enemy was advancing & that our cavalry piquets had been obliged to pass the Vadillo. The regiment in consequence of this information, marched directly . . . & halted in a wood full half a league from the ford; at sunset moved forward & occupied a camp of the 3rd Caçadores.'[530] The 2nd Brigade marched from its billets near El Sahugo at noon and stopped at Martiago. About 4pm it continued towards Villarejo and occupied positions overlooking the Badilla river from Castro de Lerilla[531] to opposite La Atalaya.

Believing that Marmont had no intention of anything other than resupplying Ciudad Rodrigo, Wellington did not want to unnecessarily concentrate his forces and instead kept his army spread out over a 25km front from Almeida in the north to Fuenteguinaldo in the south.

156

BORDER ALARMS AND SICKNESS, SEPTEMBER–OCTOBER 1811

On 23 September he sent orders to his commanders that should the French advance, they were to avoid becoming engaged and should withdraw. The Light Division was 'to remain in its present situation, but Major Gen. Craufurd will be in communication with the troops at El Bodon; and in the event of these troops being drawn back, he will immediately move back also to Robleda.'[532] Later that night the QMG sent further clarification to Craufurd and emphasized that he was not to commit his force to fight and must keep the 3rd Division's commander informed of his actions:

> You will be so good as to understand, from the instructions transmitted to you yesterday, that it is not intended that any part of the army should be seriously committed with the enemy, unless particular orders are given to that effect. You will be so good, therefore, as to withdraw your advanced posts behind the great ravine between Zamarra and Martiago as soon as you see occasion for it; and retire also with the whole division upon Robleda whenever it seems expedient to do so, even although the troops at El Bodon may not have been withdrawn. In such case you will, of course, apprise the officer commanding at El Bodon, as expeditiously as possible, of your being obliged to move back upon Robleda, reporting, at the same time, to head quarters likewise.[533]

The next day, 24 September, was quiet until about 10am, when a French column of about 1,800 infantry and cavalry arrived at La Atalaya. They occupied the village and sent cavalry piquets to a wooded hill overlooking the Badilla river, but otherwise did not advance towards the Light Division's positions.[534] The following day the French were much more aggressive. About noon they started probing the outposts and Craufurd, in obedience to his orders, ordered the division to withdraw at about 2pm:

> About midday the enemy made a slight reconnaissance of our position, directing his attention principally to that part of it occupied by the 52nd. There was also a very heavy cannonade & firing of musketry heard in the direction of El Bodon, the result is not known. About 2 pm a sudden order arrived for the baggage to be sent to the rear & about 4 the troops moved from their ground & marched, covered by the piquets to Cespedosa, where the whole division & where the cavalry assembled & remained during the night. The enemy instantly perceived our retreat & a party of horse moved down to the ford before our last piquet quitted its ground. A little before we entered Agallas the rear of their infantry was observed moving down the hill to the ford over the Vadello.[535]

First to depart was the baggage train. Unable to take the direct road to Martiago because of the French threat a few kilometres away on the far side of the Agueda river, instead, it 'had to work round their flank to rejoin the main body. The baggage had to make a still greater detour through the woods, and under the mountain. Our baggage guard consisted of the two batmen belonging to each company, with some others belonging to the staff, an officer of each battalion having the command. The mules of each company being tied together, were led by one of the batmen, the other being thus left free to act as circumstances might require.'[536]

At 4pm the brigades began withdrawing and marched about 20km to Cespedosa de Agadone. As night fell, Craufurd chose to stop there rather than marching another 12km to Robledo in the dark over poor roads. At Cespedosa he received orders for the next day:

> The Light division and other troops with Major Gen. Craufurd will pass the Agueda at the ford on the road from Peña Parda to Fuente Guinaldo, and will halt about a mile from the ford towards Fuente Guinaldo. Gen. Craufurd will be so good as to send forward to head quarters to report the progress of his march, and when he has reached his destination. He will send his baggage to Ligiosa.[537] But if Major Gen. Craufurd should perceive that the troops retire this day from Fuente Guinaldo he will in that case continue to fall back, by the right bank of the Agueda, and pass the river, either at Puente Villar, or higher up as he may find expedient.[538]

The division was on the road before daybreak[539] on 26 September and marched to El Sahugo and then on to Robledo, where the men learned that French cavalry had been there but left before the division's baggage had passed through. They marched on to Villasrubias and then headed west on the road to Casillas de Flores. The route took them through an oak wood and after 3km they crossed the Agueda river at the Cabeza ford.[540] 'The road down to the river is steep & rugged but very practicable for artillery. The river is here broad and mostly knee deep, even at the ford & in the middle somewhat deeper.'[541] They reached Fuenteguinaldo about 3pm after marching 32km.[542] Last to arrive was the Right Wing of the 95th Rifles, which had been serving as the rear guard. Upon reaching the village Rifleman Costello wrote: 'we found the greater part of the army assembled under Lord Wellington, together with the remainder of our light division, who loudly cheered us as we made our appearance, a report having arisen amongst the rest of the troops that we had been taken prisoners'.[543]

It was at Fuenteguinaldo that the division learned about the events at El Bodón. Captain Ewart wrote in his diary that:

> yesterday General Colville's Brigade, with only six squadrons of our cavalry had been very hotly engaged with a very superior force and had behaved famously near El Bodon; particularly 2nd Battalion 5th, and 77th regiments charging several squadrons of French cavalry and retaking some Portuguese guns. They afterwards retired in a square over the plain to Guinaldo, supported by the 83rd, 94th, and 21st Portuguese while General Picton retired on their left with the 45th and 88th from La Encina, the 74th crossed the Agueda and came by Robleda and Penaparda. About the same time some squadrons of Polish lancers attacked the 14th and 16th Light Dragoons near Espeja, but were soon driven back with considerable loss.

Soon gossip began to circulate condemning Craufurd for not marching quickly to reach Fuenteguinaldo. Francis Larpent, the Judge Advocate of the Army, wrote that Craufurd

> remained across a river by himself; that is, with his own division only, nearly a whole day after he was called in by Lord Wellington. He said he knew that he could defend his position. Lord Wellington, when he came back, only said, 'I am glad to see you safe, Craufurd.' To which the latter replied, 'Oh, I was in no danger, I assure you.' 'But I was, from your conduct,' said Lord Wellington. Upon which Craufurd observed, 'he is d___ crusty today'.[544]

Larpent's diary entry has been accepted as the truth and has been used in several histories of the Peninsular War, including Fortescue's and Oman's. However, there is a problem with this anecdote. Larpent did not join the Army until October 1812 and he wrote this on 7 April 1813, nineteen months after it allegedly occurred. We could find no other source that supports his allegations. This was not the first time that Craufurd was the object of malicious gossip owing to the jealousy of his peers at Army HQ.[545] To make it worse, of course, Craufurd could not respond since he had been dead for 15 months.

Wellington did not intend to fight at Fuenteguinaldo and issued orders that evening for the army to withdraw southeast to new positions near Bismula and Soito via the main road to La Alberguería de Argañán. The Light Division and the 1st KGL Hussars would form the rear guard. Their orders were as follows: 'the Light division will move off at 12 o'clock, and will march by Casillas de Flores to Forcalhos. Major Gen. Alten's brigade of cavalry will join and remain with the Light Division.'[546]

The division formed up at 11.30pm and moved out at midnight. Their march in the early hours of 27 September was not pleasant. It was very cold and extremely dark, for the quarter moon had set soon after they moved out. Between the cold and the pitch blackness, the division marched at less than 2km an hour and arrived at Casillas de Flores at daybreak, about 5am. They continued marching until they reached Forcalhos, where they halted at noon.[547] There they waited until 2pm and then headed south. Shortly after leaving the village, they heard firing coming near the rear. Craufurd had chosen to ride with the 1st KGL Hussars forming the rear guard, and was observing the advancing French cavalry. He and his escort waited too long to withdraw and were nearly caught by the enemy. They quickly turned their horses around and galloped down the road to Forcalhos. The Right Wing of the 1st Battalion, 95th Rifles, once again formed the division's rearguard and the men 'were marching carelessly along the road, [when] he and his dragoons galloped right into our column, with a cloud of French ones at his heels. Luckily, the ground was in our favour; and, dispersing our men among the broken rocks, on both sides of the road, we sent them back somewhat faster than they came on. They were, however, soon replaced by their infantry, with whom we continued in an uninteresting skirmish all day.'[548] The rear guard was soon reinforced with some companies from the 3rd Caçadores.[549]

After leaving Forcalhos, the division came across its baggage train and halted to allow it to continue unmolested by the enemy. The division finally halted at about 5pm on a wooded hill about 2km east of Alfaiates near the Sacaparte Convent; although they had marched 40km, which was not unusual in itself, and the weather was good and the countryside flat, the troops were exhausted. As one officer put it: 'this day was the most harassing retreat we experienced and as we were constantly moving from half past eleven at night to about 5 pm & though the distance was not considerable, yet the fatigue was great owing to the frequent short halts & to the slow pace of the march. About seven pm there was an alarm occasioned by the enemy attacking the piquets. The division changed its ground & formed in position ready to repel any attack.'[550]

Lieutenant Simmons wrote in his diary that 'our first line formed and also moved forward some paces, the Light Division throwing out skirmishers towards the woods. This manœuvre induced the enemy to give up the project, at least for the night. Immediately after dark the other divisions of the army retired.'[551] The division remained under arms during a very cold night. Fortunately for them it did not rain.[552]

For some reason, Wentworth Parker, the division's chaplain, did not march with the division when it pulled out of Fuenteguinaldo at midnight. He had gone

> into a house to make himself comfortable for the night, and slept very pleasantly. Some time after daybreak he heard strange noises within doors, and soon after, a French Dragoon entered his room. Giving his sword two or three menacing flourishes, he asked him for his money. He was followed by others, who were apt scholars in imitating a good example; pillage and rapine they glory in. The poor parson found himself stripped of everything, and, almost naked, was driven over rugged ground for twenty miles without shoes, and then put into a prison amongst a group of others and left to cogitate upon his hard fortune and upon his own stupidity for sliding away to make a lodgment in a house unknown to any one in such critical times.[553]

However, the French only held him for a 'couple of days, and finding that, however gifted he might have been in spiritual lore, he was as ignorant as Dominie Sampson[554] on military matters; and, conceiving good provisions to be thrown away upon him, they stripped him nearly naked and dismissed him, like the barber in Gil Blas,[555] with a kick in the breech, and sent him in to us in a woeful state'.[556]

The division formed up at 2am on 28 September, then marched to Alfaiates and on to Soito, a distance of 20km. They arrived there at 6am and bivouacked in a grove of chestnut trees on the far side of the village. There 'the walls . . . were lined by our riflemen; though we expected that the enemy would attack us during the whole day, not a shot was fired, only a few squadrons of their cavalry hung upon our rear'.[557] These riflemen were probably the Right Wing of the 1st Battalion, 95th Rifles, who had been serving as the rear guard. The rest of the army was in position on the hills behind the village. Rumour had it that Wellington intended to fight should the French advance.[558]

The next day, although they were expecting the French to attack, it was very quiet. It soon became apparent that the French had withdrawn towards Ciudad Rodrigo. During the lull Captain Ewart took the opportunity to explore Soito:

This unfortunate village was now for the third time within a few months near the scene of action of the two armies, and indeed was in a wretched state, the houses gutted and the inhabitants flying half starved and naked. We heard that Sabugal was in a similar state, as the whole of the baggage and commissariat of our army was collected near it since the twenty sixth and we were very glad to get ours this evening, as it was ascertained that the whole French force had retired towards Ciudad Rodrigo, after having gained their object in relieving that place, and taken a few prisoners, with some of the baggage of General Picton's Division, the chaplain of the Light Division and two servants with horses of the Prince of Orange's.[559]

The division stayed at Soito on 30 September and by the end of the day had received orders to move into cantonments the next day. Due to the lack of fodder for the animals, the division's officers had been taking it from the village. That night, when the villagers returned, they were reimbursed by Charles Purcell, the division's commissary officer. The division bivouacked in the open and it was a very chilly night, but with no rain.[560]

Table 13.2 Light Division, Other Ranks Sick, 24 September 1811

Unit	Strength	Sick	% Sick	Dead
43rd Foot	1,230	269	22	5
1st Bn, 52nd Foot	867	189	22	5
2nd Bn, 52nd Foot	548	222	41	5
1st Bn, 95th Rifles	727	142	20	11
2nd Bn, 95th Rifles*	90	8	9	0
3rd Bn, 95th Rifles	413	150	36	5
Total	3,875	980	25	31

Source: WO17/2468.
* Does not include Adams' company.

Despite being in a healthier location for two months, the number of sick in the division continued to go up, with 138 more men in the hospital than in August (see Table 13.2). The number of those who died from non-combat deaths, most likely from malaria, increased by 50 per cent to 31. Because the disease was intermittent, it is difficult to determine how many of the sick were new cases or those previously stricken who had got better and then relapsed. Although we do not have any data for officers, sergeants and musicians, they too began to fall ill. Duffy wrote in his diary on 1 September that in the 43rd Foot 'we have sent 10 officers to the rear this last week'.[561] Lieutenant Colonel McLeod, commander of the 43rd Foot, wrote to his father on 3 September and commented that both of his 'field officers[562] are sick in the rear and several other officers'.[563] Among the sick officers was Surgeon John Maling of the 52nd Foot. Initially the men were kept in a hospital in Castanheira, but later on they were sent to a hospital in Celorico.[564]

October

The division's organization had changed slightly in September (see Table 13.3). The companies from the 2nd Battalion, 95th Rifles, commanded by Captains Mitchell and Hart were likely attached to the Right Wing of the 1st Battalion, 95th Rifles, for administrative purposes and during operations. On 30 September Major General John Ormsby Vandeleur was assigned to the division and took command of the 2nd Brigade.[565] He was not a logical choice to command a light infantry brigade, because he was a light cavalry officer and had not served in the infantry since 1792. Furthermore, he wanted to command a light cavalry brigade, but none was available in the autumn of 1811.[566]

Table 13.3 Organization of the Light Division, 1 October 1811

Division HQ	Major General Robert Craufurd	Commander
	Lieutenant Charles Wood, 52nd Foot	ADC
	Lieutenant James Shaw, 43rd Foot	ADC
	Lieutenant John Bell, 52nd Foot	DAQMG
	Major Charles Rowan, 52nd Foot	AAG
	Charles Purcell	ACG
	Wentworth Parker	Chaplain
1st Brigade	Lieutenant Colonel Andrew Barnard, 95th Rifles	Acting Commander
	Captain Charles Beckwith, 95th Rifles	Brigade Major
1st Bn, 43rd Foot	Lieutenant Colonel Charles McLeod	Commander

(Continued)

Right Wing, 1st Bn, 95th Rifles	Brevet Lieutenant Colonel Dugald Gilmour	Commander
Company, 2nd Bn, 95th Rifles	Captain Samuel Mitchell	Commander
Company, 2nd Bn, 95th Rifles	Captain John Hart	Commander
Right Wing, 3rd Bn, 95th Rifles	Captain William Percival*	Acting Commander
3rd Caçadores Bn	Lieutenant Colonel George Elder	Commander
2nd Brigade	Major General John Vandeleur	Commander
	Lieutenant Harry Smith, 95th Rifles	Brigade Major
	Lieutenant William Armstrong, 19th Light Dragoons	ADC
1st Bn, 52nd Foot	Major Edward Gibbs	Commander
2nd Bn, 52nd Foot	Major John Hunt	Commander
Left Wing, 1st Bn, 95th Rifles	Major Peter O'Hare	Commander
1st Caçadores Bn	Lieutenant Colonel Jorge Avilez	Commander

* Percival returned to the battalion in September.

Marmont had achieved his mission of resupplying Ciudad Rodrigo and at the end of September he ordered his army to return to the vicinity of Salamanca. With the immediate threat from the French gone, and having no intentions of conducting offensive operations, Wellington placed his army in winter quarters. The 1st Brigade was to occupy Alfaiates and Aldeia da Ponte, while the 2nd Brigade was in Quadrazais, Souto, and Nave. The division assembled at Forcalhos on 2 October and moved to its various different quarters. The men would stay in these villages for several weeks (see Table 13.4).[567]

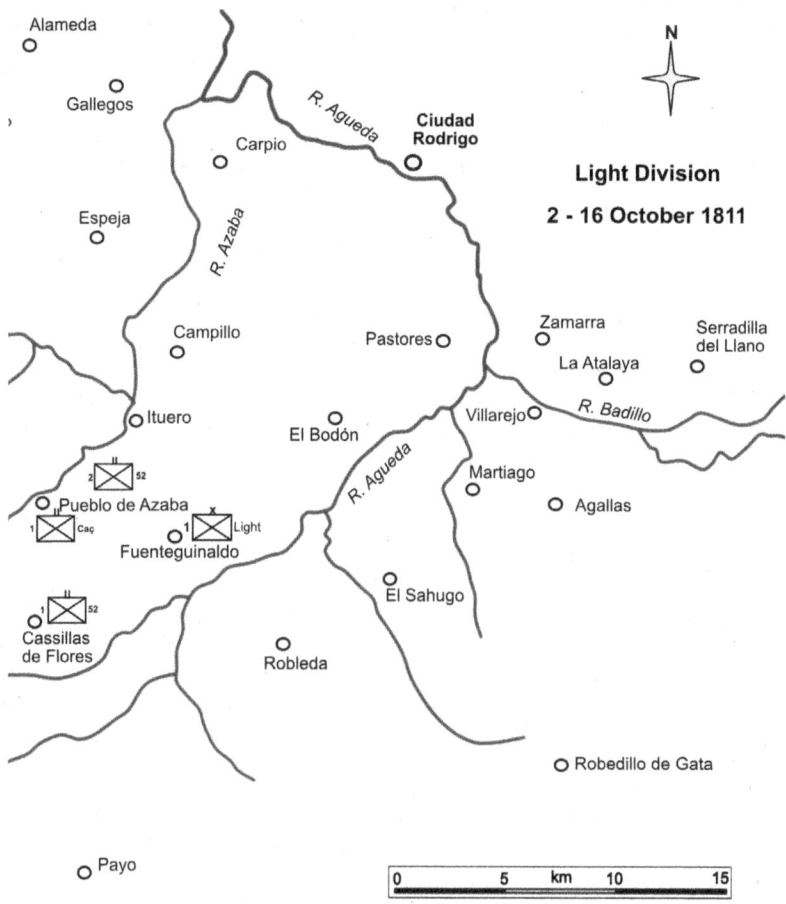

Table 13.4 Location of the Light Division, 2–16 October 1811

Division HQ	Fuenteguinaldo
1st Brigade	Fuenteguinaldo
2nd Brigade HQ	Casillas de Flores
1st Bn, 52nd Foot	Casilas de Flores
2nd Bn, 52nd Foot	Puebla de Azaba
Left Wing, 1st Bn, 95th Rifles	Castillejos de Azaba*
1st Caçadores Bn	Puebla de Azaba?

Sources: Ewart, pp. 43-4; Oglander, p. 97; Simmons, p. 204.
* Simmons says Castillejos de Duas Casas, which is 50km north of where the rest of the 2nd Brigade was billeted. He probably meant Castillejos de Azaba.

For the next ten days the division stayed put and tried to rest. The weather was good, so the officers had time to explore the area and to hunt. A group of officers in the 1st Brigade formed an amateur thespian troop and put on the play *Hamlet* on 30 October in a small chapel outside Fuenteguinaldo.[568] Cricket was also played.[569] Mail had not caught up with the division yet, so reading letters and newspapers from home was not an option. Furthermore, there were few books to read for those who were so inclined. Captain Leach explained why:

> Books were quite out of the question. Some few individuals of a corps might possibly possess a small pocket volume or two; but when it is considered that the first and most necessary point, and that which occupied our chief attention, was to procure, by some means or other, forage for our horses and mules, that the baggage which contained our few comforts and necessaries might be carried with us from place to place, it will readily be comprehended that a portable library was deemed less essential for our existence than a portmanteau containing a few changes of linen, boots, &c. &c., to say nothing of tea, sugar, chocolate, rice, bread, meat, a pig's-skin of wine, a keg of spirits, cigars, spare horse-shoes and nails, &c. &c., – that is to say, when any of these good things could be procured for love or money, which very frequently was not the case. Our half-starved animals had more than enough to do in scrambling along with such matters on their backs, without the additional weight of libraries, even had it been possible to have procured books.[570]

Little evidence remains on what the soldiers did to relax, although some got into mischief, and some unauthorized foraging occurred. Complaints from the locals reached Craufurd and on 11 October he formed up the division at Fuenteguinaldo and 'spoke to them some time about plundering &c.'[571]

On 15 October the French appeared to be stirring again and the division was given orders to be ready to move at a moment's notice. Nothing came of this, but the 2nd Brigade's 2nd Battalion, 52nd Foot, and the Left Wing of the 95th Rifles were moved to Villasrubias.[572] Two days later the 2nd Brigade was ordered forward to prevent the French garrison in Ciudad Rodrigo from foraging in the countryside. The 1st Brigade sent the Right Wing of the 95th Rifles and the 3rd Caçadores to occupy El Bodón (see Table 13.5).

Table 13.5 Locations of the Light Division, 17–31 October 1811

Division HQ	Fuenteguinaldo
1st Brigade HQ	Fuenteguinaldo
43rd Foot	Fuenteguinaldo
Right Wing, 1st Bn, 95th Rifles	Fuenteguinaldo
2 Companies, 2nd Bn, 95th Rifles	Fuenteguinaldo
Right Wing, 3rd Bn, 95th Rifles	El Bodón
3rd Caçadores Bn	El Bodón
2nd Brigade HQ	Martiago
1st Bn, 52nd Foot	Zamarra
2nd Bn, 52nd Foot	Puebla de Azaba
Left Wing, 1st Bn, 95th Rifles	La Atalaya and Guadapera
1st Caçadores Bn	Martiago

Sources: Oglander, p. 101; Ewart, pp. 44–5.

The 2nd Brigade now had to provide piquets and be ready to respond to any French foragers. The 1st Battalion 52nd Foot, at Zamarra, was the most forward of the units and the living was rough. Captain Ewart described it as 'a very bad village to be quartered in from having been often plundered and destroyed, only two short leagues from Ciudad Rodrigo, of which we have a fine view from a hill near, beyond which, half a mile in a ravine, we are ordered to have a captain's picquet'.[573] Compounding the hard living, the weather turned cold and rainy in the last week of the month, so outside recreation was curtailed.

Guadiana Fever still ravaged the ranks of the division during October, despite the men being back in the relatively disease-free region of northern Portugal. The number of dead British troops dropped by 50 per cent from the previous month, although the number of hospitalized among the British troops increased by 22 per cent (see Table 13.6).

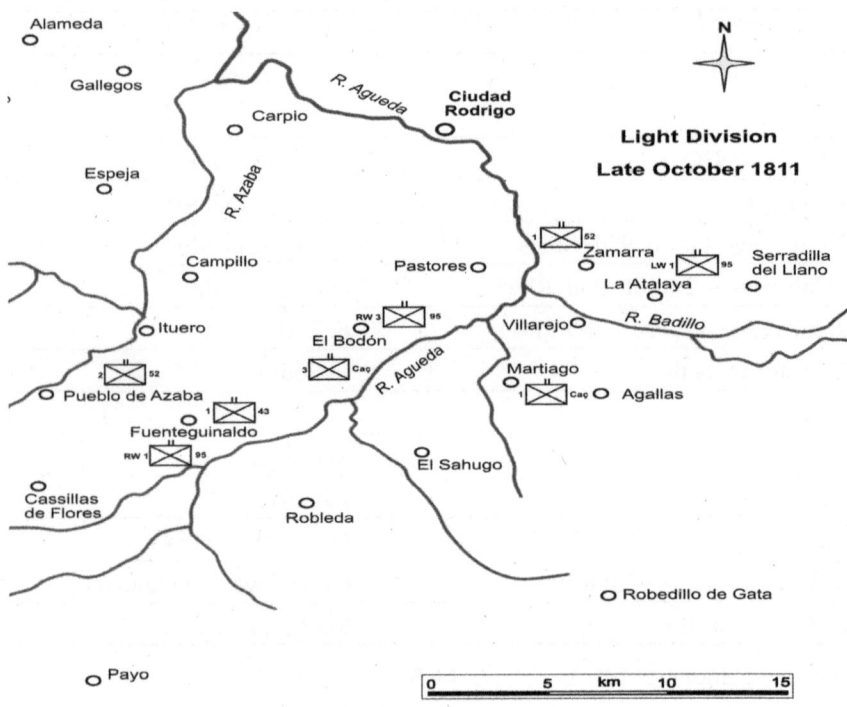

Table 13.6 Light Division, Other Ranks Sick, 24 October 1811

Unit	Strength	Sick	% Sick	Dead
43rd Foot	1,218	301	25	4
1st Bn, 52nd Foot	869	225	26	2
2nd Bn, 52nd Foot	580	276	48	7
1st Bn, 95th Rifles	722	162	22	3
2nd Bn, 95th Rifles	190	38	20	0
Right Wing, 3rd Bn, 95th Rifles	407	173	42	4
1st Caçadores	600	85	14	2
3rd Caçadores	600	77	13	1
Total	5,186	1,337	26	23

Sources: WO17/2468; WO17/2466.

Lieutenant John Cooke of the 43rd Foot was one of those who fell sick in July and spent many months in the hospital.[574] He left a gruesome description of what it was like to become sick and be sent to a hospital:

I became blind with ophthalmia, was seized with violent rheumatic pains in the soles of my feet. I took to my bed. My legs and knees swelled to an enormous size, first turning red, then blue, and I was no longer able to move.

Many other officers became sick, and were ordered to the rear; I for one, mattress and all, was shoved into a Spanish car. I was in my shirt, with my legs enveloped in bandages. Our feelings during the passage of the Agueda were indescribable . . . dragged along by bullocks sometimes forced into a run, owing to the steepness of the adamantine roads . . . first over one rock, then over another.

I could no longer bear the terrible pain. Being quite helpless and blind, I begged and entreated to be lifted out, but to get on a mule's back was quite out of the question, for my legs and knees were so inflamed. Some sick soldiers offered to try and carry or rather drag me from rock to rock. First I got a jolt on one side, then an unintentional bump on the other; the men were exhausted. I entreated them to hold up my feet, while my head lay in the road, for I could not bear them on the ground.

At the end of the second day's tormenting journey, we entered Castel Nero. The cars were drawn round a stone fountain. While waiting for our billets from the *Juez de Fora*, the howling of wolves was distinctly heard in all directions, amid the surrounding woods and rocks.

From morning until nightfall, for five burning days, we travelled at the rate of a mile an hour. The heat of the weather was almost past endurance. Each night I was dragged out of the car, mattress and all, shoved into some horrible recess that was alive with vermin. In the morning I was replaced in my uneasy vehicle for the continuation of the journey. On the fifth day, when within two leagues of Celorico (our destination), we drew up, as Major Elers of our regiment requested that he might rest for a short time – he could no longer bear the jolting of his vehicle. In a few minutes however he expired, and his body was carried forward and interred.

On our arrival at Celorico, an empty room was my quarter, and the floor was my resting place. I remained 60 days nearly immoveable, my only covering a filthy blanket, stained all over from my mule's sore back. On the journey it had been placed under the animal's pack saddle to save its back by day, while I had the benefit of it as a covering by night. In this miserable plight, what with bleeding and blistering, and long confinement, I had become a perfect skeleton, and reduced to the most wretched condition.

Five medical officers came, and having examined my now lank legs, and big feet, held a consultation at the foot of my mattress. They held no hope of a speedy recovery, and even doubted whether I should again be enabled to straighten my right leg, the knee of which had become contracted during the pains of my rough, painful journey. The staff doctors tried to persuade me to go to England, by offering a spring waggon to convey me to Lisbon. My suffering had been great, my arms hung nearly useless by my side, but my legs refused their office, for I still cherished the hope, that they would again, carry me forward. Doctor MacLean[575] most kindly pressed me to acquiesce in their advice, but without effect. I understand this poor gentleman died a few days subsequently of a fever.

How could I leave the army, whom I found amongst mountains feeding on hard biscuit and drinking rum impregnated with the mosquitoes? A pretty warlike story to recount at home! The very thought was frightful! More bleeding and blistering were therefore resorted to. By this means, and aided by a good constitution, at the expiration of another month I was able, with the assistance of crutches to reach my window. The trellis work of which being thrown open and offered me ineffable delight: I could once more enjoy the sight of a few living objects in the street.

The rain now fell in torrents for days together. Thousands of British and Portuguese soldiers crowded the churches which had been converted into hospitals. They were dying by hundreds, of fever produced by the sickly season. The excruciating torments, suffering and privations of the common soldiers were such, that an adequate description is impossible. Many of them stretched out on the pavement, lingering in raging fevers, the straw that had been placed for their comfort, having worked from under them during their agonies, while hundreds of flies settled on and blackened their dying faces. So stationary did these tormentors become, that those who still maintained sufficient power were obliged to tear them from off their faces, and squeeze them to death in their hands.

Cars piled up, and loaded with the remains of these unfortunate victims, daily passed through the streets for the purpose of pitching their bodies into some hole by way of interment. The medical officers were overpowered by the numbers of sick, fell ill themselves. Notwithstanding their strenuous efforts, it was impossible to surmount all difficulties, and pay attention to all that could have been wished. The hospital orderlies were exhausted by attending, burying, and clearing away the dead. These scenes of misery cannot be fancied.[576]

Chapter 14

WINTER QUARTERS, NOVEMBER–DECEMBER 1811

November
On 1 November word had reached the army that the French were about to resupply Ciudad Rodrigo. The 1st Battalion of the 52nd Foot was already at Zamarra, but the 2nd Battalion was at Puebla de Azaba, 40km away. For some reason the 1st Battalion of the 52nd was ordered to withdraw from Zamarra and move to Martiago, where it joined the 1st Caçadores. The Left Wing of the 1st Battalion, 95th Rifles, moved into Villarejo.[577] The 1st Brigade did not march until the morning of 2 November. It formed up near El Bodón, moved on to El Encina and finally stopped at Pastores. That night the 95th Rifles and 3rd Caçadores remained at Pastores, while the 43rd Foot returned to El Bodón. The 2nd Brigade returned to Zamarra during the afternoon. The division was too late to intercept the French convoy which dropped off the provisions and left the town three hours after arriving.[578]

The division remained in those positions until 4 November, when it returned to its cantonments. The weather turned colder, but it was mostly sunny, although it rained hard during the night of 9 November. As the month progressed the weather turned colder and by 16 November there was a frost every morning. The division finally received mail on 20 November and the following day newspapers arrived from England. On 23 November the division was alerted that another French convoy was nearing Ciudad Rodrigo. Once again the division moved to action. The 1st Brigade formed on El Bodón, while the 2nd Battalion, 52nd Foot, joined the 1st Battalion at Zamarra, and the 1st Caçadores moved to La Atalaya. The next day the 1st Brigade was ordered to Zamarra, but the orders were countermanded and

171

the men were halted at Martiago. The 3rd Caçadores were already at Zamarra when they received the orders to return to Martiago.[579]

The division stayed in the advanced positions until 28 November, when it was again ordered into cantonments (see Table 14.1). There was more good news that day when 'an order was received for Regimental Paymasters to repair to Malhada Sorda, to receive a [issue?] of pay on account of the month from 25 August to 24 September. Thus, the army, from the smallness of the issue, will still remain a quarter in arrear, a longer period than was ever before known. The muleteers of the Commissariat have however been paid up to 8 months arrears. They are always kept long in arrear, to prevent their quitting the service.'[580]

Table 14.1 Location of the Light Division, 28 November 1811

Division HQ	Fuenteguinaldo
1st Brigade HQ	Martiago
43rd Foot	Martiago
Right Wing, 1st Bn, 95th Rifles	Pastores, La Encina and Villarejo*
2 Companies, 2nd Bn, 95th Rifles	
Right Wing, 3rd Bn, 95th Rifles	
3rd Caçadores Bn	Martiago
2nd Brigade HQ	Martiago
1st Bn, 52nd Foot	Zamarra
2nd Bn, 52nd Foot	Serradilla del Llano
Left Wing, 1st Bn, 95th Rifles	La Atalaya
1st Caçadores Bn	Las Agallas

Sources: Oglander, p. 106; Ewart, p. 48; Simmons, p. 206.
* Simmons unfortunately did not specify which unit was where.

The wintry weather caused relapses in the health of soldiers who had appeared to have recovered from Guadiana Fever. Among those was Lieutenant George Simmons. He wrote on 7 November that he was hit hard with the ague. His next entry was nine days later: 'Had the ague daily, and kept my bed from its debilitating influence. I took bark [quinine] in very large doses, combined with opium, and placed a hot stone on my bosom and two at the soles of my feet as soon as there was any appearance of the cold fit. From treating myself in this way I soon dislodged this insidious enemy from my body and gradually recovered.'[581] The overall number of other ranks in the hospital had declined slightly from 1,337 in October to 1,167 in November. However, the mortality rate increased by 26 per cent (see Table 14.2).

Table 14.2 Light Division, Other Ranks Sick, 24 November 1811

Unit	Strength	Sick	% Sick	Dead
43rd Foot	1,193	256	21	11
1st Bn, 52nd Foot	863	201	23	5
2nd Bn, 52nd Foot	571	256	45	8
1st Bn, 95th Rifles	713	129	18	1
2nd Bn, 95th Rifles	188	37	20	1
3rd Bn, 95th Rifles	398	134	34	7
1st Caçadores	600	75	13	1
3rd Caçadores	600	79	13	4
Total	5,126	1,167	23	38

Sources: WO17/2468; WO17/2466.

December

There were few changes in the organization of the division, with one notable exception. On 5 December Lieutenant Colonel John Colborne arrived to take command of the 1st Battalion 52nd Foot (see Table 14.3).

Table 14.3 Organization of the Light Division, 5 December 1811

Division HQ	Major General Robert Craufurd	Commander
	Lieutenant Charles Wood, 52nd Foot	ADC
	Lieutenant James Shaw, 43rd Foot	ADC
	Lieutenant John Bell, 52nd Foot	DAQMG
	Major Charles Rowan, 52nd Foot	AAG
	Charles Purcell	ACG
	Wentworth Parker	Chaplain
1st Brigade	Lieutenant Colonel Andrew Barnard, 95th Rifles	Acting Commander
	Captain Charles Beckwith, 95th Rifles	Brigade Major
1st Bn, 43rd Foot	Lieutenant Colonel Charles McLeod	Commander
Right Wing, 1st Bn, 95th Rifles	Brevet Lieutenant Colonel Dugald Gilmour	Commander

Company, 2nd Bn, 95th Rifles	Captain Samuel Mitchell	Commander
Company, 2nd Bn, 95th Rifles	Captain John Hart	Commander
Right Wing, 3rd Bn, 95th Rifles	Captain William Percival	Acting Commander
3rd Caçadores Bn	Lieutenant Colonel George Elder	Commander
2nd Brigade	Major General John Vandeleur	Commander
	Lieutenant Harry Smith, 95th Rifles	Brigade Major
	Lieutenant William Armstrong, 19th Light Dragoons	ADC
1st Bn, 52nd Foot	Lieutenant Colonel John Colborne	Commander
2nd Bn, 52nd Foot	Major John Hunt	Commander
Left Wing, 1st Bn, 95th Rifles	Major Peter O'Hare	Commander
1st Caçadores Bn	Lieutenant Colonel Jorge Avilez	Commander

The weather for the first several days was sunny, but on 4 December it turned colder and for the next ten days it alternated between rain, sleet, snow and sunshine, with occasional fog. The latter half of December was cold but sunny. The rainy weather caused the Agueda river to rise and on 12 December the division received orders to move to the east side of the river lest it should continue to rise and make the fords impassable.[582] The poor weather kept the division in its cantonments. After two consecutive days of sunshine, Craufurd ordered a review of the division's British regiments to take place on 20 December. The location was in a field between Fuenteguinaldo and El Bodón and the men were to be there by 10am. For some units this was 25km away and they were formed up at 4am in order to get there on time. Craufurd spent a few minutes inspecting the troops and then ordered them to return to their quarters. The march back was so fatiguing for the 1st Battalion, 52nd Foot, that Colborne stopped it at El Sahugo for the night after marching 20km.[583]

By mid-month it had become very apparent that the army would soon be besieging Ciudad Rodrigo. Large numbers of heavy artillery were seen moving to Almeida, as well as material to build a bridge.[584] Before long the division was tasked to provide soldiers to build fascines and gabions. Supervising the work was quite popular among the officers because they were paid an extra 4 shillings per day.[585] This was quite a bonus for a lieutenant who only made 6 shillings 6 pence per day.

Moving the tons of supplies and ammunition needed to besiege Ciudad Rodrigo required thousands of carts, waggons and mules. There was only a limited number of carts available, since most had already been hired by the Commissary Department to keep the army supplied with its daily requirements for food and ammunition. Once those carts that had not already been hired were taken, the only source left was to take those that were in use by the divisions. This had some unforeseen consequences, for if the food could not be brought to the troops, they would go hungry. Before long, food for both humans and animals was difficult to find. Oglander of the 43rd Foot explained:

> This scarcity is occasioned by the want of conveyance for the stores formed in the rear and by the high price of corn in Spain, which prevents the natives from providing our commissaries with bread, except for ready money. Forage is also very scarce, nearly all the chopped straw in these districts being consumed and it is an article of too great bulk to be brought from any distance. No corn has been issued for the horses of the officers, excepting for the General's Staff, which is indeed regularly supplied. The Regimental Staff [get] their issues extremely irregularly; even the artillery attached to this division & the cavalry doing the outpost duty are badly off.[586]

In the 52nd Foot there was a 'lack of Bread. Our poor fellows have not had any bread for some time, not until the last 3 days & then only half rations and at a time when they have no money, 3 months' pay due to them & have been obliged to feed themselves upon chestnuts & acorns. The inhabitants refuse to bring bread to market as the commissary prefer it and pays only by paper, a receipt for it. The men have 1½ or 2lb of meat when they have no bread, but without salt or potatoes & they would prefer ½lb of bread.'[587]

Shortage of food was not the only problem. The men's uniforms were becoming ragged and although new clothing had arrived in Lisbon, few waggons or carts were available to bring it forward. Surprisingly, the biggest problem was in the 2nd Battalion, 52nd Foot, which had only been in country for nine months. Lieutenant Charles Dawson wrote in early December that in his company the men's 'clothing [was] in poor shape. Our 2nd Battalion naked and have been excused outlying picquet. We cannot muster 30 shirts amongst them, no stockings, coats & pantaloons patched like harlequins, but we are expecting cloathing [sic] every day.'[588] Unfortunately for them, Dawson was overly optimistic. Lieutenant George Barlow, also of the 2nd Battalion, 52nd Foot, was shocked at how bad the situation was by the end of December and wrote home that 'lack of clothing and food I regret however continuance in these quarters, for the sake of the men. They are literally in rags for want of new clothing, which the paucity of bullocks and the still more wretched nature of the roads, added to our current distance from Lisbon of 280 miles, prevent from reaching our division. It has been actually some weeks on the route & in the meanwhile some of our company cannot come to parade on account of nakedness.'[589]

The 43rd was in marginally better shape. Lieutenant Oglander wrote on 20 December that 'we have not got ours, yet it is on its way up & the detachment that joined in July last received theirs previously to quitting England & that of the rest of the men is not yet by any means bad'.[590] Like Dawson in the 52nd Foot, Oglander was also overly optimistic. Corporal Thomas Garretty described how he

> was charged with a mission to fetch clothing from Lisbon for the use of the regiment. One description of article was flannel shirts, of which I received six hundred, for the approaching winter wear. On returning, I met with an accident, which had nearly deprived me of sight. One of our party, with consummate carelessness, placed his powderhorn upon the table, fully charged, and by some accident the whole quantity exploded.[591]

Garretty made no comment about how the damaged and scorched clothing was received by the men when he returned to the regiment.

Entertainment

When not on duty, the officers filled their time with a variety of activities. Hunting was still popular and some of the senior officers and those on the staff had brought foxhounds with them.[592] Captain Leach, having heard that there were woodcock in the area, formed an overnight expedition on 11 December to hunt them. He took with him

> two of my brother-officers, to a solitary farm-house in the mountains beyond the Vadillo, where we slept. We took with us our servants, a mule laden with provisions, portmanteaus, &c. &c., and the Irish piper

belonging to the band. In the evening we danced boleros, fandangos, and Irish jigs, with the farmers' daughters, and early the next morning attacked the woodcocks, which I never remember to have seen more numerous. We had capital sport, and returned late at night to our quarters at Atalaia. One of our party, who was a better performer at the dance than with a gun, fired thirty shots, at least, without killing a single bird; and towards evening, by way of putting a finishing stroke to the day's work, he let fly at an enormous wild cat, which was perched on a tree above his head, not twenty yards distant, and the animal escaped unhurt. This was a standing joke against him ever after.[593]

After the success of their performance of *Hamlet* in October, the thespians in the division decided to put on another Shakespeare play:

Every morning the officers were engaged rehearsing their different parts, or superintending the making of theatrical dresses (as the tragedy of Henry IV was to be performed by various officers) and scene painting. The latter was principally executed by Bell[594] (the assistant quarter master general of the division) in an old chapel, within one hundred yards of the village, which had been gutted of its ornaments by the French or the priests. The night of performance arrived. Written bills of the play having been distributed throughout the village, which was filled like a beehive with officers with flowing camlet cloaks, and mounted on *boricos* [donkeys], mules, and ragged-maned stallions; [sic] They came a considerable distance, from other divisions of the army. Tickets being issued for pit and boxes, we moved in Bacchanalian groups towards 'theatre'. It was crammed to excess, as we had not forgotten to reserve some room for the soldiers. The curtain no sooner drew up, than the wonder of the *Muchachas* knew no bounds, and they became so loquacious in admiration of the scenery and dresses, and in disputing among themselves which was the prince, and which the various characters the officers were to personify, that it was a considerable time before they could be so far tranquillized as to permit the performance to proceed, which, however, went off with great eclat.[595]

William Freer left a review of the final performance: 'the scenery and dresses are excellent and among the company several excellent performers, the last performance was honoured by officers from all parts of the army. Lord Wellington was to have been there but something occurred that put it off.'[596]

The most popular activity for the officers was attending dances, especially if there were young women available. John Cooke described one such dance:

The officers, therefore, put on their best uniforms, and decorated themselves with all the precision and care used when about to attend a ball of a more enlightened circle. On entering the room we observed the females decorated in their best attire and trinkets. The band struck up a *bolero*. That being concluded, the male peasantry retired, leaving their mistresses to hop down our country dances, and to instruct us in those figures we had attempted to teach them. Generals, and all ranks, mixed in these rustic dances, where a variety of little coquetries were practised on the half-enamoured swains. The smell of garlic was scarce tolerable; but these were no times for niceties.'[597]

Captains William Mein and John Ewart rode 25km through the mountains on a steep and slippery paved road from Agallas to Robledillo de Gata to attend a dance hosted 'by two officers of the 1st Cacadores and a ball after, at which their band attended, where we danced till past 10pm with some ladies and their attendants, fugitives from Ciudad Rodrigo. The weather very fine, but much milder on this side of the sierra and about Ciudad Rodrigo.'[598]

Christmas

Despite the food shortages, the officers appeared to gather enough to share among themselves.[599] This was usually done at the company messes or by combining the resources of two messes. In the 43rd Foot 'every effort was exerted to do ample justice to Christmas. The different officers' messes dined alternately with each other, to partake of lean roast beef and plumb [sic] pudding. A four pound loaf cost a dollar;[600] moist sugar three *pecetas*[601] a pound, and every other commodity equally expensive; still the festive board was well supplied, and the evenings most joyfully spent.'[602] In the 52nd Foot Captain Ewart of the 1st Battalion went to Las Agallas, where he ate with Captain James Currie of the 2nd Battalion, and 'dined on roast beef, plum pudding and turkey, with a ham'.[603] Lieutenant Kinloch of the 1st Battalion wrote to his mother that he ate a '1st course gravy soup, sirloin of beef roasted, curried fowl, vegetables; 2nd course, roast hare, boiled turkey with white sauce, three couples of woodcocks; besides a good pudding & English cheese; we had dinner for seven people'.[604] In the same letter home, he complained about how expensive his mess bill[605] was and remarked that he had asked Colonel Colborne if he could be transferred to another company:

The fact is that I have been completely drawn into this expense without almost knowing it myself, ever since I was transferred from Captain [John] Douglas's company I have of course [been] living at the mess of the company to which I belonged & as hardly anything in the way of pay was issued, every body laid out money as they had it & the other day when accounts were settled I found myself on the debit side much beyond what I possibly could have conceived. On this I was obliged to draw on my uncle for the £50, besides this I was put to the expense of purchasing another animal to carry my baggage, this of itself was £50, before this Douglas was always so good as to carry it for me. After finding out all this you may be sure I was anxious to return to my old company, & upon mentioning this to Colonel Colborne he removed me back again.[606]

Newly arrived in country Lieutenant George Barlow of the 2nd Battalion, 52nd Foot, alluded to how expensive life was in a letter home on 3 December, and explained what he was doing to keep expenses down: 'Our mess consists of but four & is as moderate as possible, we drink little or no wine, take a cup of hot chocolate or tea and generally go to bed by ten or eleven at latest. I seldom or ever play at cards & when that happens we play but shilling points . . . that I am the only officer who possesses any books & indeed who use them much; as the earlier part of the day is generally employed by them in coursing or shooting, both of which diversions are to be had hereabouts in the highest perfection.'[607]

Despite the wintry weather and the paucity of food, being in winter quarters did improve the division's overall health. There were 982 other ranks still in the hospital, a decrease of 3 per cent from the previous month. However, the mortality rate was still rising, with another 69 deaths. In the past six months the division had lost 180 British other ranks from disease, plus another eighty sent home broken in health. This was 8 per cent of its strength lost without engaging in combat. Going into 1812, it could field fewer than 3,000 other ranks among its British troops (see Table 14.4).

Table 14.4 Light Division, Other Ranks Sick, 24 December 1811

Unit	Strength	Sick	% Sick	Dead
43rd Foot	1,176	208	18	16
1st Bn, 52nd Foot	850	166	20	7

WINTER QUARTERS, NOVEMBER–DECEMBER 1811

Unit	Strength	Sick	% Sick	Dead
2nd Bn, 52nd Foot	555	223	40	20
1st Bn, 95th Rifles	702	113	16	5
2nd Bn, 95th Rifles	185	36	19	2
3rd Bn, 95th Rifles	375	109	29	13
1st Caçadores	600	78	13	2
3rd Caçadores	600	49	8	4
Total	5,043	982	19	69

Sources: WO17/2468; WO17/2466.

Throughout the month the division continued to rotate units between the forward outposts and the quiet billets in the rear (see Table 14.5).

Table 14.5 Locations of the Light Division, 31 December 1811

Division HQ	Fuenteguinaldo
1st Brigade HQ	Fuenteguinaldo
43rd Foot	Fuenteguinaldo
Right Wing, 1st Bn, 95th Rifles	Pastores and La Encina
2 Companies, 2nd Bn, 95th Rifles	
3rd Bn, 95th Rifles	
3rd Caçadores Bn	Fuenteguinaldo
2nd Brigade HQ	Martiago
1st Bn, 52nd Foot	Martiago
2nd Bn, 52nd Foot	Agallas
Left Wing, 1st Bn, 95th Rifles	La Atalaya
1st Caçadores Bn	Robledillo de Gata

Sources: *With the 43rd*, p. 92; Ewart, p. 53.

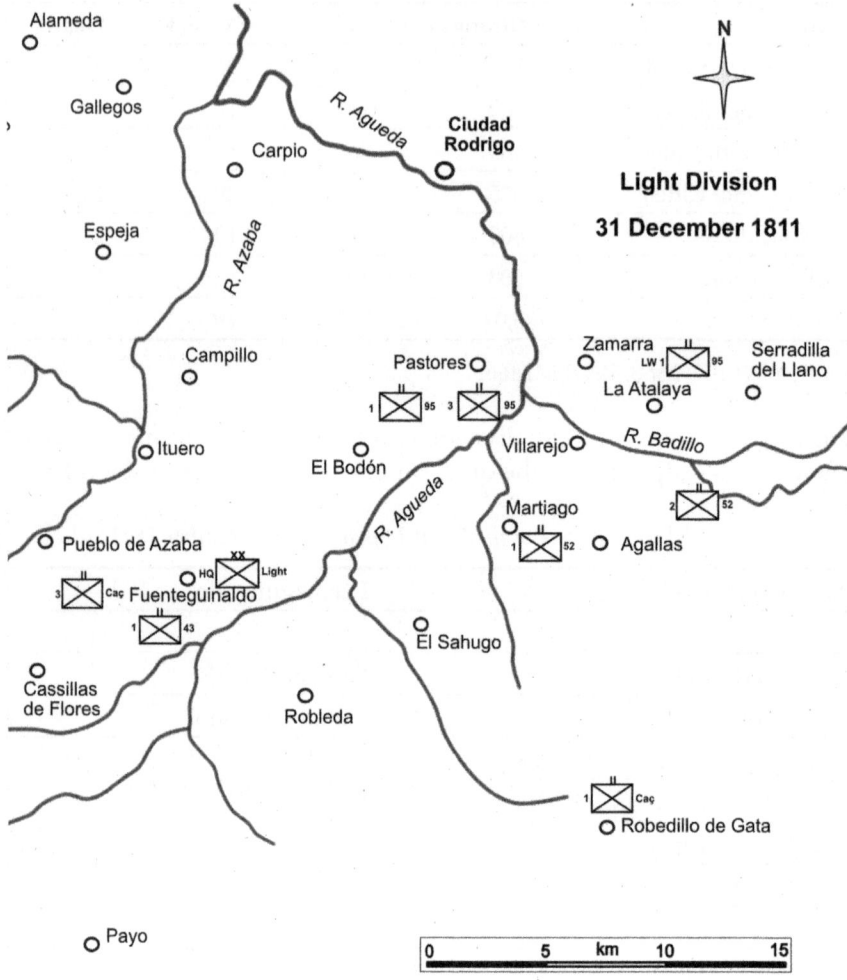

The final days of 1811 were cold and quiet. The officers and men continued to rest and party, knowing that within a few weeks they would once more be in the middle of the action. If it was anything like the previous 18 months, they knew that many of them would be killed or wounded during the sieges and campaigns. But that is the lot of a soldier, and a story for another time.

Chapter 15

WHAT HAPPENED TO THEM

We are always curious about what happened to the officers and men of the Light Division who feature so prominently in our books, and this volume is no exception. Most of the officers and men continued to fight with their regiments over the next forty months. Some were killed and many others were seriously wounded. Many of those who survived went on to attain senior rank in the British Army.

Note: the names of the battles for which medals were awarded are given as they appeared on the medals or clasps.

Division Staff

Barnard, Andrew Francis: continued to temporarily command the 1st Brigade until May 1813. After General Craufurd died from his wounds on 24 January 1812, Barnard temporarily commanded the Light Division until May 1812. He commanded the 3rd Battalion, 95th Rifles, at Waterloo. He moved up through the ranks and was promoted to full general in 1851. He died on 17 January 1855. He was awarded the AGC with four clasps[608] and the Waterloo Medal. He was created a KCB in 1815 and a GCB in 1840.

Craufurd, Robert: was severely wounded in the storming of Ciudad Rodrigo on 19 January 1812. He died on 24 January and was buried in the walls of Ciudad Rodrigo the next day. He was awarded the AGM with a clasp for Busaco and Ciudad Rodrigo.

Erskine, Sir William: Commanded the 5th Division from April to May 1811 and then the cavalry with Lieutenant General Rowland Hill's detached Corps from May to June 1811. He commanded the 2nd Cavalry Division from June to December 1811, April to November

1812, and in February 1813. He died on 13 February 1813 from injuries sustained by falling off a balcony in Lisbon.

Vandeleur, John Ormsby: commanded the 2nd Brigade until he was seriously wounded at the assault on Ciudad Rodrigo on 19 January 1812. He returned to the division in May 1812. In July 1813 he left the Light Division to take command of a light cavalry brigade and led it through to the end of the war. He commanded the 4th Cavalry Brigade at Waterloo. He was promoted to lieutenant general in 1821 and general in 1838. He died in Dublin on 1 November 1849. He was created a KCB in 1815 and a GCB in 1833. He was awarded the AGC for Ciudad Rodrigo, Salamanca, Vittoria and Nive, and the Waterloo Medal.

43rd Foot

Cooke, John Henry: was slightly wounded at Badajoz in 1812 and was wounded again at Vittoria in 1813. He continued to serve with his battalion until the peace in 1814. He had fought in the War of 1812, and served in France after Waterloo until 1818. He was promoted to captain in 1823, brevet major in 1838, exchanged into the 25th Foot in 1838 and into the 21st Foot in 1855. He retired as a brevet lieutenant colonel by the sale of his commission in 1855. He was a Yeoman of the Guard in 1862 and knighted in 1867. He died on 13 January 1870. He received the MGSM with eight clasps.[609]

Duffy, John: was slightly wounded at the siege of Ciudad Rodrigo in January 1812. He returned to England in May 1812 but went back to the Peninsula in February 1813. He was promoted to major on 13 June 1813. He was slightly wounded at Vittoria. He returned to England in January 1814. He died in 1855 having been promoted to lieutenant general in 1851. He received the MGSM with six clasps.[610]

Fergusson, James: was severely wounded at Ciudad Rodrigo and Badajoz. He was promoted to major in the 79th Foot in December 1812. A month later he exchanged into the 85th Foot and remained in the Peninsula until the end of the war in April 1814. Over the next forty-six years he would be promoted through the ranks till he became a full general in 1860. He died in 1865. He received the MGSM with seven clasps.[611]

Freer, William: continued to serve with the 1st Battalion until he lost his right arm at the assault on Badajoz in April 1812. He returned to the Peninsula in February 1813 and was wounded again at Nivelle in

November 1813. He was promoted to captain on 1 December 1813, and was eventually promoted to lieutenant colonel. He was in command of the 10th Foot on Corfu when he died on 2 August 1836.

Garretty, Thomas: was with his company at the siege of Ciudad Rodrigo and was seriously wounded in the left thigh at the assault on Badajoz on 6 April 1812. He returned to England in 1813 and was medically retired in 1817. He was recalled to duty in 1819 and found fit for service in a veterans' battalion. He retired in 1823 after seventeen years of service. His date of death is unknown; however, he was still alive in 1848 and received the MGSM with four clasps.[612]

McLeod, Charles: was killed during the assault on Badajoz on 6 April. He received the AGM and clasp for Ciudad Rodrigo and Badajoz.

Napier, William: returned to the 1st Battalion in April 1812 and assumed command upon the death of its commander at Badajoz on 6 April. He was promoted to major in May 1812 and remained in command of the battalion until March 1814. He went on half-pay in 1819. He is best known for writing the six-volume *History of the War in the Peninsula and in the South of France*. He died in 1860. He received the AGM and clasps for Salamanca, Nivelle and Nive and the MGSM with three clasps.[613]

Oglander, Henry: continued to serve with the 1st Battalion until he was seriously wounded at Badajoz, where he lost his left arm. He returned to the Peninsula as a captain in the 47th Foot in February 1813. He was seriously wounded at San Sebastian in 1813, where he was shot in the body and lost the index finger on his right hand. Due to his wounds, he received an annual pension of £450. He stayed in the army and commanded the 26th Foot until his death at sea in 1840. He was awarded the AGM for San Sebastian.

52nd Foot
Barlow, George Ulrick: was seriously wounded in the right arm and slightly wounded in the hip at Badajoz and returned to England in June 1812. He went back to Portugal in the spring of 1813 and was severely wounded in the foot at the Nivelle. He left the Peninsula in December 1813 and was promoted to captain in the 69th Foot at the end of the year. He fought at Waterloo. He exchanged into the 4th Light Dragoons in 1821 and died in India in 1824. He received the Waterloo Medal.

Colborne, John: was wounded at Ciudad Rodrigo, but continued to command the 1st Battalion and occasionally temporarily the 2nd Brigade until the peace in 1814. He commanded the battalion, and temporarily a brigade, at Waterloo in 1815 and served in France until 1818. He was promoted through the years, eventually becoming a field marshal in 1860. He served as the Commander-in-Chief of Canada from 1836 to 1839 and as Commander-in-Chief of Ireland from 1855 to 1860. He died on 17 April 1863 at the age of 85. He was awarded the AGC with three clasps,[614] the MGSM with five clasps,[615] and received the Waterloo Medal. He was created a KCB in 1815, a GCB in 1838 and Baron Seaton in 1839.

Dawson, Charles: served with the regiment through the rest of the Peninsular War. He was severely wounded in the lower leg at Badajoz and in the lung at Waterloo. He died from complications of his wound in France on 3 June 1817. He was awarded the Waterloo Medal.

Dawson, Henry: was promoted to captain in 1812 and was killed by a musket ball to the chest at San Munoz on 17 November 1812.

Dobbs, John: served with the regiment until 1813, when he was seconded to the 5th Caçadores and promoted to captain in the Portuguese Army. He was severely wounded at Bayonne in April 1814 and returned to the 52nd Foot on 13 October 1814. He was promoted to captain in 1816, but it was backdated to 25 October 1814. He went on half-pay in 1816 and exchanged into the 6th Foot in 1835. He retired in 1835 and died on 23 August 1880 at the age of 89. He received the MGSM with ten clasps.[616]

Ewart, John Frederick: was wounded in the arm during the taking of Fort Picurina at Badajoz. He fought with the regiment throughout the campaign of 1812 but returned to England in December 1812 after being promoted to major in the Royal York Rangers. He stayed in the army and was promoted to lieutenant general in 1854. He died on 23 October 1854. He received the MGSM with five clasps.[617]

Kinloch, Charles: was promoted to captain on 18 March 1812 and seriously wounded in the back at Badajoz. He returned home to recuperate in May. His wound never healed properly, and he would be plagued by pain from it for the rest of his life. He purchased a captaincy in the 99th Foot on 18 March 1813 and exchanged back into the 52nd Foot on 22 July 1813. He rejoined Wellington's Army in southern

France in December 1813 as an ADC to General John Hope and served in that position until the end of the war. He missed Waterloo but joined the 52nd Foot in Paris in July 1815. He went on half-pay in July 1816. He died on 22 October 1822 at the age of 34.

Napier, George: lost his right arm leading the Light Division's storming party at Ciudad Rodrigo. He spent the next two years recovering. He returned to his battalion in the Peninsula in January 1814. He was promoted to major general in 1837 and to general in 1854, and died in 1855. He received the AGM for Ciudad Rodrigo and the MGSM with four clasps.[618]

95th Rifles

Beckwith, Thomas Sydney: became the AQMG of the British forces in Canada in 1812. He commanded a brigade in the 1813 Chesapeake campaign. He was promoted to major general on 4 June 1814 and appointed Quartermaster General of the British forces in Canada. In 1829 he became the commander of the East India Company's Bombay Army, and in 1830 was promoted to lieutenant general. He died of a fever in 1831. He received the AGM with clasps for Vimiera, Corunna and Busaco.

Costello, Edward: fought with the 1st Battalion in the Peninsula until April 1814 when peace was declared. He ended the war as a sergeant. His trigger finger was shot off at Quatre Bras and he was pensioned out of the army in 1818. In 1835 he was commissioned as a captain in the British Legion and fought in Spain during the Carlist War. He returned to England in 1838 and was appointed a Yeoman Warder of the Tower of London. He died in 1869 at the age of 81. He was one of the most decorated soldiers in the 95th Rifles. He was awarded the Waterloo Medal and the MGSM with eleven clasps.[619]

Cox, John: stayed with the 1st Battalion until the war ended in April 1814. He was severely wounded at Ciudad Rodrigo, suffering a compound fracture of his left arm, and at Tarbes in March 1814, when his left leg was broken by a musket ball. Despite five years of continuing campaigning, including fighting at Waterloo, he was not promoted to captain until 1819. Eighteen years later he was promoted to lieutenant colonel and in 1855 he was promoted to major general. He died in 1863. He was awarded the Waterloo Medal and the MGSM with ten clasps.[620]

Kincaid, John: served with the 1st Battalion through the rest of the Peninsular War and was its adjutant at Waterloo. He was promoted to captain in 1826 and retired in 1831. For his service he was appointed Exon in the Yeomen of the Guard in 1844. He died on 22 April 1862. He received the MGSM with nine clasps[621] and the Waterloo Medal.

Leach, Jonathan: commanded his company until the end of the Peninsular War. During that time he fought in twenty-one battles and sieges. Despite being wounded, he assumed command of the 1st Battalion at Waterloo after the two senior officers above him became casualties. He was promoted to brevet major in 1813 and brevet lieutenant colonel on 18 June 1815. He was promoted to major in the Rifle Brigade on 9 September 1819 and retired on 24 October 1821. He was created a CB in 1815. He received the MGSM with twelve clasps[622] and the Waterloo Medal. He died on 14 January 1855.

O'Hare, Peter: died in the assault on Badajoz on 6 April 1812. He was awarded the AGM with clasps for Fuentes d'Onor, Ciudad Rodrigo and Badajoz.

Simmons, George: was with the battalion until the end of the war in 1814. He was severely wounded at Waterloo and promoted to captain in 1828 and major in 1838; he retired in 1845. He died in 1858 at the age of 72. He received the MGSM with eight clasps[623] and the Waterloo Medal.

Smith, Harry: was appointed brigade major of the 2nd Brigade of the Light Division in March 1811 and served in that position until the end of the war in April 1814. He was promoted to captain on 28 February 1812. After the Peninsular War was over, he went to North America and served on the staff during the Chesapeake and New Orleans campaigns. He returned to Europe in time to participate in the Waterloo campaign and served as the brigade major of the 10th British Brigade. He was promoted to major in 1826 and lieutenant colonel in 1830. From 1828 to 1840 he served in South Africa and fought in the Kaffir War. He was sent to India in 1840, where he served as the adjutant general. He fought in the Gwalior campaign of 1843, commanded a division in the 1st Sikh War and won the battle of Aliwal on 28 January 1846. He was promoted to major general and returned to South Africa in 1847, where he was appointed governor of the Cape of Good Hope. He served in that position until 1852. During that time he led the British forces in the 7th and 8th Kaffir Wars between 1847 and 1851. He returned to Britain and served on the Home Staff, and was promoted to lieutenant general in 1854. He retired in 1859 and died on 12 October 1860. For his service he was made a CB on 22 June 1815, a KCB on 2 May 1844 and a GCB on 7 April 1846. In July 1846 he was created a baronet. He received the MGSM with twelve clasps[624] and the Waterloo Medal.

Appendix I

STRENGTH OF THE LIGHT DIVISION, JANUARY–DECEMBER 1811[625]

Every infantry battalion and cavalry regiment in the British Army was required to submit a report to the Horse Guards of its strength on the 25th of each month. For those battalions in Britain, the strength return was submitted by the regiment. For battalions on active service, the return was sent up through its chain of command to the headquarters of the relevant theatre. A return was also sent to its regiment in Britain. The regimental returns usually did not contain as much information as those from the theatre headquarters. Furthermore, because of the delay of receiving the returns from active theatres, the information in the regimental returns could be one or two months out of date.

The returns are divided into four categories:

- Officers Present: this reflected the officers who were present for duty with the battalion. It did not include officers who were assigned to the battalion but were on the army staff.
- Staff Officers: like Officers Present, this section only included officers who were present for duty with the battalion and not those who were performing temporary duty on the staff of the army.
- NCOs: this included sergeants but not corporals. Musicians such as drummers, buglers and trumpeters were also included in this section.
- Rank and File: this section included all soldiers who were not officers, sergeants or musicians. It did not differentiate by rank.

The first three categories are further subdivided by rank. The last category was further subdivided by function or status:

- Fit for Duty: the total number of soldiers available to perform their duty. Some returns refer to this category as Present or Present Fit for Duty. This number was known as the effectives.
- Sick: the number of soldiers who were incapacitated due to injury, illness or wounds. The returns did not break the numbers down by cause of incapacity. In some returns it might be further divided into those who were sick in their quarters and those who were hospitalized.
- On Command: the number of soldiers assigned to the battalion but detached for duty in another location.
- Total: the total of rank and file soldiers assigned to the battalion, regardless of their status.
- Dead: the number of soldiers who died from disease, injury or combat.
- Deserters: the number of deserters since the previous month. It also listed those soldiers thought to have been taken prisoner.
- Sent Home: the number of other ranks sent home, usually due to poor health.

Abbreviations:

1LT	First Lieutenant
2LT	Second Lieutenant
Adj	Adjutant
Bu	Bugler
Cor	Cornet
CPT	Captain
Dr	Drummer
Ens	Ensign
LT	Lieutenant
Maj	Major
NCO	Non-Commissioned Officer
Pay	Paymaster
QM	Quarter-master
SGT	Sergeant

Table Al.1 1st Battalion, 43rd Foot, January–December 1811

Date	Officers Present						Staff Officers				NCOs		Rank and File						
	LTC	Maj	CPT	LT	Ens	Pay	Adj	QM	Surgeon	Assistant Surgeon	SGT	Dr	Fit for Duty	Sick	On Command	Total	Dead	Deserted	Sent Home
January	1	9	21	6	1	1	1	1	1	2	56	23	781	153	24	958	5		
February	1	9	18	6	1	1	2	1	1	2	63	23	791	130	29	950		1	
March	1	9	18	6	1	1	1	1	1	2	64	23	736	179	34	949			
April	2	9	16	6	1	1	1	1	1	2	64	23	668	216	45	919	13		
May	2	8	16	6	1	1	1	1	1	2	64	23	668	223	52	923	5		
June	2	8	16	6	1	1	1	1	1	2	64	23	662	199	46	907	3	1	
July	3	11	24	8	1	1	1	1	1	2	70	24	1,022	185	36	1243	8		4
August	2	11	23	4	1	1	1	1	1	2	70	23	911	269	54	1234	7		
September	1	11	23	7	1	1	1	1	1	2	68	24	919	269	42	1230	5		
October	1	7	10	4	1	1	1	1	1	2	68	23	872	301	45	1218	4		
November	2	11	24	6	1	1	1	1	1	2	67	23	900	256	37	1193	11		
December	1	6	13	3	1	1	1	1	1	2	67	23	933	208	35	1176	16		1

Table AI.2 1st Battalion, 52nd Foot, January–December 1811

Date	Officers Present					Staff Officers				NCOs		Rank and File			Total	Dead	Deserted	Sent Home
	LTC	Maj	CPT	LT	Ens	Pay	Adj	QM	Surgeon	Assistant Surgeon	SGT	Dr	Fit for Duty	Sick	On Command				
January	1	2	8	18	6	1	1	1	1	2	58	21	844	109	18	971	3	2	19
February	1	1	8	19	7	1	1	1	1	2	57	21	856	97	14	967	2		3
March	1	1	8	16	7	1	1	1	1	2	58	20	768	164	20	952	14		1
April	1	1	8	15	9	1	1	1	1	2	59	20	738	176	29	943	7		
May	1	2	8	15	6	1	1	1	1	2	58	22	744	147	29	920	10		12
June	1	1	8	14	8	1	1	1	1	2	56	22	716	169	28	913	7		1
July	1	1	8	15	7	1	1	1	1	2	66	21	713	150	26	889	6		13
August	1	2	8	18	7	1	1	1	1	2	66	21	652	179	52	883	5		1
September	1	2	8	17	7	1	1	1	1	2	67	20	650	189	28	867	5		10
October	1	1	9	17	8	1	1	1	1	2	64	20	601	225	43	860	2		
November	1	1	6	16	8	1	1	1	1	1	66	20	626	201	36	863	5		
December	1	1	9	17	9	1	1	1	1	1	66	21	640	166	44	850	7		5

Table A1.3 2nd Battalion, 52nd Foot, March–December 1811

Date	Officers Present					Staff Officers				NCOs			Rank and File						
	LTC	Maj	CPT	LT	Ens	Pay	Adj	QM	Surgeon	Assistant Surgeon	SGT	Dr	Fit for Duty	Sick	On Command	Total	Dead	Deserted	Sent Home
March	2		7	15	6	1	1	1	1	2	39	19	459	68	5	562	1		
April	2		7	15	6	1	1	1	1	2	49	18	449	235	4	588	2		
May	2		6	15	7	1	1	1	1	2	49	18	458	115	13	586	4		
June	2	1	6	17	3	1	1	1	1	2	47	18	389	107	9	505	8		2
July	1		6	16	4	1	1	1	1	2	47	18	402	150	7	559	11		9
August	1		6	14	2	1	1	1	1	2	46	18	363	169	20	552	5		3
September	1		6	16	1	1	1	1	1	2	45	18	316	222	10	548	5		
October	1		6	17	1	1	1	1	1	1	46	18	293	276	11	580	7		7
November	1	2	11	24	6	1		1	1	2	47	18	306	256	9	571	8		
December	1		7	16	1	1	1	1	1	1	47	17	322	223	10	555	20		

Table A1.4 1st Battalion, 95th Rifles, January–December 1811

Date	Officers Present					Staff Officers					NCOs		Rank and File			Total	Dead	Deserted	Sent Home
	LTC	Maj	CPT	1LT	2LT	Pay	Adj	QM	Surgeon	Assistant Surgeon	SGT	Bu	Fit for Duty	Sick	On Command				
January	1*	2	3	16	6	1	1	1	1	2	49	16	687	88	16	791	9		3
February		2	8	15	5	1	1	1	1	1	50	15	700	75	12	787	5		
March		1	8	15	6		1	1	1	1	49	15	652	109	15	776	7		4
April		1	8	14	5	1	1	1	1	1	48	15	641	115	14	770	3		4
May		2	7	16	5	1	1	1	1	1	49	15	638	107	18	763	3	1	1
June		2	8	15	4	1	1	1	1	1	49	15	646	103	11	760	2		1
July		2	8	15	3	1	1	1	1	1	49	15	638	88	18	744	1		15
August		2	7	14	4	1	1	1	1	1	48	15	580	136	25	741	3		1
September		2	7	13	5	1	1	1	1	1	49	15	570	142	15	727	11		2
October		2	7	16	6	1	1	1	1	1	47	14	545	162	15	722	3		4
November		2	7	16	5	1	1	1	1	1	48	15	568	129	16	713	1	2	11
December		1	7	16	6		1	1	1	1	48	17	578	113	11	702	5	3	2

* LTC Thomas Beckwith was serving as the commander of the 1st Brigade.

Table AI.5 2nd Battalion, 95th Rifles, January–December 1811*

Date	Officers Present					Staff Officers					NCOs		Rank and File			Total	Dead	Deserted	Sent Home
	LTC	Maj	CPT	1LT	2LT	Pay	Adj	QM	Surgeon	Assistant Surgeon	SGT	Bu	Fit for Duty	Sick	On Command				
January		1		2							6	2	66	31		97	2		
February		1		2							6	2	69	24		93	1		
March		1		2							6	3	68	28		96			
April		1		2	1						6	2	66	29		95	1		
May		1		2	1						6	2	76	19		95			
June		1		2	1						6	2	80	10		88	1		4
July		1		1	2						6	2	81	7	1	89	1		
August		1		2	1						6	2	77	9	3	89			
September		1		2	1						6	1	82	8		90			
October		2		4	1						12	2	152	38		190			
November		2		4	1						10	2	151	37		188	1		3
December		2		4	1						10	2	148	36	1	185	2	1	

* One company until October 1811, when a second company is included.

Table AI.6 Right Wing,* 3rd Battalion, 95th Rifles, August–December 1811

Date	Officers Present					Staff Officers					NCOs		Rank and File						
	LTC	Maj	CPT	1LT	2LT	Pay	Adj	QM	Surgeon	Assistant Surgeon	SGT	Bu	Fit for Duty	Sick	On Command	Total	Dead	Deserted	Sent Home
August 1	1		5	8	5					1	29	10	300	80	34	414			
September 1			4	11	2					1		10	255	150	8	413	5		
October 1	1	1	4	11	2				1	1	28	10	220	173	14	407	4		
November 1	1	1	4	11	3					1	28	10	254	134	10	398	7		
December 1	1	1	6	11	4						27	20	258	109	8	375	13		9

*Five companies.

Table A1.7 Brunswick Oëls,* January–March 1811

Date	Officers Present					Staff Officers					NCOs		Rank and File					
	LTC	Maj	CPT	LT	EN	Pay	Adj	QM	Surgeon	Assistant Surgeon	SGT	Dr	Fit for Duty	Sick	On Command	Total	Dead	Deserted
January	2	9	21	10	1	1	1	1	1	1	55	25	751	157	30	958	24	36
February	2	8	21	9	1	1	1	1	1	1	55	25	791	122	2	921	19	1
March	2	7	18	8	1	1	1	1	1	1	55	25	737	168	15	920	2	

* The Brunswick Oëls had twelve companies, but only its HQ and nine of the companies were assigned to the Light Division. The table above reflects the state of the whole regiment and not just those companies assigned to the Light Division. To determine the approximate number of those fit for duty, divide the number of those fit for duty by twelve and then multiply by nine.

Table AI.8 Approximate number of Brunswick Oëls Assigned to the Light Division Who Were Fit for Duty, January–March 1811

Month	Fit for Duty
January	563
February	593
March	553

Appendix II

STRENGTH OF THE 1ST AND 3RD CAÇADORES, 1811

Every infantry regiment, caçadore battalion and cavalry regiment in the Portuguese Army was required to submit a report to the Army HQ of its strength on the 25th of each month. The below returns were found in the National Archives at Kew and are in WO17/2466 (Portugal, 1810–1812). Unfortunately the archives only had returns for the four months given below.

The returns are likewise divided into categories:

- Staff: the officers, sergeants and specialists who were present for duty with the battalion.
- NCOs: this included sergeants, but not corporals. Buglers were also included in this section.
- Rank and File: this section included all soldiers who were not officers, sergeants or musicians. It did not differentiate by rank.
- ○ Present: the total number of soldiers available to perform their duty. This is the same as the British Effectives.
- ○ Sick: the number of soldiers who were incapacitated due to injury, illness or wounds. Most were sent to higher level hospitals.
- ○ Detached and On Command: the number of soldiers who were assigned to the battalion but were detached for duty in another location.
- ○ Changes from the previous month.
- ○ Former Deserters. From time to time the Government issued an amnesty decree as an incentive to deserters to return to their units. Most deserters were soldiers returning home. Many times they remained hidden by their families. If they were arrested they were returned to the unit without further punishment unless they were NCOs or corporals, who were demoted to privates. Initially Beresford court-martialled and shot some deserters to make an example but

- soon gave up because it did not deter the men. Instead, he asked the Government to pressure the local magistrates to be more active in tracking and arresting the deserters and returning them to their units.
  - From Punishment. Men that were court-martialled and punished with some sentence that took them out of the unit, such as forced labour. Once they completed their sentence, they were returned to their unit.

At the end of the NCOs and Other Ranks section is Total. This is the total of all officers, NCOs, and other ranks assigned to the battalion, regardless of their status.

Abbreviations

Adj	Adjutant
AdjS	Adjutant Sergeant
AS	Assistant Surgeon
AWOL	Absent without Leave
BD	Bandmaster
BH	Sick, but with the battalion
BM	Bugle Major
Bug	Buglers
CH	Chaplain
Cor	Coronheiro was an artificer who worked on maintaining the musket's wooden parts
CPT	Captain
Det	Detached
Ens	Ensign
Esp	Espingadeiro was an artificer who worked on maintaining the musket's metal parts
Fur	Furriel were junior sergeants. This rank did not exist in the British Army
Hos	Sick in Army Hospital
Leave	Authorized absence
LT	Lieutenant
LTC	Lieutenant Colonel
Maj	Major
Mus	Musicians who formed the battalion's band
NCO	Non-Commissioned Officer
Pay	Paymaster
QM	Quartermaster
QMS	Quartermaster Sergeant
SGT	Sergeant
Sur	Surgeon

Table AII.1 1st Caçadores, 1811

Staff															Company Officers		
	LTC	Maj	Adj	Pay	QM	AdjS	QMS	Ch	Sur	AS	Cor	Esp	BD	Mus	BM	CPT	LT	En
Feb	1	1	1		1	1	1		1	2	1	1	1	8	1	4	5	10
Oct	1	1	1	1	1	1	1		1	2	1	1		8	1	5	5	5
Nov	1	1	1	1	1	1	1		1	2	1	1		8	1	5	5	5
Dec	1	1	1	1	1	1	1		1	2	1	1		7	1	5	6	5

NCOS and Buglers			Rank and File				Sick		Absent			Recruits	Total
	SGT	Fur	Bug	Present	Det	On Command	Arrested	Hos	BH	Leave	AWOL			
Feb	25	5	10	470		28	3	35				12	628
Oct	28	5	12	401	42	30		84	1		4	38	679
Nov	29	4	12	402	44	31		58	17		1	47	668
Dec	28	4	12	387	49	36		57	21			50	679

Changes from Previous Month

	New Soldiers			Returnees		Discharges		Deserters	Dead
	Volunteers	Conscripts		Former Deserters	From Punishment	Unfit for Duty	Bad Conduct		
February	4	7			1			1	
October	2	33						2	2
November	1	2						20	1
December	1							40	2

Table AII.2 3rd Caçadores, 1811

Staff															Company Officers			
	LTC	Maj	Adj	Pay	QM	AdjS	QMS	Ch	Sur	AS	Cor	Esp	BD	Mus	BM	CPT	LT	En
Feb	1	1	1	1	1	1	1	1	1	2	1	1	1	8	1	5	5	10
Oct	1	1	1	1	1	1	1	1	1	1	1	1	1	7	1	4	6	6
Nov	1	1	1	1	1	1	1	1	1	1	1	1	1	7	1	4	5	6
Dec	1	1	1	1	1	1	1	1	1	1	1	1	1	8	1	5	6	5

	NCOS and Buglers		Rank and File				Arrested	Sick		Absent		Recruits	Total
	SGT	Fur	Bug	Present	Det	On Command		Hos	BH	Leave	AWOL		
Feb	25	5	10	481		4		55				12	628
Oct	25	6	12	443	17		4	77				59	679
Nov	25	6	12	452	14		7	72				55	678
Dec	26	6	12	468		16	5	49				62	681

Changes from Previous Month

	New Soldiers		Returnees		Discharges		Deserters	Dead
	Volunteers	Conscripts	Former Deserters	From Punishment	Unfit for Duty	Bad Conduct		
February	7		33					
October	11		3		1	1		2
November	2		3				6	4
December	1		2				4	4

NOTES

1. Cooke, pp. 77–8.
2. *Wellington's Light Division in the Peninsular War: the Formation, Campaigns, and Battles of Wellington's Famous Fighting Force, 1810* (Frontline Books, 2020).
3. All five of these diaries were published in 2023 by the author.
4. These were light battalions, called caçadores. Later the 2nd Caçadores were replaced by the 3rd Caçadores.
5. General Orders, 22 February 1810.
6. Robert Stewart, Viscount Castlereagh.
7. Vane, vol. 7, p. 69.
8. Ibid.
9. Verner, vol. 2, p. 72.
10. *Riflemen*, p. 97.
11. Captain William Napier, who was on the march, said in his *History* that they marched 62 miles (100km) in 26 hours. However, he said they started from Malpartida, some 39km from Navalmoral. The distance using twenty-first-century maps from Google Maps is 65km.
12. Gifford was never appointed temporary commander of the brigade, but as its senior lieutenant colonel, he would command it in Craufurd's absence.
13. Horward, pp. 10–12.
14. *Riflemen*, p. 176; Simmons, p. 47.
15. Lieutenant Colonel George Elder commanded the 3rd Caçadores Battalion.
16. WD, vol. 5, p. 559.
17. *Riflemen*, p. 192.
18. WD, vol. 6, pp. 26–7.
19. Horward, p. 50; Oman, vol. 3, pp. 532–7.
20. Horward, p. 55.
21. *General Orders*, p. 124.
22. An infantry brigade was authorized a major general as its commander.
23. WD, vol. 3, pp. 503–4.
24. Only its HQ and nine of its companies were assigned to the division, while three companies were assigned to other divisions.
25. WD, vol. 7, pp. 34–5.
26. The 95th Rifles' strength number is a combination of strength for the eight companies of the 1st Battalion and the company from the 2nd Battalion.
27. Simmons, p. 136.
28. Garretty, p. 113.
29. Leach, p. 186.
30. Gurwood, p. xlv.

31 Napier, *Early Military Life*, pp. 140–1.
32 Leach, p. 186.
33 His captain, Peter O'Hare, was the senior captain in the regiment.
34 Costello, pp. 47–8.
35 Brandy.
36 Gurwood, pp. xliii–xliv.
37 Leach, pp. 187–8.
38 A waterproof cloth made of camel hair.
39 Hay, pp. 20–1.
40 Kinloch, pp. 63–4.
41 Hay, p. 20.
42 Leach, pp. 189–90.
43 Ibid, pp. 188–9; Kinloch, p. 63.
44 Gurwood, p. xliv.
45 Leach, p. 191.
46 Costello, pp. 43–4.
47 Kinloch, pp. 63–4.
48 Leach, pp. 187–8.
49 WSD, vol. 7, p. 38.
50 Costello, pp. 46–7.
51 Duffy, p. 104.
52 Napier, *Early Military Life*, pp. 141–2.
53 There is no record of Corporal Fleming being convicted by a brigade court-martial. He was probably convicted by a regimental court-martial. Unfortunately, no records could be found of any regimental courts-martial conducted by the 95th Rifles prior to 1812.
54 Costello, pp. 46–7.
55 WD (enlarged edn), vol. 4, p. 535.
56 General Order, 23 January 1811.
57 Information on the courts-martial was provided by noted historian Dr Zachary White, who has studied extensively the British military justice system of the Napoleonic Wars.
58 Riflemen, p. 105.
59 Napier, *Early Military Life*, pp. 165–7.
60 General Order, 5 March 1811. However, they marched with the 6th Division. WD (enlarged edn), vol. 4, p. 655.
61 An unpublished paper by Nicholas Haynes lays out a strong case for him being so.
62 WND, vol. 4, p. 552.
63 Brevet Lieutenant Colonel, 4th Dragoons.
64 WND, vol. 4, p. 558.
65 Oman, vol. 3, p. 206.
66 Ibid, p. 230.
67 Pelet, pp. 234–5.
68 Oman, vol. 4, p. 609.
69 Ibid, p. 609 and vol. 5, p. 543.
70 McGuigan & Burnham, p. 101.
71 General Order, 5 March 1811.
72 Ibid.
73 Duffy, p. 106.
74 Simmons, p. 136.
75 Duffy, p. 106.

NOTES

76 Sunrise was at 6.22am.
77 Costello, p. 48.
78 Ibid, pp. 49–50.
79 Leach, pp. 195–6.
80 Garretty, pp. 114–15.
81 Kincaid, *Adventures*, pp. 39–40.
82 Duffy, p. 107.
83 Costello, p. 49.
84 Napier, *Early Military Life*, pp. 157–8.
85 Simmons, p. 137.
86 Duffy, p. 107.
87 Napier, *Early Military Life*, pp. 149–50.
88 Brown, p. 134.
89 Simmons, p. 138.
90 Duffy, p. 107.
91 Simmons, pp. 138–9.
92 Duffy, p. 108.
93 This would not be the last time Wellington used smoke and mirrors to keep a junior officer in command within the Light Division. In August 1811 Colonel Beckwith, the 1st Brigade commander, was invalided home and was replaced by Lieutenant Colonel Andrew Barnard, 95th Rifles. Barnard was a very junior lieutenant colonel and it would be impossible to give him permanent command of the brigade, since the position was supposed to be filled by a major general. He temporarily commanded the brigade until May 1813. Until then, Wellington, not having a suitable senior candidate available to formally replace Beckwith, maintained the illusion of Beckwith returning as late as 15 October 1812. To achieve this, Barnard was never officially placed in command with a General Order and the brigade was referred to as Beckwith's Brigade in official correspondence. Barnard commanded the 1st Brigade for 21 months. At one point, shortly after the capture of Badajoz in April 1812, Barnard actually commanded the division for about a month.
94 WSD, vol. VI, p. 582.
95 Unpublished private letter from Lieutenant Colonel Henry Torrens to Wellington, 19 September 1810.
96 Letter dated 24 April 1811. WD (enlarged edn), vol. 4, pp. 771–2.
97 WD, vol. 4, p. 315.
98 Contemporary accounts called it the Soure river. It flows north past Pombal to the town of Soure and thence into the Mondego river. In the nineteenth century the river was called the Arunca until it reached the town of Soure, and from there it was called the Soure. It is now known as the Arunca river.
99 O'Hare's 3rd Company and Leach's 2nd Company.
100 Costello, p. 50.
101 Fririon, p. 144.
102 Patrick Fleming was a corporal in December 1810.
103 Costello, p. 51.
104 Ibid.
105 Fririon, p. 145.
106 Oman, vol. 5, p. 614.
107 PT AHM-DIV-1-14-12-3 ms 33.
108 PT AHM-DIV-1-14-223-2 ms 45.
109 Fririon, p. 145.
110 Martinien, p. 401.

111 Pierre Soult was the brother of Marshal Jean Soult.
112 Kincaid, *Random Shots*, p. 80.
113 Costello, p. 52. A Spanish dollar was worth 4.5 shillings.
114 Rifleman John Palmer, 7th Company.
115 Rifleman Thomas Tracey, 3rd Company.
116 Costello, p. 50.
117 Kincaid, *Adventures*, p. 41; Duffy, p. 108.
118 Why the attack was split between the two brigades, instead of having just one brigade do it, is unknown.
119 Duffy, p. 108.
120 Moorsom, p. 132.
121 Ibid.
122 Simmons is incorrect: it was the Anços river.
123 Simmons, p. 140.
124 Duffy, p. 108.
125 Costello, p. 52.
126 Leach was still in Lisbon, confined to his sick bed.
127 Lieutenant Leigh Heppenstall.
128 Smith, pp. 41–2.
129 Kincaid, *Adventures*, pp. 49–50.
130 Lieutenant William Johnstone.
131 Smith, pp. 42–3.
132 Ibid.
133 Garretty, p. 121.
134 Simmons, p. 141.
135 Kincaid, *Adventures*, pp. 51–2.
136 Duffy, p. 109.
137 Costello, p. 53.
138 Napier, *Early Military*, p. 176.
139 Ibid, p. 177.
140 Costello, p. 53.
141 Ibid, p. 54.
142 Former.
143 Costello, p. 54.
144 Ibid.
145 We could find no record of a Muckston serving in the Rifles.
146 Simmons, p. 141.
147 Costello, p. 53.
148 Including Lieutenants John Winterbottom and John Cross. Winterbottom, the battalion's adjutant, was grazed in the leg by a cannonball. "The shot had done him more injury than he expected, and he was laid up in hospital with that wound six or seven months, and suffered a great deal of pain." Napier, George. *Early Military Life...* p. 153. Ensign Richard Lifford died of his wounds on 10 July 1811.
149 Lieutenant Robert Beckwith.
150 Oman, vol. 4, p. 614.
151 Captain William Chapman, who was a 95th Rifles officer serving with the 1st Caçadores. Some sources erroneously list him as a Rifles casualty.
152 PT AHM-DIV-1-14-12-3 ms 33.
153 Fririon, p. 149.
154 Pelet, p. 446.
155 Martinien, pp. 183, 232, 253, 388, 447, 462.

NOTES

156 Pelet, p. 443.
157 Oman, vol. 4, p. 145.
158 Pelet, p. 448.
159 Ibid, p. 447.
160 Duffy, p. 109.
161 A small ridge.
162 Pelet, pp. 442–3.
163 The use of a French term to refer to their own light troops by Wellington's staff is very unusual.
164 WD (enlarged edn), vol. 4, p. 664. This is one of the few orders for a battle that has survived.
165 Kincaid, *Adventures*, p. 27.
166 Duffy, p. 109.
167 Ibid.
168 Simmons, p. 142.
169 Costello, p. 55.
170 Sunset was at 6.01pm.
171 Duffy, p. 109.
172 The modern-day N342 road.
173 WD (enlarged ed.), vol. 4, p. 665.
174 Ibid.
175 For more information on the length of a march column, see Burnham & McGuigan, pp. 61–2.
176 Smith, p. 44.
177 Duffy, p. 110.
178 Napier, *Early Military Life*, p. 155.
179 Ibid, pp. 155–6.
180 Lloyd was in the 43rd Foot.
181 Napier, *Life of General*, pp. 56–7. The failure of the two companies to go with him was a rare example of cowardice in the Light Division. It bothered William Napier greatly and during the months spent recovering from his wound he gave it much thought. He wrote: 'The excuses for the soldiers were – 1st. That I had not made allowance for their exertions in climbing from the ravine up the hillside with their heavy packs, and they were very much blown. 2nd. Their own captains had not been with them for a long time, and they were commanded by two lieutenants, remarkable for their harsh, vulgar, tyrannical dispositions, and very dull bad officers withal, and one of them [Lieutenant John Creighton] exhibited on this occasion such miserable cowardice as would be incredible if I had not witnessed it. I am sure he ordered the men not to advance, and I saw him leading them the second time to the right. This man was lying down with his face on the ground, I called to him, reproached him, bade him remember his uniform, nothing would stir him, until losing all patience I threw a large stone at his head. This made him get up, but when he got over the wall he was wild, his eyes staring, and his hands spread out. He was a duellist [sic], and had wounded one of the officers some time before. I would have broke him but before I recovered my wound sufficiently to join he had received a cannon-shot in the leg, and died at the old, desolate, melancholy mill below Sabugal. [He died on 12 May 1811.] Everything combined to render death appalling, yet he showed no weakness. Such is human nature, and so hard it is to form correct opinions of character.'

182　The village has since been incorporated into Condeixa and is not named on Google maps. It can be found by following the N342 road for 6km until you see the Capela do Casal Novo at coordinates 40°05′37.8″N, 8°27′03.7»W
183　Napier, *History*, vol. 3, p. 54.
184　They were in Captain Charles Beckwith's 6th Company of the 2nd Battalion 95th Rifles.
185　Kincaid, *Random*, pp. 82–3.
186　Napier, *Early Military Life*, p. 156.
187　Ibid, p. 157.
188　Riflemen, p. 106.
189　Napier, *Early Military Life*, p. 161; Smith, p. 43.
190　Simmons, p. 143.
191　Costello, p. 55.
192　Ibid, pp. 56–7.
193　Sprünglin, p. 471.
194　Captain John Douglas's and Captain James Reynett's companies, the latter being commanded by Lieutenant James Love. Reynett was serving as a DAQMG at the time.
195　Moorsom, p. 134.
196　Napier, *Passages*, pp. 184–5.
197　Simmons, p. 154.
198　*Redcoats*, p. 128.
199　Napier, *Early Military Life*, p. 161
200　Kincaid, *Adventures*, pp. 55–6.
201　Simmons, p. 143.
202　Kincaid, *Adventures*, pp. 54–5.
203　*Redcoats*, p. 128.
204　WD, vol. 7, p. 347.
205　Oman, vol. 4, pp. 152–3, 611.
206　Napier, *Passages*, p. 185.
207　Died of wounds, 16 March 1811.
208　Died of wounds, 31 March 1811.
209　WD (enlarged edn), vol. 4, p. 668.
210　Letter from Sir John Morillyon Wilson to H.A. Bruce in Napier, *Life of General*, vol. 1, pp. 58–60. Wilson did not know who Napier was. Years later he was attending a party and 'the gentlemen were speaking about "handsome men", and I said, of all the handsome men I had ever seen in the various parts of the world where I had been, there was none to be at all compared with the one whom I then described to them as above written. Napier sprang from his chair, put his arms round me, and exclaimed, "My dear Wilson, was that you? that glass of tea and brandy saved my life!" And a few tears trickled from his bright and animated eyes, expressive of his grateful recollection of the good service I had rendered him in that hour of his need and painful suffering.'
211　Napier, *Early Military Life*, p. 158.
212　Ibid, p. 159.
213　Ibid, p. 161.
214　Ibid, p. 162.
215　Duffy, p. 110.
216　Costello, pp. 59–60.
217　Sprünglin, pp. 470–1.
218　Pelet, p. 465.
219　Sprünglin, p. 470.

NOTES

220 Pelet, pp. 468–9.
221 Ibid.
222 Sutlers who provided food, drink and other items to the soldiery. Each regiment had its own and often the women were married to soldiers within the regiment.
223 Pelet, pp. 468–9.
224 Ponte da Mucela.
225 Pelet, pp. 468–9.
226 Three battalions.
227 Two battalions.
228 Three battalions.
229 Marcel, p. 130.
230 Pelet, p. 446; Sprünglin, p. 471; Fririon, p. 155.
231 Duffy, p. 110.
232 Simmons, p. 144.
233 Duffy, pp. 110-111.
234 Costello, p. 57.
235 The penalty for looting from the peasants was hanging.
236 Costello, pp. 57–8.
237 WD (enlarged edn), vol. 4, p. 670.
238 O'Hare was still a captain at this point.
239 Costello, p. 58.
240 Duffy, p. 111.
241 Simmons, p. 145.
242 Kincaid, *Adventures*, pp. 57–8.
243 Marcel, p. 130.
244 Letter from Ney to Masséna dated 16 March; Bonnal, vol. 3, pp. 507–8.
245 Bonnal, vol. 3, p. 507.
246 Sprünglin, pp. 471–2.
247 The eagle was lost in the river but was found later by some Portuguese civilians when the water levels dropped.
248 Guingret, p. 165.
249 Ibid, pp. 166–7.
250 Marcel, p. 130.
251 Sunset was at 6.02pm.
252 Kincaid, *Random*, p. 84.
253 Bonnal, vol. 3, p. 508.
254 Simmons, p. 146.
255 Costello, p. 61.
256 Kincaid, *Adventures*, pp. 59–60.
257 Costello, p. 60.
258 Kincaid, *Random*, p. 85.
259 Guingret, p. 173.
260 General Order, 16 March 1811.
261 On a modern map Alçapema is on the opposite side of the bridge from Foz de Arouce. The ford is about 200m downstream of the bridge.
262 General Order, 17 March 1811.
263 Costello, p. 60.
264 Duffy, p. 111.
265 Kincaid, *Random*, p. 86.
266 Duffy, p. 111.
267 Ibid.
268 19 March.

269 Duffy, p. 112.
270 Simmons, p. 148.
271 General Order, 18 March 1811.
272 Kincaid, *Adventures*, pp. 61–2.
273 Ibid., p. 62.
274 Duffy, p. 112. After a while so many prisoners were being taken that they were slowing the advance of the lead divisions. A collection point was established for prisoners at Ponte da Mucela, where the divisions were to send their prisoners. The General Order did not designate who was responsible for guarding prisoners there. General Order, 20 March 1811.
275 General Order, 20 March 1811.
276 Kincaid, *Adventures*, p. 63.
277 Duffy, p. 112.
278 Simmons, p. 148.
279 Duffy, p. 113.
280 This battalion was assigned to the Light Division by General Order, 5 March 1811.
281 Ewart, pp. 5–9.
282 Ewart, p. 11.
283 Kincaid, *Adventures*, p. 64.
284 British Army slang for a French soldier.
285 Lieutenant James Stewart
286 Simmons, pp. 159–60.
287 Kincaid, *Random*, pp. 152–3.
288 Simmons, p. 160.
289 Kincaid, *Random*, p. 153.
290 Duffy, p. 114.
291 Ewart, p. 12.
292 Simmons, pp. 160–1.
293 General Order, 16 March 1811.
294 Kent served in the 5th Battalion, 60th Foot, for the rest of the war, having fought in twelve battles and sieges after leaving the 43rd Foot. He was promoted to lieutenant on 2 September 1812 and became the battalion adjutant on 31 December 1812. He went on half pay on 25 December 1818 and died around 1822.
295 Mitchell was appointed adjutant of the 1st Battalion, 88th Foot, on 26 September 1811 and was promoted to lieutenant on 13 November 1813. He was severely wounded at Orthes on 27 February 1814. He retired on full pay in 1821 and died around 1822.
296 Simpson was seconded to the Portuguese Army on 3 July 1811 and immediately promoted to lieutenant and appointed adjutant of the 9th Caçadores. He was promoted to captain in the Portuguese Army on 13 December 1813 and returned to the British Army on 13 October 1814. While with the Portuguese, he was promoted to lieutenant in the British Army on 17 June 1813. He went on half-pay in 1815.
297 WD, vol. 7, p. 432.
298 Ney was relieved of his command by Masséna on 22 March for insubordination,
299 Duffy, p. 115.
300 30km. The British Army marched at a rate of 4km per hour.
301 Simmons, p. 161.
302 Ewart, p. 13.
303 Simmons, p. 161.

NOTES

304 Kincaid, *Random*, p. 95.
305 Kincaid, *Adventures*, pp. 66–7.
306 Ewart, p. 13.
307 Duffy, p. 115.
308 Ewart, p. 13.
309 WD [enlarged edn], vol. iv, p. 719.
310 *Men*, p. 47.
311 Duffy, p. 116.
312 We have not been able to determine which regiment these two squadrons belonged to.
313 Garretty, p. 125.
314 *Men*, p. 70.
315 Duffy, p. 116; *Men*, p. 70.
316 Lipscombe, p. 160.
317 Lieutenant John Hopkins claimed that it was Major Patrickson, the commander of the 43rd Foot, who gave the order to charge. *Men*, p. 51.
318 Duffy, p. 116.
319 Ibid.
320 Hopkins was in command because its commander, Captain Joseph Wells, was on detached duty.
321 Ruvina is about 6km north of Sabugal.
322 *Men*, p. 48,
323 Harrison, p. 76.
324 *Men*, p. 49.
325 Simmons, p. 162.
326 Duffy, p. 116.
327 *Men*, p. 70.
328 Garretty, p. 127.
329 *Men*, p. 49.
330 Kincaid, *Random*, p. 98.
331 Ibid., pp. 98–9.
332 Duffy, p. 117.
333 *Redcoats*, p. 167.
334 Duffy, p. 117.
335 Ibid.
336 This anecdote was recorded by William Moorsom, and it is not attributed to any source. However, this and other anecdotes probably came from Peninsular War veteran James Frederick Love, who was on the committee with Moorsom that oversaw the writing of the *Historical Record of the Fifty-Second Regiment*, pp. 138–9.
337 Dobbs, p. 18.
338 Major Edward Gibbs.
339 *Men*, p. 50.
340 Ibid.
341 Mellish was only a major and at this time the DAAG.
342 Dobbs, p. 21.
343 This was the same howitzer that the 43rd Foot initially captured. Its ownership changed hands several times but at the end of the battle it was held by the 1st Battalion, 52nd Foot. This would be the cause of much contentious debate between the two regiments and at one point Wellington was asked to confirm which regiment's claim was valid, which he declined to do.
344 *Redcoats*, p. 175.

345 Smith, p. 46.
346 Costello, p. 63.
347 Oman states they lost 769 men, of whom 186 were captured. Oman, vol. iv, p. 617.
348 Oman, vol. 4, p. 202.
349 Duffy, p. 118; Simmons, p. 163.
350 Ewart, p. 15.
351 Simmons, p. 163.
352 Smith, p. 47.
353 Unauthorized foraging and looting were forbidden and the Provost Marshal was known to hold drumhead courts-martial and hang the offending soldiers.
354 Garretty, pp. 129–30.
355 Duffy, p. 119; Ewart, p. 16; Simmons, p. 163.
356 Coxen was part of the company from the 2nd Battalion, 95th Rifles.
357 Simmons, p. 164.
358 Ewart, p. 17.
359 Duffy, p. 120; Ewart, p. 17.
360 Duffy, p, 120; Ewart, p. 17.
361 Duffy, p. 120.
362 General Order, 22 April 1811.
363 Napier, *Early Military Life*, pp. 180, 189.
364 Smith, p. 45.
365 Kinloch, p. 70.
366 *Redcoats*, p. 131.
367 Ibid.
368 This account was written by Lieutenant John Dobbs, the brother of Captain Dobbs who was sent to reinforce the piquets and push the French back. Dobbs, pp. 24–5.
369 Ensign Samuel Pritchard.
370 WD [enlarged edn], vol. iv, p. 781.
371 Modern-day Villar de Argañán.
372 Duffy, p. 120.
373 Modern-day Saelices el Chico.
374 Ewart, p. 19.
375 Duffy, p. 120.
376 Reynett was away on the Staff as a DAQMG.
377 *Redcoats*, p. 131.
378 WD [enlarged edn], vol. iv, p. 770.
379 In July 1809 the British sent an expedition to the Low Countries to destroy the naval base and stores at Antwerp. Over the next four months the army was plagued with Walcheren Fever, a combination of typhoid, typhus and malaria. Thousands of troops died and those who survived the fever were often physical wrecks. It would take years for them to recover their health and be fit for campaigning. Five companies of the 2nd Battalion, 52nd Foot, took part in that expedition. The large number of sick after a month of campaigning in Portugal and Spain was likely a direct result of the soldiers not being fully recovered from the disease.
380 *Redcoats*, p. 142.
381 Leach, p. 211.
382 Modern-day Rio Tourões.
383 Modern-day La Almedilla.
384 Lieutenant General Stapleton Cotton commanded the outposts.

NOTES

385 WD, vol. 4, p. 779.
386 Ewart, p. 20.
387 Consisting of the 16th Light Dragoons and the 1st KGL Hussars. The brigade was commanded by Lieutenant Colonel Friederich von Arentschildt, since Anson himself was on leave.
388 Freer, p. 67.
389 Kincaid, *Random*, p. 110.
390 Duffy, p. 121.
391 Cavalry videttes would ride in a circle as a visible signal that the enemy was advancing.
392 *With the 43rd*, p. 67.
393 Duffy, p. 121.
394 San Cristoval Hill is 819m high and towered 150m above the land to the east. It is 4km southwest of Espeja and 4km south of Highway E-80. It is about a kilometre south of the 1st Brigade's position.
395 Modern-day Poço Velho, about 7km from the 1st Brigade's position.
396 WD, vol. 4, p. 783.
397 Ewart, p. 20.
398 Duffy, p. 122.
399 This is the Dehesa el Águila farm, which is 4km south of E-80 and 4km east of Poço Velho.
400 Duffy, p. 122.
401 Kincaid, *Random*, pp. 110–11.
402 WD, vol. 4, p. 784.
403 Oman, vol. 4, pp. 618–21.
404 Duffy, p. 122.
405 The writer of the orders meant Caria not Caril. The road to Caria is N332.
406 WD, vol. 4, p. 784.
407 Oman, vol. 4, pp. 625–8.
408 About 11,000 men.
409 About 4,700 men.
410 Duffy, p. 122.
411 Sunset was at 7.09pm though nautical twilight was at 8.15pm.
412 Simmons, p. 179.
413 *Men*, pp. 71–2.
414 Garretty, pp. 131–2.
415 *Men*, p. 72.
416 One Spanish dollar was equal to 4 shillings 6 pence.
417 Garretty, p. 132.
418 *Redcoats*, p. 151.
419 Costello, p. 66.
420 Duffy, p. 127.
421 PT-DIV-14-189-43 m005.
422 The four companies did some skirmishing near Fort Concepcion. Leach, p. 215.
423 About 4.30am.
424 Duffy, p. 127.
425 Kincaid, *Adventures*, p. 37.
426 Costello, p. 67.
427 *Redcoats*, p. 151.
428 Napier, *History*, vol. 3, p. 520.
429 Simmons, p. 169.
430 Costello, pp. 67–8.

431 Kincaid, *Adventures*, p. 38.
432 Dobbs, p. 25.
433 *Redcoats*, p. 152.
434 On a road in march column, the British soldier marched at a speed of 4km per hour. Over rough terrain it was considerably slower.
435 Simmons, p. 169.
436 Freer, p. 69.
437 Kincaid, *Adventures*, p. 38.
438 Leach, p. 214.
439 Ewart, p. 22.
440 Leach, p. 216.
441 Simmons, p. 172.
442 Duffy, p. 128.
443 Kincaid, *Adventures*, p. 39.
444 Costello, pp. 68–9.
445 Ewart, p. 22.
446 Dobbs, p. 26.
447 Kincaid, *Adventures*, p. 41.
448 Dobbs, p. 28.
449 Duffy, p. 129; Ewart, p. 23; Freer, p. 71.
450 Duffy, p. 129; Ewart, p. 24.
451 4:38am.
452 Freer of the 43rd Foot says it was the 3rd Caçadores, while Cox and Simmons said it was the Rifles who fired.
453 Ewart, p. 25.
454 Duffy, p. 130.
455 The Light, 1st, 5th and 6th Divisions.
456 Duffy, p. 130.
457 Ewart, p. 26.
458 Oglander, p. 72.
459 Freer, p. 73.
460 Leach, p. 220.
461 Duffy, p. 132.
462 *With the 43rd*, p. 73.
463 Duffy, p. 132; Simmons, p. 187.
464 Ewart, p. 28.
465 *With the 43rd*, p. 74.
466 John McDermid and Simmons were both seriously wounded at the Combat of the Coa on 24 July 1810.
467 Simmons, p. 188.
468 Kincaid, *Adventures*, pp. 42–3.
469 Smith, p. 50.
470 Oglander, p. 76.
471 Simmons, p. 189; Duffy, p. 133.
472 During hot weather the division would normally begin its march in the dark, cool hours of early morning and stop for the day by noon.
473 Duffy, p 134.
474 Oglander, p. 78, said it took 45 minutes for the 43rd Foot to cross.
475 Ewart, p. 29.
476 Duffy, p. 134.
477 Oglander, p. 78.
478 Leach, p. 221.

NOTES

479 Kincaid, *Random*, p. 129.
480 Kincaid, *Adventures*, p. 49.
481 WD, vol. 8, p. 10.
482 Kinloch, p. 76.
483 Oglander, p. 81.
484 Kincaid, *Random*, pp. 129–30.
485 Email from Doctor Michael Crumplin, FRCS.
486 This number was for the Other Ranks, i.e. corporals and privates. It does not include the officers, sergeants and musicians. WO17/2468.
487 Ross, pp. 17–18.
488 Leach, p. 224.
489 Dobbs, p. 29.
490 Ibid.
491 Oglander, p. 83; Ewart, p. 33.
492 4.41am.
493 Oglander, p. 84.
494 Cooke, pp. 77–8.
495 Kincaid, *Adventures*, p. 44.
496 Leach, pp. 224–5.
497 Cooke, pp. 82–3.
498 James Gilchrist, 43rd Foot.
499 Oglander, p. 86.
500 Ibid.
501 Ross, p. 18.
502 *Redcoats*, p. 136.
503 Oglander, p. 87.
504 Ewart, p. 37.
505 Duffy, p. 136.
506 The Monastery of La Caridid.
507 Duffy, p. 136.
508 Kincaid, *Adventures*, p. 45.
509 Costello, pp. 71–2.
510 Beckwith was sent home to recover his health. We could not determine the exact date when he left, but Cox records in his diary on 21 August that he was still there. Riflemen, p. 109.
511 Unpublished letter provided by Dr Rory Muir.
512 The exact date Barnard was given command of the 1st Brigade is not known, but it was probably no earlier than 31 August.
513 *Redcoats*, p. 136.
514 Moore Smith, p. 165.
515 Napier, *Passages*, p. 207.
516 Leach, pp. 230–1.
517 Riflemen, pp. 109-10. It landed in Lisbon on 14 August.
518 *Men*, p. 15.
519 A severely inflamed throat, often caused by strep throat or diphtheria.
520 Smith, p. 50.
521 Duffy, p. 137.
522 Ewart, p. 39.
523 Costello, pp. 72–3.
524 *Men*, p. 154.
525 Oglander, p. 93.
526 Duffy, p. 137; Oglander, pp. 93–4.

527 Oglander, p. 93.
528 This river flows west out of the El Gata mountains into the Agueda river. It is called the Agadón from its source in the mountains, but after flowing past La Atalaya it joins the Las Vegas river, and its name becomes the Badilla.
529 Simmons, p. 199; Duffy, p. 137.
530 Oglander, p. 94.
531 Ewart, p. 39. Ewart called it the Quinta d'Urquisa. It is an old Visigoth fort that overlooks the bridge.
532 WD, vol. 5, p. 285.
533 Ibid., p. 287.
534 Duffy, pp. 137-8; Oglander, p. 563.
535 Oglander, p. 95.
536 Dobbs, p. 30.
537 Lageosa, Portugal, about 20km southeast of Fuenteguinaldo.
538 WD, vol. 5, p. 288.
539 Nautical twilight was 5am.
540 Duffy, p. 138. The ford is at 40°21'16.6"N, 6°41'12.1"W.
541 Oglander, p. 95.
542 Ewart, p. 40; Oglander, p. 95.
543 Costello, p. 74.
544 Larpent, *p. 85.
545 The source of this jealousy, and other attacks on Craufurd's character, can be traced back to his appointment, as a very junior brigadier general, to command the Light Division in 1810. To read more about this, see our *Wellington's Light Division in the Peninsular War*, pp. 27–8, 242–6.
546 WD, vol. 5, p. 289.
547 Duffy, p. 138.
548 Kincaid, *Adventures*, p. 47.
549 Riflemen, p. 110.
550 Oglander, p. 96.
551 Simmons, p. 201.
552 Duffy, p. 139; Ewart, p. 41.
553 Simmons, pp. 296–7.
554 Dominie Sampson was a poor schoolmaster who never accomplished much in Walter Scott's *Guy Mannering*.
555 The novel *The Adventures of Gil Blas* was first published in English in 1748, but remained popular among the British officers in the Peninsula.
556 Kincaid, *Adventures*, pp. 46–7.
557 Ewart, p. 41.
558 Oglander, p. 96.
559 Ewart, pp. 41–2. The Prince of Orange was serving on Wellington's staff.
560 Ibid., p. 42.
561 Duffy, p. 137.
562 Majors Richard Elers and Daniel Hearn. McLeod had not yet learned of Elers's death on 29 August.
563 Mac Innes, p. 187.
564 Duffy, p. 137; *Redcoats*, p. 154.
565 General Order, 30 September 1811. Oglander, p. 97. Oglander wrote in his diary on 2 October that he had been with the 2nd Brigade for several days, so he likely took command the same day the orders were published.
566 McGuigan & Burnham, pp. 285–7.
567 Ewart, pp. 43–4.

NOTES

568 Duffy, p. 140.
569 Ewart, p. 44.
570 Leach, p. 239.
571 Ewart, p. 44.
572 Ibid.
573 Oglander, p. 101, Ewart, pp. 44–5.
574 According to Dr Michael Crumplin, based on the symptoms described, he was probably suffering from reactive arthritis.
575 Assistant Surgeon Charles Maclean, 53rd Foot. In fact he survived the war.
576 Cooke, pp. 92–4.
577 Ewart, p. 46.
578 Duffy, p. 140.
579 Oglander, p. 106; Ewart, p. 47.
580 Oglander, p. 106.
581 Simmons, pp. 205, 206.
582 Oglander, p. 109. They were never ordered to do so.
583 Ewart, p. 49.
584 Oglander, p. 109.
585 *Redcoats*, p. 155.
586 Oglander, p. 107.
587 *Redcoats*, p. 156.
588 Ibid.
589 Barlow, p. 118.
590 Oglander, p. 110.
591 Garretty, p, 143.
592 *With the 43rd*, p. 93.
593 Leach, p. 242.
594 Lieutenant John Bell, 52nd Foot.
595 Cooke, pp. 98–9.
596 *With the 43rd*, p. 93.
597 Cooke, p. 97.
598 Ewart, pp. 50–1.
599 The enlisted soldiers celebrated too, but we could find no references describing what they did.
600 A dollar was equivalent to 4 shillings 6 pence.
601 The peseta was a Spanish coin equivalent to 3 shillings 7 pence.
602 Cooke, p. 97.
603 Ewart, p. 50.
604 Kinloch, pp. 86–7.
605 The 52nd Foot was one of the most fashionable infantry regiments outside the Foot Guards, and its officers expected to live better than their peers in other regiments.
606 Kinloch, p. 87.
607 Barlow, pp. 108–9.
608 Barrosa, Ciudad Rodrigo, Badajoz, Salamanca, Vittoria, Nivelle, Orthes and Toulouse.
609 Ciudad Rodrigo, Badajoz, Salamanca, Vittoria, Pyrenees, Nivelle, Nive and Toulouse.
610 Fuentes d'Onor, Ciudad Rodrigo, Vittoria, Pyrenees, Nivelle and Nive.
611 Vimiera, Corunna, Busaco, Fuentes d'Onor, Ciudad Rodrigo, Salamanca and Nive.
612 Busaco, Fuentes d'Onor, Ciudad Rodrigo and Badajoz.

613 Busaco, Fuentes d'Onor, and Orthes.
614 Corunna, Albuhera, Ciudad Rodrigo, Nivelle, Nive, Orthes and Toulouse.
615 Maida, Benevente, Busaco, Pyrenees and Egypt.
616 Corunna, Fuentes d'Onor, Ciudad Rodrigo, Badajoz, Salamanca, Vittoria, Pyrenees, San Sebastian, Nivelle and Nive.
617 Vimiera, Fuentes d'Onor, Ciudad Rodrigo, Badajoz and Salamanca.
618 Corunna, Busaco, Orthes and Toulouse.
619 Busaco, Fuentes d'Onor, Ciudad Rodrigo, Badajoz, Salamanca, Vittoria, Pyrenees, Nivelle, Nive, Orthes and Toulouse.
620 Roleia, Vimiera, Busaco, Fuentes d'Onor, Ciudad Rodrigo, Vittoria, Pyrenees, Nive, Orthes and Toulouse.
621 Fuentes d'Onor, Ciudad Rodrigo, Badajoz, Salamanca, Vittoria, Pyrenees, Nivelle, Nive and Toulouse.
622 Roleia, Vimiera, Busaco, Fuentes d'Onor, Ciudad Rodrigo, Badajoz, Salamanca, Vittoria, Pyrenees, Nivelle, Nive and Toulouse.
623 Fuentes d'Onor, Ciudad Rodrigo, Badajoz, Salamanca, Vittoria, Pyrenees, Nivelle and Toulouse.
624 Corunna, Busaco, Fuentes d'Onor, Ciudad Rodrigo, Badajoz, Salamanca, Vittoria, Pyrenees, Nivelle, Nive, Orthes and Toulouse.
625 WO17/2467; WO17/2468.

BIBLIOGRAPHY

National Archives at Kew:
WO17/2466 (Portugal, 1810–1812)
WO17/2467 (1811, Jan–June) Theatre Returns
WO17/2468 (1811, July–Dec) Theatre Returns

Arquivo Histórico Militar (AHM)
(Portuguese Military Archives):
  PT AHM-DIV-1-14-12-3
  PT AHM-DIV-1-14-12-3 ms 33
  PT AHM-DIV-1-14-12-4
  PT AHM-DIV-1-14-12-5
  PT AHM-DIV-1-14-223-2
  PT AHM-DIV-1-14-256-03
  PT AHM-DIV-1-14-270-01
  PT DIV-14-189-43 m005
  PT DIV-3-8-2-26

Print and Internet Sources
Barlow, George Ulrich. *A Light Infantryman with Wellington: The Letters of Captain George Ulrich Barlow, 52nd and 69th Foot, 1808–1815*, ed. Gareth Glover (Solihull (UK): Helion, 2018)
Bonnal, Henri. *La Vie Militaire du Maréchal Ney, Duc d'Elchingen, Prince de la Moskowa.* 3 vols (Paris, Chapelot, 1911–14)
Brown, Steve. *Wellington's Redjackets* (Barnsley: Frontline, 2015)
Brumwell, John. *The Peninsular War, 1808–1812. Letters of a Weardale Soldier, Lieutenant John Brumwell*, ed. William Egglestone (Delhi: Facsimile, 2019)
Burnham, Robert. *Wellington's Light Division in the Peninsular War: the Formation, Campaigns & Battles of Wellington's Famour Fighting Force, 1810* (Barnsley: Frontline 2020)
Burnham, Robert and Ron McGuigan. *Wellington's Foot Guards at Waterloo* (Barnsley: Frontline, 2018)

Compilação das Ordens do Dia, Quartel General do Exercito Portuguez Concenentes a Organização, Disciplina, e Economia Miitares na Campanha de 1810.

Cooke, John. *A True Soldier Gentleman: the Memoirs of Lt. John Cook 1791–1813* (Swanage: Shinglepicker, 2000)

Costello, Edward. *The Peninsular and Waterloo Campaigns* (Hamden: Archon Books, 1968)

Craufurd, Robert. 'Action near Almeida', *Royal Military Chronicle*, January 1811

Craufurd, Robert. *Standing Orders, as Given Out and Enforced by the Late Major-Gen. Robt. Craufurd for the Use of the Light Division during the Years 1809, 1810, and 1811*, ed. William Campbell and James Shaw (Godmanchester: Ken Trotman, 2006)

Dobbs, John. *Recollections of an Old 52nd Man* (Staplehurst: Spellmount; 2000)

Ewart, John. *The Peninsular War Diary of Captain John Frederick Ewart, 52nd Light Infantry, 1811–1812*, ed. Gareth Glover (Godmanchester: Ken Trotman, 2010)

Fririon, François. *Journal Historique de la Campagne de Portugal . . . (15 septembre 1810 au 12 mai 1811)* (Paris: Librairie Militaire de Leneveu, 1841)

Garretty, Thomas. *Memoirs of a Sergeant Late in the Forty-third Light Infantry Regiment previous to and during the Peninsular War* (Cambridge: Ken Trotman; 1998)

General Orders: Spain and Portugal, vol. 2 (London: Egerton Military Library, 1811)

Gordon, Alexander. *At Wellington's Right Hand: the Letters of Lieutenant Colonel Sir Alexander Gordon, 1808–1815*, ed. Rory Muir (Stroud: Sutton, 2003)

Gray, Charles. 'Memoirs of the Peninsular War', in Kenneth Dutton, *That Gallant Gentleman: the Remarkable Story of Colonel Charles George Gray* (Rockhampton: Central Queensland University, 2010)

Green, William, *Where Duty Calls Me: The Experiences of William Green of Lutterworth in the Napoleonic Wars*, ed. John and Dorothea Teague (West Wickham: Synjon Books, 1975)

Guingret, Pierre. *Relation Historique et Militarie de la Campagne de Portugal sous le Maréchal Masséna, Prince d'Essling* (Limoges: Bareas, 1817)

Gurwood, John (ed.). *General Orders of Field Marshal the Duke of Wellington in Portugal, Spain, and France, from 1809 to 1815; in the Low Countries and France in 1815; and in France, Army of Occupation from 1816 to 1818 . . .* (London, 1838)

Harrison, Samuel. *The Peninsular War Journal of Sergeant Samuel Harrison of the 43rd Foot 1796–1812*, ed. Gareth Glover (Godmanchester: Ken Trotman, 2017)

Hay, William. *Reminiscences 1808–1815 Under Wellington* (Cambridge: Ken Trotman, 1992)

Horward, Donald. *Napoleon and Iberia: the Twin Sieges of Ciudad Rodrigo and Almeida, 1810* (London: Greenhill, 1994)

Journals of Majors John Duffy and John Maxwell Tylden 43rd Foot, ed. Gareth Glover and Robert Burnham (Godmanchester: Ken Trotman, 2023), [Referenced as Duffy].

Kincaid, John. *Adventures in the Rifle Brigade in the Peninsula, France, and the Netherlands from 1809–1815* (Staplehurst: Spellmount, 1998)

Kincaid, John. *Random Shots from a Rifleman* (Philadelphia: E.L. Carey & A. Hart, 1835)

Kinloch, Charles. *A Hellish Business: the Letters of Captain Charles Kinloch 52nd Light Infantry 1806–1816*, ed. Gareth Glover (Godmanchester: Ken Trotman, 2007)

BIBLIOGRAPHY

Larpent, Francis. *The Private Journal of Judge Advocate Larpent* (Staplehurst: Spellmount, 2000)

Leach, Jonathan. *Rough Sketches of the Life of an Old Soldier* (Cambridge: Ken Trotman, 1986)

Levinge, Richard. *Historical Records of the Forty-third Regiment Monmouthshire Light Infantry 1739 to 1867* (Uckfield: Naval & Military, 2014)

Lipscombe, Nick. *Wellington's Guns: the Untold Story of Wellington and His Artillery in the Peninsula and at Waterloo* (Bodey: Osprey, 2013)

London Chronicle, 29 October 1810.

Mac Innes, John. *Brave Sons of Skye* (London: Eyre & Spottiswoode, 1899)

Marcel, Nicolas. *Campagnes du Capitaine Marcel, du 69e de Ligne, en Espagne et en Portugal* (Paris: Plon-Nourrit, 1913)

Martinien, Aristide, *Tableaux par Corps et par Batailles des Officiers Tués et Blessés pendant les Guerres de l'Empire (1805–1815)* (Paris: Éditions Militaires, n.d.)

McGuigan, Ron and Robert Burnham. *Wellington's Brigade Commanders* (Barnsley: Pen & Sword, 2017)

Men of Wellington's Light Division: Unpublished Memoirs of the 43rd (Monmouthshire) Regiment in the Peninsular War, ed. Gareth Glover and Robert Burnham (Barnsley: Frontline, 2022)Moorsom, William. *Historical Record of the Fifty-Second Regiment* (London: Richard Bentley, 1860)

Moore Smith, George. *The Life of John Colborne, Field-Marshal Lord Seaton* (London: J. Murray, 1903)

Muir, Rory. *Life of Wellington* (Online, 2022)

Napier, George. *The Early Military Life of General Sir George T. Napier*, ed. William Napier (London: John Murray, 1886)

Napier, George. *Passages in the Early Military Life of General Sir George T. Napier*, ed. William Napier (London: John Murray, 1884)

Napier, William. *Life of General Sir William Napier*, ed. H.A. Bruce, 2 vols (London: John Murray, 1864)

Napier, William. *History of the War in the Peninsula and in the South of France*, 6 vols (New York: W.J. Widdleton, 1864)

Noel, Jean Nicolas Auguste. *Souvenirs militaires d'un officier du Premier Empire (1795–1832)* (Paris: Berger-Levrault, 1895)

Oglander, Henry. *The Journals of Captain Henry Oglander of the 43rd & 47th Foot in the Copenhagen, Corunna & Peninsular Campaigns*, ed. Gareth Glover and Robert Burnham (Godmanchester: Ken Trotman, 2022)

Oman, Charles. *A History of the Peninsular War*, 7 vols (Oxford: AMS, 1980)

Pelet, Jean. *The French Campaign in Portugal 1810–1811* (Minneapolis: University of Minnesota, 1973)

Redcoats of Wellington's Light Division: Unpublished & Rare memoirs of the 52nd (Oxfordshire) Regiment of Foot, ed. Gareth Glover and Robert Burnham (Barnsley: Frontline, 2022)

Riflemen of Wellington's Light Division in the Peninsular War: Previously Unpublished & Rare Memoirs of the 95th Rifles 1808 - 14, ed. Gareth Glover and Robert Burnham (Barnsley: Frontline, 2023). [Referenced as *Rifleman*].

Ross, Hew D. *Memoir of Field-Marshal Sir Hew Dalrymple Ross, G.C.B., Royal Field Artillery with a New Introduction by Howie Muir* (Godmanchester: Ken Trotman, 2008)

Simmons, George. *A British Rifleman: Journals and Correspondence during the Peninsular War and the Campaign of Wellington* (London: Greenhill, 1986)

Sprünglin, Emmanuel. 'Souvenirs'. *Revue hispanique*, 1904, vol. 11, pp. 299–537

Tomkinson, William. *The Diary of a Cavalry Officer in the Peninsular War and Waterloo: 1809–1815* (London: Frederick Muller, 1971)

Vane, Charles (ed.). *Correspondence, Despatches, and Other Papers of Viscount Castlereagh, second Marquess of Londonderry* (London: William Shoberl, 1851)

Verner, Willoughby. *History & Campaigns of the Rifle Brigade: 1800–1813*, 2 vols (London: Buckland & Brown, 1995)

Wellington, Duke of. *The Dispatches of Field Marshal the Duke of Wellington, During his Various Campaigns in India Denmark, Portugal, Spain, the Low Countries, and France, from 1799 to 1818*, ed. Lt-Col. John Gurwood (London: John Murray, 1834–9) [Referenced as 'WD']

Wellington, Duke of. *Dispatches of Field Marshal the Duke of Wellington, During his Various Campaigns in India Denmark, Portugal, Spain, the Low Countries, and France*, ed. Lt-Col. John Gurwood (London: Parker, Furnivall & Parker, 1844–7 [Referenced as 'WD (enlarged edn)']

Wellington, Duke of. *Supplementary Dispatches, Correspondence, and Memoranda of Field Marshal Arthur Duke of Wellington, K.G*, ed. 2nd Duke of Wellington (London: John Murray, 1860–71) [Referenced as 'WSD']

With the 43rd in the Peninsula: the Letters of William Freer, Edward Freer and Daniel Gardner of the 43rd Foot (1808–15), ed. Gareth Glover and Robert Burnham (Godmanchester: Ken Trotman, 2022). [Referenced as *With the 43rd*]

NAME INDEX

The Name Index consists of those individuals mentioned in the text.

Algeo, John, 119
Allen, Humphrey, 49, 50
Alten, Victor, 160
Anson, George, 114, 215
Arbuthnott, Duncan, 102
Arentschildt, Friedrich von, 115, 215
Armstrong, William, 164, 175
Avilez, Jorge, 12, 14, 29, 38, 119, 154, 164, 175

Balvaird, William, 49
Barclay, Robert, 7, 8
Bardet, Marital, 72
Barlow, George, 177, 180, 185
Barnard, Andrew, 149, 150–3, 155, 163, 174, 183, 207, 217
Beckwith, Charles, 29, 37, 76, 88, 153, 174, 210
Beckwith, Robert, 208
Beckwith, Thomas, 7, 8, 14, 29, 37, 40, 50, 57, 63, 64, 75, 88, 92–7, 100–2, 115, 130, 151, 152, 187, 207, 217
Bell, John, 11, 29, 37, 153, 163, 174, 178, 219
Beresford, William, 37, 201
Binner, Captain, 72, 76, 77, 79
Breunig, Anthony, 127
Bull, Robert, 94
Burke, Richard, 35

Cameron, Alexander, 107
Campbell, Alexander, 24, 83, 84
Campbell, Patrick, 102
Campbell, Robert, 109, 110
Campbell, William, 11, 29, 37
Carroll, Richard, 65
Castlereagh, Lord, 1, 205
Chapman, William, 208
Colborne, John, 152, 174, 175, 179, 180, 186
Cole, Galbraith, 3
Colville, Charles, 118, 159
Conroux, Nicolas, 27
Cooke, John, xvii, 142, 145, 168, 178, 184
Costello, Edward, xvii, 15, 19, 20, 30, 31, 33, 41, 46, 49, 50, 55, 70, 71, 81, 102, 120, 122, 125, 155, 158, 187
Cotton, Stapleton, 108, 111, 113, 214
Cox, John, 107, 187, 216
Coxen, Edward, 107
Craufurd, Robert, 1–9, 11, 24, 28, 36, 108, 118, 121, 124, 125, 129, 131, 134, 135, 137, 140, 142, 144–6, 153–160, 163, 164, 166, 174, 175, 183, 205, 218
Creighton, John, 102
Cross, John, 208
Currie, James, 179

Dalzell, Robert, 65, 102
Dawson, Charles, 112, 121–3, 155, 176, 177, 186
Dawson, Henry, 63, 64, 109, 110, 186

Delabassée, Mathieu, 72
Dobbs, John, 99, 123, 126-7, 129, 141, 186
Dobbs, Joseph, 58, 59, 101, 109, 110
Douglas, John, 180, 210
Drouet, Jean, 27, 91
Drummond, George, 14, 24, 28, 29, 36, 37, 64, 119, 133, 154, 155
Duffy, John, 21, 30, 32, 44, 69, 74, 83, 85, 94–96, 99, 115, 117, 132, 163, 184
Dundas, David, 47
Dupont, Pierre, 20
Dutoya, Chief of Battalion, 78

Eeles, Charles, 109, 110
Elder, George, 4, 11, 29, 38, 64, 154, 164, 175, 205
Elers, Richard, 150, 169, 218
Emery, Henry, 66
Erskine, William, 36, 37, 39, 56, 57, 58, 60, 61, 93, 108, 183
Ewart, John, 87, 92, 129, 159, 161, 167, 179, 186

Ferey, Claude, 72, 77
Fergusson, James, 94, 96, 118, 184
Fleming, Patrick, 21, 22, 206, 207
Fonseca Joaquim da, 65
Freer, William, 102, 132, 178, 184, 216
Fririon, François, 41, 51
Fririon, Joseph, 40–2, 72, 77, 78, 79

Garretty, Thomas, 14, 32, 48, 96, 106, 118, 177, 185
Gibbs, Edward, 29, 38, 152, 154, 164, 213
Gifford, Theophilus, 61, 65
Gifford, William, 2, 205
Gilchrist, James, 145, 217
Gilmour, Dugald, 11, 29, 35, 37, 46, 61, 64, 88, 153, 164, 174
Gomm, William, 102
Graham, Thomas, 152
Gray, Charles, 152, 154

Guingret, Pierre, 78, 82
Gurwood, John, 15, 16, 18, 101, 102

Haggup, William, 102
Harrison, Samuel, 95
Hart, John, 155, 163, 164, 175
Hay, William, 17
Hearn, Daniel, 218
Heppenstall, Leigh, 208
Hertzberg, Frederick, 12
Heudelet, Étienne, 97, 103
Hopkins, John, 95, 96, 98–100, 213
Hopwood, John, 41, 42
Houston, William, 119
Hunt John, 154, 164, 175

Johnstone, William, 47, 208
Jones, William, 65
Junot, Jean, 5, 39, 45, 91

Kent, James, 89, 212
Kincaid, John, 32, 43, 47, 48, 55, 60, 63, 64, 76, 79, 83–5, 87, 88, 92, 114, 115, 120, 125, 126, 140, 149, 188
Kinloch, Charles, 17, 109, 139, 179, 180

Lamotte, Auguste, 72, 77
Lamour, François, 78
Larpent, Francis, 159
Leach, Jonathan, 14, 17, 31, 46, 113, 124, 141, 154, 166, 177, 188, 207, 208
Leighton, Burgh, 24
Lifford, Richard, 208
Light, William, 67
Liverpool, Lord, 20, 22
Lloyd, Thomas, 59, 209
Loison, Louis, 72, 85, 91
Love, James, 101, 111, 210, 213
Lowe, Patrick, 99

Mackenzie, John, 2
Mackinnon, Henry, 119
Maclean, Charles, 170, 219
Maling, John, 163
Marcel, Captain, 78

NAME INDEX

Marchand, Jean, 40, 45, 49, 59, 61, 62, 72, 78, 121
Marmont, Auguste de, 131, 134, 139, 155, 156, 164
Masséna, André, 5, 19, 20, 25–7, 31, 33, 34, 41, 53, 54, 69, 70, 72, 81, 83, 89, 91, 105, 111, 116, 118, 127
McCullock, John, 79
McDermid, John, 102, 133, 216
McDonald, Sergeant, 108
McLeod, Charles, 7, 11, 14, 153, 163, 174, 185, 218
Mein, William, 44, 49, 65, 179
Mellish, Henry, 37, 78, 100, 101, 108, 213
Merle, Pierre, 94
Mermet, Julian-Augustin, 45, 61, 62, 72, 77
Mitchell, James, 89, 212
Mitchell, Samuel, 147, 153, 155, 163, 164, 175

Napier, Charles, 66
Napier, George, 15, 21, 23, 33, 49, 58, 60, 61, 64–6, 108, 109, 152, 187
Napier, William, 58, 60, 65, 66, 122, 185, 203
Ney, Michel, 3, 5, 6, 39, 40, 41, 42, 45, 46, 51, 52, 54, 55, 61, 62, 65, 70–2, 75, 78, 80, 82–4, 212
Nightingall, Miles, 75

Oglander, Henry, 135, 176, 177, 185
O'Hara, Robert, 101
O'Hare, Peter, 43, 46, 47, 49, 75, 76, 120, 124, 152, 154, 164, 175, 188, 206, 207, 211

Pack, Denis, 8, 39, 46, 54, 142
Palmer, John, 43, 208
Parker, Wentworth, 153, 161, 163, 174
Patrickson, Christopher, 29, 37, 64, 102, 213
Pelet, Jean, 26, 51, 54, 72
Percival, William, 164, 175, 3

Picton, Thomas, 3, 39, 106, 159, 162
Pinto de Silveira, Manuel, 11
Powell, Thomas, 154
Pritchard, Samuel, 214
Purcell, Charles, 11, 29, 37, 153, 162, 163, 174

Reynett, James, 111, 210, 214
Reynier, Jean, 5, 39, 81, 97, 101
Ridewood, Henry, 12, 28, 29
Ross, Hew, 94
Ross, John, 12, 28, 29, 37, 57, 58, 64, 101, 151, 152
Rouse, John, 60
Rowan, Charles, 12, 29, 37, 153, 163, 174
Rylance, Thomas, 102

Shaw James, 153, 163, 174
Simmons, George, xvii, 14, 30, 44, 47, 48, 55, 61, 63, 64, 73, 76, 80, 88, 106, 107, 118, 125, 132, 160, 165, 173, 188, 216
Simpson, Andrew, 89, 212
Smith, Harry, xvii, 11, 29, 37, 46, 47, 57, 102, 109, 133, 154, 155, 164, 175, 188
Snodgrass, Kenneth, 107
Soult, Jean, 2, 28, 131, 208
Soult, Pierre, 43, 97, 208
Spencer, Brent, 109, 130–2, 134
Sprünglin, Emmanuel, 70, 71
Stewart, James, 11, 29, 37, 88, 212
Stewart, John, 12, 29, 38, 46, 57, 60–2, 64, 65, 67, 109
Stopford, Edward, 119
Strode, John, 63, 65

Todd, Alexander, 34
Torrens, Henry, 36, 37, 151, 207
Tracey, Thomas, 43, 208
Travers, James, 149

Vandeleur, John, 163, 164, 175, 184

Wellington, Duke of, ix, xvii, xviii, 1–8, 11, 17, 20, 22–4, 26, 28, 30, 35–9, 45, 46, 54–6, 59, 61, 64–6, 70–2, 75, 77, 81–5, 87, 89, 91, 93, 95, 102, 105, 107, 110, 111, 113, 116, 117, 119, 121, 130, 131, 134, 137, 139–141, 147–9, 151, 152, 155, 156, 158, 159, 161, 164, 178, 186, 207, 209, 213, 218
Wells, Joseph, 150, 213
Wilson, John, 66
Winterbottom, John, 208
Wood, Charles, 153, 163, 174
Wynch, James, 8, 14

PLACE INDEX

Principal locations mentioned in the text.

Agadon, 218
Agallas, 156, 157, 179, 181
Aguas, 146
Agueda river, 3–5, 105, 107, 108, 111, 113, 114, 130
Alameda, 114–17
Albuera, 107
Alça Pema, 83, 211
Aldea da Ribeira, 116
Aldehuela, 154
Aldeia da Ponte, 131, 132, 147, 164
Aldeia de Santo Antonio, 92
Alemquer, 8
Alentejo, 142
Alfaiates, 91, 101, 105, 106, 131, 132, 147, 160, 161, 164
Alhandra, 27
Almaraz, 3
Almedilla, 113, 214
Almeida, 3, 6, 7, 25, 91, 105, 107, 108, 111, 113, 116, 117, 127, 129, 130, 133, 156, 176
Almoster, 87
Alpalhão, 136, 137
Alva river, 83, 84
Alverca da Beira, 87, 88
Alviela river, 34
Anços river, 44, 208
Arronches, 136, 137, 140
Arunca river, 40, 207
Atalaia, 178
Atayala, 150
Aveiro, 1

Avelãs de Ambom, 89
Azaba river, 4, 5, 107, 108, 110, 111, 114–18, 110, 129, 165, 167, 171
Azambuja, 8
Azava, 110–14

Badajoz, xviii, 129–37, 139–40, 184–6, 188, 207, 219, 220
Badillo river, 148
Bailén, 20
Baraçal, 7, 87
Barba del Puerco, 5, 108, 130
Barquilla, 110
Barrosa, 219
Bemposta, 144, 146
Benevente, 220
Bismula, 91, 159
Busaco, 7, 26, 65, 183, 187, 219, 220

Cabeza Ford, 258
Cadiz, 20, 149, 151
Campo Maior, 3, 136, 137
Caria, 215
Caril, 116, 215
Carpio, 109, 111, 114, 129, 130
Cartaxo, 8, 22
Carvalhal Benfeito, 87
Casal Novo, 56–67, 108, 122, 210
Casillas de Flores, 158, 160, 165
Castanheira, 163
Castelo Bom, 119
Castelo Branco, 135, 137, 146
Castelo de Vide, 142, 143

229

Castillejos de Azaba, 165
Castro de Lerilla, 148, 156
Caya river, 136
Celorico, 87, 163, 169 Cespedosa de Agadone, 258 Ciera river, 70, 72
Ciudad Rodrigo, xix, 3–6, 25, 91, 105, 107–14, 129–31, 141, 147, 148, 150, 156, 161, 162, 164, 166, 167, 171, 175, 176, 179, 183–8, 219, 220
Côa, 3, 4, 6, 7, 91–3, 96, 103, 105, 113, 116, 130, 132, 216
Coimbra, 7, 39, 45, 53, 67
Condeixa, 53–5, 57, 66, 67, 210
Condeixa-a-Nova, 45, 53
Corunna, 28, 127, 220
Costelo de Vide, 140, 146

Dos Casas river, 113, 116
Douro river, 4

El Bodón, 156, 157, 159, 166, 167, 171, 179
El Gata Mountains, 156, 218
El Payo, 4
El Sahugo, 147, 150, 156, 158, 175
Escalos de Cima, 135
Espeja, 135, 137, 146
Esphinal, 39

Forcalhos, 106, 160, 164
Fort Concepcion, 116, 215
Foz de Arouce, 69–80, 82, 211
Freixedas, 88
Fuente Guinaldo, 158
Fuenteguinaldo, 146, 147, 155, 156, 158, 159, 161, 165–7, 173, 175, 181, 218
Fuentes de Oñoro, xviii, 106–8, 111, 113–27, 129, 132
Furcalhos, 113

Galizes, 86, 87
Gallegos de Argañán, 107
Golegã, 2, 39
Guadapera, 167

Guadiana river, xviii, 140, 167, 173
Guarda, 89, 91

La Alameda de Gardon, 107
La Alamedilla, 214
La Albergueria de Argañán, 106, 147, 159
La Agallas, 150
La Atalaya, 155–7, 167, 171, 173, 181, 218
La Calzada, 2
La Encina, 159, 173, 181
Lamarosa, 34
Lamas, 56, 63
Lariquella, 147, 150
Las Agallas, 173, 179
Las Erias, 154
Leiria, 35, 39, 40, 87
Ligiosa, 158, 218
Lisbon, 2, 7, 11, 14, 17, 18, 25–8, 31, 74, 86, 112, 170, 177, 184, 208, 217
Lousa, 146

Maior river, 11, 14, 18, 87
Malhada Sorda, 172
Malpartida, 205
Marialba, 108, 109, 111
Marialva, 109, 110, 114
Martiago, 147, 150, 154, 156–8, 167, 171–3, 181
Meimoa, 134, 135, 145–7
Melo, 81
Melon, 87
Miranda do Corvo, 54, 56, 61, 62, 70, 73, 74, 87
Moimenta da Serra, 86
Molino Carbonero, 5
Molinos dos Flores Ford, 114
Monasterio de La Caridad, 148
Mondego river, 1, 39, 45, 53, 54, 207
Monte Agraço, 27
Monte Reguengo, 136, 137, 140
Murcella, 83

Navalmoral, 3, 205
Nave d'Aver, 113, 115

PLACE INDEX

Nave de Haver, 116, 131, 132
Nisa, 136, 137, 143
Nogueira do Cravo, 87

Oporto, 1
Oropesa, 2

Paialvo, 35
Pastores, 33
Pedrogao de Sao Pedro, 134
Pega, 91, 93
Penamacor, 130, 134, 135
Peña Parda, 1
Pernes, 32–4
Pinhanços, 86, 87
Pinhel, 3, 4
Plasencia, 2
Poço Velho, 119, 120, 215
Poços, 87
Pombal, 35, 39–43, 51, 87, 207
Pombeiro, 84
Ponte da Mucela, 83, 84, 87, 211, 212
Ponte de Murcella, 72
Portalegre, 136, 137, 143
Pozo Velho, 115
Puebla de Azaba, 165, 167, 171
Puente de Larilla, 148
Puerto de Banos, 132

Quadrazais, 106, 145, 147, 164
Quinta da Aguila, 115
Quintas de São Bartolomeu, 91

Redinha, 42–51
Robleda, 157, 159
Robledillo de Gata, 154, 179, 181
Rocamondo, 89
Roleia, 220
Rovena, 95

Sabugal, 89, 91–103, 105, 112, 116, 130, 132, 162, 209, 213
Sacaparte Convent, 160
Salamanca, 3, 105, 108, 129–31, 156, 164, 184, 185, 219, 220
San Cristoval, 115, 215

San Felices Chico, 110
Sancti Spiritus, 108
Santarém, xviii, 2, 8, 11, 14, 18, 27, 30–4, 39
Santiago, 86
Sao Miguel de Acha, 134, 136
São Paio, 87
São Pedro, 107
São Pedro Rio Seco, 107
Sarnadas, 137, 143
Sarradillo del Llano, 173
Serra de Estrella, 134, 135
Sexmiro, 108, 110
Sobral, 7, 27
Soito, 106, 132, 146, 147, 159, 161, 162
Soure river, 44, 207

Tagus river, 2, 3, 27, 28, 135, 136, 143
Talavera, 2, 28, 31
Tancos, 2
Tomar, 39
Torres Novas, 34, 39
Torres Vedras, 7, 8, 26, 27
Turones river, 113, 116, 121, 124

Vadello, 157
Vadillo, 156, 177
Val de Espinho, 106
Vale de Santarém, 39
Venda Nova, 39
Vila Franca de Xira, 86, 87
Vila Seca, 56
Vila Velha, 135, 137, 143
Vilar Formoso, 207
Villar de Ciervo, 4
Villar de Puerco, 110
Villar Maior, 116
Villar Torpim, 4
Villarejo, 147, 150, 155, 156, 171, 173
Villasrubias, 158, 166
Vimiera, 28, 187, 219, 220
Vitigudino, 3

Zamarra, 148, 150, 157, 167, 171–3

Dear Reader,

We hope you have enjoyed this book, but why not share your views on social media? You can also follow our pages to see more about our other products: facebook.com/penandswordbooks or follow us on Twitter @penswordbooks

You can also view our products at www.pen-and-sword.co.uk (UK and ROW) or www.penandswordbooks.com (North America).

To keep up to date with our latest releases and online catalogues, please sign up to our newsletter at: www.pen-and-sword.co.uk/newsletter

If you would like a printed catalogue with our latest books, then please email: enquiries@pen-and-sword.co.uk or telephone: 01226 734555 (UK and ROW) or email: Uspen-and-sword@casematepublishers.com or telephone: (610) 853-9131 (North America).

We respect your privacy and we will only use personal information to send you information about our products.

Thank you!